Remembering America's Heroes is a 501(c)(3) non-profit organization based in Milwaukie, Oregon. RAH's mission is to educate our youth and the community about the high cost of freedom and the sacrifices made by our country's military veterans.

Under the leadership of Executive Director Ken Buckles, Remembering America's Heroes (RAH) provides education to youth and the community so they can understand and appreciate the value of freedom and its cost.

www.rahusa.us

REMEMBRANCE

BY
KENNETH BUCKLES

BENJAMIN BLAIR

Copyright © 2022 by Kenneth W. Buckles

All rights reserved. No part of this book may be reproduced or used in any manner without written permission of the copyright owner except for the use of quotations in a book review. For more information, address: www.rahusa.us
First paperback edition October 2022

Cover design by Benjamin Blair
Cover concept by Malinda Buckles

ISBN 9798849302348

www.rahusa.us

This book is dedicated to…

Jerry Pero
    for his dedication and devotion to Oregon's Vietnam Memorial.

Gunny Brandon
    for his friendship, loyalty, and support.

Jim Gadberry
    for his undying support and invaluable friendship.

"Honor to the soldier and sailor everywhere, who bravely bears his country's cause. Honor, also, to the citizen who cares for his brother in the field and serves, as he best can, the same cause."

~ Abraham Lincoln

CONTENTS

Preface	1
Introduction	2

HONORING VIETNAM VETERANS ACROSS AMERICA

Medal of Honor
Larry Gilbert Dahl	12

MARINES
Percy 'Gunny' Brandon	20
Jerry Pero	28
Robert Delsi	32
John Stofiel	34
Jay Lillie	39
Ed Contreras	47
Aaron Contreras	47
John Hays Sr.	51
Charles Person	55
Loren Corpuz	61
Vic Ganuelas Sr.	63
Rene Garcia	66
Mike Goldade	71
George Winslow	75

ARMY
Maj Gen Raymond F. Rees	80
Terry Piestewa	86
Walter 'Joe Bear' Running Crane	87
Charlie Gonzales	98
Mel Garten	106
Ralph Colin	108
Joe Mendoza	110
Richard Garza	113
Ron Cannon	117
Mike Breshears	126
Norman Haugk	127

Terry Low	133
Al Blain Sr.	139
David Branham	146
Larry Bussey	153
Mark Derry	156
Jim Glennon	159
Michael Coon	166
Mike McMillon	170
Robert Haltiner	173
Herb Hirst	178
James 'Doc' Wilson	182
Randall Joshua	189
Jerry Gomes	192
Milton Jackson	203

NAVY

John 'Mike' McGrath	207
Doug Bomarito	212
Jose Hernandez	215
Ann Copeland	218
Tim Myers	224
Vic Wood	234
Wayne Scott	238

AIR FORCE

Lt. General Russell C. Davis	241
Jim Willis	247
Ron Koenig	254
Bob Boyer	256
Norm Maves Jr.	257

TEACHERS-COACHES-ADMINISTRATORS

Jim Gadberry	265
Len Kauffman	276
Tom W. Doud	282
Bob Hofer	284

Ed Burton	288
Dan Rom	297
Mike Zagyva	303
Sam Whitehead	312
Dave Wood	317

THE BROTHERS JOHNSON

Michael W. Johnson	322
Andrew S. Johnson	322

THE BROTHERS ANGELL

Grant Angell	338
Curt Angell	338

INSPIRATION AT IT'S FINEST

Kim Phuc Phan Thi	343
William Hanh Vuong	345

LEST WE FORGET - GOLD STAR ALUMNI

Hallie 'Bud' William Smith	355
Warner 'Craig' Jacobson	358
David F. Popp.	360
Wayne Conrad Reinecke	362
Larry Iannetta	365
Martin Dietrich	368
William Block	370
Rodney 'Keith' Arnold	379
Michael Greeley	381
Donald Schafer	383
Larry E. Dikeman	385
Daniel Irvin Mambretti	387

IMPORTANT ACKNOWLEDGEMENTS ..392

MHS GOLD STAR ALUMNI ..398

Lest We Forget

They sent me
  and my friends
    and my generation
to Vietnam to die
  and some of us did.
The rest of us have been dying
  in bits and pieces
    since the first day they sent us
      home.
            ~Unknown

First Encounter

You have stopped for a break, stand up
to put your gear on and hear shots,
see the flash of the muzzles.
You have been followed.
The whiteness of the branches
that have been cut along the way
tells you you're on a new trail,
but the sergeant is a stateside G.I.:
barracks inspections, rules and regs.
You are probably surrounded.
There are five others beside you.
You are twenty-three.
You look quickly around you:
the sky, the trees.
You're far from home.
You know now that your life
is no longer yours.

~Leroy V. Quintana
Army Airborne 1967-68

PREFACE

Remembrance Volume III follows the releases of Remembrance Volume I in 2020 and Volume II in 2021. As was the case with in the first two volumes with all the WWI, WWII, and Korean War veteran, every Vietnam veteran hereafter I either knew or became friends with. I am grateful that they were able to share with me, and now you, their experiences.

I'm also very grateful to the many, many friends and veterans who gave me names and contacts of people asking me to be interviewed and include them in this volume. Many of whom told me that I would not understand what happened. We may not be able to comprehend, but we have to listen so that we can understand the reasons why we as a nation need to apologize to these great men.

I would like to also apologize to the many Vietnam veterans I was unfortunately unable to include in this book. You all deserve to be remembered and apologized to by everyone.

So why focus on wanting to apologize to Vietnam veterans in Volume III and include an apology on the back cover? The answer is simple. I asked every single Vietnam veteran the same question, "How were you treated when you came back home?" And the majority of veterans' responses included in some way, shape or form: disdain, revile, and disregard.

You will read how many veterans I interviewed experienced being spit at, screamed at, cussed at, and of course called, 'Baby Killers'. Some had rotten eggs, urine, or feces thrown at them. There were those who were lucky as they returned to a military base, but many went through hell.

Upon their return home our Vietnam veterans suffered from PTSD just like the veterans of the past WWI, WWII, and Korean War conflicts as well as Iraq and Afghanistan veterans. However, the similarity stops there for they also suffered from their horrible treatment coming back home, only adding to their PTSD. For them it is still a deep wound that has only been bandaged but never healed.

This is unacceptable! And has been swept under the carpet for over fifty years! It's not right! I strongly believe we Americans and our nation need to apologize, and this book is a start to that apology.

INTRODUCTION

Dear Vietnam Veterans,

   I'm so sorry for how you were treated when you came back home.

If you have read the previous two Volumes of Remembrance, you will know how for over twenty-five years, I have brought American veterans from all over the United States to high schools in Oregon to share their military experiences during times of war with students. Those events were named Living History Days.

Since I started asking veterans to join us for our Living History Days (LDH), one of my most difficult challenges was getting Vietnam veterans to attend and or talk to high school students. Our very first LHD at Milwaukie High School in '96, we invited WWII veterans. Our second in '97, I reached out to invite not only WWII veterans, but also Korean War veterans.

Our third LHD still included WWII and Korean War veterans, but we planned to go all out and thank the Vietnam veterans who attended be thanked for serving, honored, and shown Milwaukie High School Mustang Love.

2

In the winter of 1998, I started searching out and calling Vietnam veterans. Many times, I was hung up on, and several times I was cussed out and then hung up on. Most however were cordial and would explain to me why they were not interested and that they had never have gotten involved with veteran organizations because of the painful memories of how they were treated when they came home.

Some told me that the WWII veterans at VFW (The Veterans of Foreign Wars) and American Legions did not want them to be members and labeled them losers. Some who were able to join were shunned and even told that Vietnam was not a war, and they did not belong in any veterans' associations.

Many admitted that they had never told their own children that they were Vietnam veterans, or they lied to them, saying they were stationed stateside. Because of this many declined to speak or attend events.

Although it was fairly easy getting most of the WWII and Korean War veterans to attend or speak to students, the Vietnam veterans were more of a challenge. If I could not convince them to attend, I thought maybe I should start asking MHS students to seek out and invite any of their parents who were Vietnam veterans.

I was shocked at the number of students who returned to me saying how stunned they were to learn their parent was a Vietnam veteran because they had kept it from their family. Students were also frustrated because they could not even get their fathers to even just attend or only come for lunch and The Assembly of Honor.

As usual, a large number of WWII and Korean War veterans we often have were able to attend the event in November. However, only a few Vietnam veterans said they would attend and attend only the last day. With what little number of Vietnam veterans we had we were excited to give them the honor they deserved.

3

The event started with the vets attending our Gold Star Assembly where all the names of Milwaukie High School Alumni who died while serving our country in the Armed Forces are read aloud and a candle is extinguished to honor them.

After the assembly, WWII and Korean War veterans were divided into groups and escorted to every classroom in the school, each group visiting two different classes for back-to-back sessions with the students. After these visits, they were escorted to the Commons and served hot lunches by the students.

This being the last day, we have our Assembly of Honor, in which all veterans line up in the school's halls leading to the incredibly decorated main gym. Entering into the gym first were the WWII veterans, followed by the Korean War veterans, and last were the Vietnam veterans.

With all our students and staff already in the main gym, our high school band started playing military anthems, and the students all stood and clapped to the music until the last veteran entered the gym, a good fifteen minutes later. We had 800 chairs on the floor with one aisle down the middle, and aisles down both outsides. I always greeted the veterans as they entered the gym so I can have the honor of seeing their reactions as they enter.

To this day the loudest cheers I've ever heard in that gym were when the Vietnam veterans were introduced and walked into the gym. Every one of them had tears in their eyes or openly wept. Many looked at me, shook their heads and said, "I have never been welcomed home by the public before, only by other Vietnam veterans."

I'll never forget when one Vietnam veteran entered the gym, and after I shook his hand, he stopped walking and looked into the gym with a look of shock, started crying and then collapsed into my arms and began sobbing. I kept saying over and over to him, "This is for you; you deserve this, and these Mustangs love you."

Over the next several years, the number of Vietnam veterans grew little by little as more started attending and also began speaking to students. Many have told me how healing our whole Living History Day was for them.

Over the years, whenever I meet a Vietnam veteran, I always ask if I can shake their hand. This act will always lead to some small talk, and always at the end of our conversations, I say, "I'm so sorry for how you were treated when you came back home." Practically every time, tears well up in their eyes and they thank me.

So why apologize?

A couple of years ago, I approached a gentleman at a restaurant in Portland, Oregon who was wearing a Vietnam veteran cap. He had a very strong accent, so I asked where he was originally from.

"I'm from New Zealand and yes, we Kiwis had troops in Vietnam just like the Aussies. We had your Yank's backs," he said laughing.

I responded with, "Wow, I had no idea! Well, I bet you weren't treated like our veterans when they came home."

He got tears in his eyes, raised his voice, and said, "Oh, hell yes. It happened to us, and the Aussies too. After a moment of silence, he then said, "I was spit on and called a baby killer."

I quickly replied, "I'm so sorry, I had no idea."

But then he smiled and proudly said, "In 2008, New Zealand had a National Vietnam Veterans Apology Day. It was so emotional, powerful, and healing. There were thousands of people there, including us veterans, hugging, and crying with each other. It was a day I'll never forget," he said with tears in his eyes.

I was blown away and said, "It would be amazing if my country would do that."

He laughed and said, "It would never happen. You Yanks have too many self-centered people."

While he might be right, but we have to try!

In 1969, when I was still in school, the United States held its first draft lottery for the Vietnam War. Young men were all given a random number corresponding to their birthdays. Any with lower numbers were drafted, told to report to induction centers, and then possibly sent to Vietnam.

The draft ended in 1972, the same year I graduated from high school. Because I was not drafted into the military, I was able to pursue my dreams of playing college football and becoming a high school PE teacher. Later I would go on to become a weight training teacher, head football coach, and assistant wrestling and track and field coach.

During the spring term of '77, my last term, I was offered a job for Columbia Distributors driving a delivery truck and making $10 an hour. Back then, that was a lot of money for a 22-year-old. My delivery route was in downtown Portland, Oregon, and I'll never forget what I witnessed during Portland's Rose Festival week.

Since 1907, the U.S. Navy has brought ships to this annual event and anchored them on the Willamette River, which divides the city of Portland. The week the Navy ships arrived, many establishments that I delivered to had posted signs stating: "Military personnel will not be served," "No Military allowed," or "Navy Sailors in uniform will not be served." Although I was disgusted by this, I said nothing.

At the time I knew little about Vietnam veterans. In the coming years, I would look back upon my personal memory of how they were treated in greater disgust and shame. Since then, I've learned many important facts about these special veterans

First, it was Vietnam veterans who came up with the saying "Welcome Home" and they always greet each with this because most Americans did not. Personally, I feel I don't have the right to say "Welcome Home" to them because I had my chance in the '70s and I didn't do it.

Second, it was a Vietnam veteran who conceived the idea for a Vietnam War National Memorial for his brothers and sisters who never came home. He personally funded the memorial's construction with his own money, as well as collecting the rest in private donations. The "Wall," as it is called, has become veterans' place to meet and gather every Veterans and Memorial Day. (Many other Vietnam War memorials built all around America were also conceived by veterans!)

Third, it was Vietnam veterans who raised awareness to most civilians that combat drastically changes veterans' lives. The term PTSD or post-traumatic stress disorder started in the 1970s in large part due to the diagnoses of Vietnam veterans.

I remember hearing civilians and veterans from other wars back in the '80s putting down Vietnam veterans over this issue. Those other war veterans would often say, "We just came back, got jobs, got married, and raised a family." They were of course also unaware of how different the trauma was for Vietnam veterans.

Most Americans now know that every veteran who has experienced combat in any war or conflict never comes home the same. The suicide rates for veterans versus civilians show how different they really are, of which the Iraq and Afghanistan veterans are even higher.

Last, the founding principle of Vietnam veterans is, "Never Again." Almost all tell me, "Never again will veterans coming home be treated like we were. Never again will one generation of veterans abandon another." And based upon this principle, all over the U.S., Vietnam veterans greeted Desert Storm, Iraq, and Afghanistan veterans at airports to welcome them home.

However, more needs to be done. For years now, I have been advocating for a formal acknowledgement of the widespread mistreatment of Vietnam veterans, and for a long-overdue formal apology to all of them and their families for the mistreatment they endured after the war.

In August of 2019, my wife and I started a Vietnam Apology cause in our small town of Canby, Oregon. We traveled around setting up a red, white, and blue canopy tent and started selling Vietnam Veteran Apology T-Shirts at various car shows. We hung poster size banners with DEAR VIETNAM VETERANS emblazoned in large letters above the Vietnam Service Patch, and under that was I'M SO SORRY FOR HOW YOU WERE TREATED WHEN YOU CAME BACK HOME.

We were not prepared for the emotional responses we received from the start. Almost every single person under the age of fifty who approached us had no idea a formal apology had never happened. Many were upset because they were totally unaware of this happening. One man was upset with me stating, "I don't believe this happened in America. Are you sure you are not exaggerating?"

A nine-year-old boy said to me, "I don't believe this can be true. Americans love veterans." His parents stepped forward and gave me permission to teach him the facts. They didn't have a clue either.

Many people wearing Vietnam veteran hats would stop and look, then walk away and soon return and demand to know what our booth was all about. Two different veterans became angry and yelled at us, "This better not be fake," and, "Why are you doing this?"

Many of the wives would approach us and say, "My husband is a Vietnam veteran and wants to know what this is all about." Many would come back later to introduce themselves and thank us. They would then tell me how they were treated when they came home. And as always, with a lot of tears.

But the most emotional encounter was at an outdoor concert at which we had set up our tent. I was visiting a friend about twenty-five yards from our tent when I noticed my wife, Malinda, frantically trying to get my attention, waving her arms over the loud music.

There was a senior citizen gentleman talking to her and his back was to me. I ran back to see what the matter was, and on returning, I started by trying to introduce myself to the man when I noticed he was sobbing. I pulled him aside to see if I could offer some comfort, and he started talking.

"Your wife told me, this apology thing you both are doing is real and sincere. I saw this over an hour ago and it took me this long to approach you guys. I was very afraid this was some kind of cruel joke."

"You see, I joined the Army in 1964 because my father served during WWII and my grandfather served in WWI. I wanted to follow their footsteps and make them proud. When I was sent to Vietnam, I truly believe it was the right thing to do, it was my turn. We must stop the spread of Communism.

"While over there, we started to hear that there were college kids protesting the draft, but we did not know how ugly it was getting. Not once did I ever hear that our troops were getting cussed and spit on. So, when I came home for the first time, we were greeted by protesters, and I was spat on.

"This devastated me. I thought, 'Is this America?' It completely destroyed me, and I crawled into a bottle for the next two years. I never made it to my parents' home. Everything I had grown up believing and living and sacrificing for my country was now turned upside down. Years of pain and anger, not being able to keep a job, destroying two marriages, lots of therapy.

"Then I see this apology banner, and wow! God Bless you and your wife. You have no idea how much this means to me. Thank you, thank you, thank you."

He then gave me a big hug, full of lots of tears, and then hugged my wife.

After that, my beautiful wife Malinda and I went around to many businesses in our hometown of Canby and asked if businesses would donate to the cause by buying T-shirts with the apology on it and then have employees wear them and let us take a picture. We also asked if they would agree to wear and have their employees wear the Vietnam Veteran Apology T-Shirt on Veterans Day, November 11, 2019.

We had wonderful responses from many Canby businesses who joined the cause...

Canby Mayor Brian Hodson, Canby American Legion, Canby High Football Team and Coaches, Cutsforth's Market, Backstop Bar & Grill, Wild Hare Saloon, Canby Police Department, Canby Fire Department, Gwynn's Coffeehouse, Northwest Furniture Outlet, Canby's Now Here This, T Advantage Mortgage Canby, Millar's Point S Tire & Auto Service, and Baker's Prairie Bakery. Thank you, Canby!

HONORING VIETNAM VETERANS ACROSS AMERICA

For many years now I have dreamed about driving across the United States with this message on a vehicle –

"DEAR VIETNAM VETERANS, WE HONOR YOU FOR YOUR SERVICE, VALOR, AND SACRIFICE AND WE ARE SORRY FOR HOW YOU WERE TREATED WHEN YOU CAME BACK HOME"

Recently my dream is becoming a reality. I am proud to announce that Weston Dealerships in Gresham, Oregon has provided a Hummer H2 SUV so we can drive across America with the message. Starting in October of 2022 in Canby, Oregon, we will first head to Weston Dealership for the kickoff, then drive across the country to the Vietnam Veterans Memorial in Washington, D.C., arriving before Veterans Day, and then return home spreading our apology message all across America as we travel.

We will be stopping in the following cities: Canby, OR, Milwaukie, OR, Hermiston, OR, Boise, ID, Ogden, UT, Cheyanne, WY, Lincoln, NE, Des Moines, IA, Springfield, ILL, Indianapolis, IN, Columbus, OH, Charlestown WV, Washington DC, Waynesboro, VA, Lynchburg, VA, Nashville, TN, Clarksville, TN, Atlanta, GA, Birmingham, AL, New Orleans, LA, Dallas, TX, Broken Arrow, OK, Amarillo, TX, Albuquerque, NM, Flagstaff, AZ, Las Vegas, NV, Orange County, CA, Fresno, CA, San Francisco, CA, Medford, OR, Canby, OR.

I know this will lead to some healing and hope and pray this cause will lead to achieving the dream of having a National Vietnam Veteran Apology Day in America!

I decided to start this book by honoring Larry Dahl, a fallen soldier. Larry is the only Clackamas County native to receive the Medal of Honor. Clackamas County is where Milwaukie High School resides. I have also decided to end the book with a 'Lest We Forget' section featuring Gold Star Alumni who gave their lives in service of our country.

LARRY GILBERT DAHL — Medal of Honor, Army

I first met Larry's mother, Theo Keene and two other family members at Remembering America's Heroes first Oregon Military Hall of Fame induction ceremony on April 14, 2007.

They were extremely grateful that Larry was again being remembered. In March of 2022, I reconnected with Theo, Larry's son Michael, and Michelle, Larry's widow, over the phone. All agreed to share their memories and thoughts for this section. I'm very grateful.

Theo Keene – Larry's mother, who is still living at 90 years of age.

"Larry was such a good boy, so very thoughtful and helpful. He mowed several neighbors' lawns to make some money and he would surprise me many, many times with roses or gifts. He was the second of six children. I had three boys and three girls. I got married at fifteen years of age, and my oldest son was born when I turned sixteen. Larry was born when I was seventeen years old on June 10, 1951.

"Larry loved to drive, to take me places, and run errands. I miss him terribly and think about him every day. I've never gotten over his death. It's still very hard."

Michelle – Larry's widow.

"I met Larry during our sophomore year in High School (Franklin High School in Seattle, Washington) through a friend one afternoon when we rode their bikes down to Lake Washington. I can honestly say it was love at first sight.

"He made a stool in shop in high school which became known as the 'Kissing Stool' which my son now possesses. I was a foot shorter than him and stood on this stool to kiss him so I wouldn't be on tip toes, nor did he have to stoop down. I'm short by the way.

"Larry did not graduate due to low grades because of his dyslexia. So, he volunteered to join the Army to get training and have a trade after his service. He also had to sign a waiver, I believe, to go to Vietnam due to his blood type, which was AB+, which is not rare, but not easily available in military hospitals in combat zones.

"After Larry's death, my father filled in admirably until his death when Michael was twelve."

In November of 2016, there was a memorial rededication ceremony for Larry Dahl that featured guest speakers from the military and a speech by Michael. He was kind enough to send me his speech which follows:

> A legacy is defined as anything handed down from the past, as from an ancestor or predecessor. My father joined the military in 1969 and went to Basic Training at Fort Lewis Washington. After completing training as a Heavy Vehicle Driver, he served in Vietnam, a conflict from which he would not return.
>
> He was posthumously awarded the Medal of Honor for saving the lives of his fellow soldiers during a fateful convoy in February of 1971. I was barely three years old. My memories of my father are fragmented, and much of what I learned about him came second hand.

There were ceremonies and events connected with what my father had done, but as a child at that time, I cannot say I fully understood everything. Perhaps in all fairness, I wasn't expected to. I didn't see my life as being different or special in any way. It was not until much later in life that things connected.

Eventually I was contacted by people who served with my father, and they began to tell their stories; some funny, some thoughtful, some tragic. By that point in time, I was serving myself, already deployed overseas, and had my own time on the ground. My own perspective gave greater meaning and value to these stories. I had learned to appreciate through my own experiences that indescribable bond soldiers have when they are together in harm's way. I had learned what it meant to look out for others and to be willing to do what was needed to get them home.

I will never forget the first convoy I took in southern Baghdad through an area known as 'Four Corners', when the lead vehicle was struck by two electronically fired projectiles, or EFP's.

I will never forget the way the gun truck escorts took charge, ensured the way forward was clear, and protected the downed vehicle. I was in the convoy commander's vehicle at the time, and I think his words were fitting: "Every time we go out it seems like there is a round out there with someone's name on it. Our crews prepare, train, and rehearse so that even when things like this happen, we can look at that round and say, 'Not today!'"

I have also learned that a legacy, if that is what we agree to call it, is not entirely about paying something back, but paying something forward. I remember the conversation I had with Anthony Diaz, whose father Hector was in the truck when my father was killed. Anthony told me how if it had not been for my father's sacrifice, Hector would not have made it home from Vietnam, and he would never have been born. Anthony himself served in both the Navy and Army and retired after twenty years of service.

He is presently in Washington State and is looking forward to a future in the Sheriff's Department where he will doubtless continue to serve. All three of my children raised their hands and served their country for a brief time, though not as long as I have done.

My own service has been a humble attempt not to somehow follow in my father's footsteps, but to make some meaningful contribution to my fellow man and to my nation in a manner my father would respect.

I have told my father's story to my fellow soldiers, not out of hubris but as a lesson in heroism and sacrifice. I have told his story in order to spread a simple message: that every person in this world has value and purpose, and we may never know when we may be called on to rise above ourselves and do something truly significant. True valor is not contained in badges or medals, but in the strength of our character, the depth of our commitment, and the power of our compassion.

My thanks once again to all those who have gathered here today as friends, family, and brothers in arms. We not only respect his sacrifice, but celebrate his life, and the way he touched the lives of others in big ways and small, and we will never forget. As Shakespeare's Hamlet said of his own father: 'He was a man, take him for all in all, I shall not look on his like again.'

Larry Gilbert Dahl was Killed in Action on February 23, 1971, and posthumously awarded the Medal of Honor which was presented to his family by Vice President Ford on August 8, 1974. He is buried at Willamette National Cemetery in Portland, Oregon.

Larry Dahl's Medal of Honor Citation

Rank and organization: Specialist Fourth Class, U.S. Army, 359th Transportation Company, 27th Transportation Battalion, U.S. Army Support Command. Place and date: An Khe, Binh Dinh Province, Republic of Vietnam, 23 February 1971. Entered service at: Portland, Oreg. Born: 6 October 1949, Oregon City, Oreg. Citation: Sp4c. Dahl distinguished himself by conspicuous gallantry and intrepidity while serving as a machine gunner on a gun truck near An Khe, Binh Dinh

Province. The gun truck in which Sp4c. Dahl was riding was sent with 2 other gun trucks to assist in the defense of a convoy that had been ambushed by an enemy force. The gun trucks entered the battle zone and engaged the attacking enemy troops with a heavy volume of machine gun fire, causing a large number of casualties. After a brief period of intense fighting the attack subsided. As the gun trucks were preparing to return to their normal escort duties, an enemy hand grenade was thrown into the truck in which Sp4c. Dahl was riding. Instantly realizing the great danger, Sp4c. Dahl called a warning to his companions and threw himself directly onto the grenade. Through his indomitable courage, complete disregard for his safety, and profound concern for his fellow soldiers, Sp4c. Dahl saved the lives of the other members of the truck crew while sacrificing his own. Sp4c. Dahl's conspicuous gallantry, extraordinary heroism, and intrepidity at the cost of his life, above and beyond the call of duty, are in keeping with the highest traditions of the military service and reflect great credit on himself, his unit and the U.S. Army.

~ The United States Army website, Medal of Honor Recipients

When I had a chance to sit down and talk with Larry's son Michael, he told me the following:

"Ken, I want to share something else with you. When I have done presentations about my father, I have often told the story of Anthony Diaz, whose father Hector was on the gun truck with my father during the ambush. Hector passed away a few years ago, but he told his son many times the story of how my father saved his father's life. Eventually we connected and he mailed me the following letter:

Sergeant Dahl,

> I know that you do not know me; my name is Anthony M. Diaz. I am currently serving my fourth tour in the Middle East. Your Father saved my father's life in Vietnam. Had it not been for this unselfish act my father would have died that day. My father and I had talked about what occurred that day. It's not too detailed but some facts you might not know...
>
> During that convoy they were ambushed. The ambush went on for a bit and during the ambush my father was on the Mini gun in the

rear...as he was shooting the mini jammed......leaving my father working on the Mini trying to unjam it...my father was standing on the left side of the mini if you were facing the front of the truck. My father had his back to your dad as he was manning the 50 on the left side of the truck (facing the front of the truck).

There was a brief end to the gun fire, and they thought it was over... and the truck began to move, and they were at the bottom of a little hill... your father was still scanning the area and at the same time checking on my Dad...

Just as the truck began to move your father saw a figure (VC) pop up. He threw the hand grenade at the exact time your Dad lit him up with the 50... my father said he got him... how he knew that I'm not sure, but he seemed pretty sure of it...

The grenade made it and bounced into the back right hand corner opposite of the side where my father was working on the mini gun.

Your father announced it being there at the same time he was jumping on it...his body shielded most of it which saved everyone in the back but some of it still went through him and hit my father in his lower legs...

My father was thrown out of the truck, lying next to your father... he described to me how he was crying and telling the door gunner that your father (the man lying next to him) had saved his life…

When my father died, he still had pieces of that grenade in him... and I think it was because he wanted a constant reminder of the love your dad showed him the day he saved his life.

I remember my father telling the story like it was yesterday... and will never forget it.

Every time my father told that story he was in tears.

I was born only three days after your father saved my father's life. Had it not been for his sacrifice, I would have never met my father.

I have to tell you that whenever I was in a situation in the Middle East, I always remembered your father after it was all over, and I kept thinking about how I wanted to make sure if that situation ever came to me, that I could be there for my buddies no matter what the cost.

I know and you will never be able to explain those feelings to anyone who has not been there, and even if you spent the rest of your life trying, they would never understand the closeness that you feel to the guys around you... knowing that no matter what differences you may have, that if the shit hits the fan, they will be there for you no matter what.

Sincerely,

Anthony M. Diaz
MA2 Diaz USN
MOBSECRON 2
Mobile Anti-terrorism Task Force Det. 22

Larry Dahl would have been 72 years old in June of 2022.

> Greater love has no one than this,
> that he lay down his life for his friends.
> ~John 15:13

In Washington D.C. at the Vietnam War Memorial there is a plaque honoring veterans who died after the war. All of whom died as a direct result of injuries they suffered in Vietnam. However, all were not eligible to be put on the Memorial Wall because of Department of Defense guidelines. Included are those who died from PTSD-related illnesses, or exposure to chemicals like Agent Orange as well as many others.

The men and women you will read about here after are just but a few of those men and women we give honor for their service, valor, and sacrifice.

MARINES

This is my rifle.
There are many like it, but this one is mine.
My rifle is my best friend. It is my life.
I must master it as I must master my life.

Without me, my rifle is useless.
Without my rifle, I am useless.
I must fire my rifle true.
I must shoot straighter than my enemy
who is trying to kill me.
I must shoot him before he shoots me. I will ...

My rifle and I know that what counts in war
is not the rounds we fire,
the noise of our burst, nor the smoke we make.
We know that it is the hits that count. We will hit ...

My rifle is human, even as I, because it is my life.
Thus, I will learn it as a brother.
I will learn its weaknesses, its strength,
its parts, its accessories, its sights, and its barrel.
I will keep my rifle clean and ready,
even as I am clean and ready.
We will become part of each other. We will ...

Before God, I swear this creed.
My rifle and I are the defenders of my country.
We are the masters of our enemy.
We are the saviors of my life.

So be it, until victory is America's
and there is no enemy, but peace!

~Marines' Creed

PERCY 'GUNNY' BRANDON

Sioux and Cree
4 Purple Hearts

I met this Marine Corps legend at a Barbecue for Marines at the Marine Corps Reserve Base in Portland, Oregon during the summer of 1998.

Gunny's father was full-blooded Sioux, and his mother was full-blooded Cree, and he was damn proud of his Native heritage. Gunny was sitting behind a table selling his book *Gunny: A Story About a Marine Gunnery Sargeant*, which I highly recommend reading for a more detailed account of Gunny's life, his time as a Marine MP, a drill instructor, and combat during the Vietnam War.

His therapist encouraged Gunny to write about his experiences as therapy for severe PTSD and he ended up writing a book. Gunny claimed it helped him tremendously. However, nightmares would still wake him up every night.

Whenever I attended any veteran-related event such as the barbecue where I met Gunny, I would invite any veterans to our next Living History Day. At this event, there were several hundred Marines in attendance, mostly reservists and many WWII, Korean War, and Vietnam Marines. Gunny however stood out the most for he was a super friendly guy and learned he was very respected by everyone.

As I started to introduce myself to Gunny and he interrupted me and said, "I know who you are. It's real impressive what you have been doing for veterans the past two years at Milwaukie High School. I've driven to Milwaukie High School the past two Living History Days. But I just park and watch all the veterans arrive and be greeted by the students."

I told him that this coming November we were honoring Vietnam veterans and I invited him. He gave me his address and phone number and for the next four years I sent him an invitation and called him, but he always said he had other commitments.

In the fall of 2003, I begged him to attend, but he told me again, "I've been coming every year; I just don't get out of my car. I just park and watch the students greet all the veterans when they arrive."

I asked why he didn't come in and he stated, "It would be too emotional."

Well, I knew we had to make it happen. I got fellow teacher Jeff Linman and his Tech Cadre students involved. They started calling him on a regular basis and convinced him they wanted to meet him and shake his hand.

The students knew when he was arriving, what kind of car he was driving, and the parking lot he was going to park in. What he didn't know was that the students were going to make him get out of his car and escort him to the commons where all the veterans were gathering for coffee and donuts. Several students were assigned to him, and all were on a mission to keep him at MHS for the entire day. Gunny was not getting out of this.

The week before LHD, we would always have a schoolwide in-service assembly to get the students prepared for the big day. I told the entire student body and staff about Gunny Brandon and how he had come seven times only to sit in the parking lot, but that this would be his first time to attend because we had a plan.

On the day of the event, after lunch, all the veterans lined up in the hallway and were escorted into the main gym where the students greeted them with a standing ovation and our band played the military anthems. The all the students started chanting, 'GUNNY, GUNNY, GUNNY'.

It was then that our plan came in to action, and two students walked up to Gunny who was sitting in his car.

21

"When I got out of my car, two pretty high school girls grabbed each arm and started escorting me to the school. They stayed at my side the entire day. If they hadn't been right, there. I probably would have snuck out of that school." He laughed when telling me.

Gunny was able to stay and even sat with the other veterans during the final honor assembly where we salute the veterans from WWII, Korea, Cold War, and Vietnam. What he didn't know was that I had another surprise for Gunny, for near the end, I was going to personally recognized him.

I got really emotional while telling everyone about Gunny Brandon and his past seven years of only sitting in his car and not attending. I then pointed him out to the crowd and asked Gunny to please stand. He received the loudest standing ovation I ever witnessed at a Milwaukie High assembly.

After a few minutes, the entire student body started chanting 'GUNNY, GUNNY, GUNNY', over and over again. Students told me Gunny was so moved he had tears running down his face. He told me later, "I was looking for a trap door to get out of there, but I was very moved by the students' display of affection."

After that first time, Gunny started to attend every LHD and Remembering America's Heroes (RAH) related event, and I was very honored that he called me a friend. Over the years I became closer to him and viewed him as another father figure. He was such an amazing man. He would give you the shirt off his back. Everyone who met or knew Gunny loved him, admired him, and respected him.

Gunny has done so much for so many. It's so hard to imagine that he had a reputation of being a bad ass. He was an intense competitive football player, boxer, wrestler, weightlifter, a tough Marine, a tough drill instructor and military police, but he was loved by so many.

Gunny is a living legend in Oregon. My wife and I are so blessed to have known Gunny Brandon. I will always love him. He is a real American Hero.

When I asked Gunny about why he joined the military he told me, "I looked up to and was inspired by my older brother Howard 'Stubby' Brandon. Stubby joined the Marines and was killed on Iwo Jima. I remember my mother crying every night for years over the loss of her son, Stubby."

Gunny was angry that his brother was killed and vowed to join the Marines to avenge Stubby's death, even though the war had ended. His mother forbade him from joining, but Gunny tried to join the Marines on his own. At the time, Gunny was only seventeen, so the Marines told him his mother needed to sign a release form allowing him to join.

He came home and asked his mother to sign the papers, and she cussed him out. "She was so mad I thought she was going to punch me, but I didn't give up pestering her and she eventually signed the papers. Instead of finishing my senior year in high school, I reported for Boot Camp."

Gunny served in the Marine Corps faithfully from 1953 to 1970 and medically retired due to severe wounds suffered while serving in Vietnam. In Vietnam, he served with the 2nd Battalion 4th Marines Fox Company known as the 'Magnificent Bastards'.

This company is famous for the battle of Dai Do, that occurred in the spring of 1968, during which about 400 Marines faced more than 3,000 North Vietnamese Army regulars. Eighty-one Marines were killed, with a large majority of the rest being wounded, including Brandon.

Despite his injuries, a few weeks later, Gunny later returned to the front lines only to be more seriously injured. He spent almost three years in the hospital learning to walk again, and still carried shrapnel from his wounds.

Gunny told me it was gruesome hand to hand fighting. Gunny was later nominated for the Bronze Star because of his heroism during that battle.

While he showed me an old photograph at his home, Gunny told me about this gruesome battle. He told me how, after the battle, he posed for the picture with his foot on the head of a dead Vietcong soldier. Gunny didn't tell me when or where he was ordered to the office of a Colonel, but he did tell me that Colonel stuck a copy of the picture in Gunny's face and yelled, "What the hell is this?"

Gunny shrugged and said, "We do what we do."

The Colonel ripped up Gunny's Bronze Star recommendation letter in his face and yelled, "You will never receive any medals if I have any say over it. Get the hell out of here!"

Gunny told me, "I'm not proud of it, but it happened. We turned into animals out there. I don't know if anyone who wasn't there would ever understand. It's hard for me to understand even after all these years. I don't know why I still keep this picture."

Gunny's tours in Vietnam earned him four Purple Hearts, with the fourth forcing him to an early retirement from the Corps. He told me he was lucky to be alive.

Whenever I walked into Gunny's home, I always felt like I was walking into a Marine Corps Museum. Almost every room was filled with memorabilia, pictures, gifts, plaques, and sculptures. He loved showing his personal museum to people.

One wall was dedicated to honoring his parents, sisters, and brothers. He was given so many amazing gifts such as a life size wooden sculpture of him in Marine Corps dress blues.

Two of the most impressive art works were a life size wooden sculpture of the Famous Flag Raisers photo from Iwo Jima. Each Marine was carved from a separate log. It was built on top of a trailer and Gunny took it to parades and veteran related events.

The second impressive artwork is located at the front of his driveway. It's a life size monument made of medal, iron, and steel re-bars hand made by Gunny himself of the Flag Raisers. Gunny built this as a memorial to his older brother, Stubby.

Sitting down with Gunny was always filled with stories many of which never made it into his book. He gave me permission to write about this story.

"I owned a tavern back in 1980. It was on a country road close to St Paul, a small town out in the country. One afternoon, after running some errands, I returned to my tavern to see two bikers had forced two Mexican men to stand in the corner while the bikers played pool and made the two men buy them beer.

"I approached them and told them to leave. The bikers said, 'Who the hell are you?' And I said, "I own this place.' They both break their pool sticks in half, started walking towards me holding the thicker half of the pool sticks like baseball bats. One of the bikers yelled, "We gonna kick your ass!' So, I pulled out my concealed handgun and ordered them to drop the sticks and get the hell out of here now.

"As they left, one of them says to me, 'You just made a big mistake, we'll be back.' A couple of days later the St. Paul Police called me and tells me that the Oregon State Police just warned them that about fifty bikers from that motorcycle gang were on their way from Portland and were headed to my tavern. They figured they would arrive in about a half hour. They advised me to close my tavern and leave. There would be no police protection because they did not have enough police on duty to deal with the situation and the state police were not going to show up either.

"I closed my tavern, but did not leave, and waited for the bikers."

I asked Gunny "What were you going to do, you were so badly outnumbered?"

"I had six rounds in my gun, and I was prepared to shoot six of the bastards before they got to me. When the biker gang showed up, the two bikers who I kicked out a few days early asked the gang's leader if they could 'beat his ass". Just then, one of the other bikers' steps forward and says, 'Hey this guy's the real deal. He's a bad ass and a Vietnam veteran.'

"The biker leader then looked at me and tells everyone, 'Leave him alone', and then he looks at me and tells me, 'We're going to drink all your beer and destroy your tavern, but you are free to go.' I said, 'I'm not leaving.' For over an hour those bikers drank everything, beer, wine, pop, and ate all the food and broke every chair, table, mirror, sign, window, and door.

"The leader yelled at everyone to stop and asked me, 'How much would it cost to replace everything?' I told him, 'Maybe around $5000.' And you know what he did, he told one of the bikers to write me a check for $5000."

Gunny was visibly upset after he told me that story. He said "I still get angry thinking about that day. I don't respect anyone who gangs up on someone in a fight. I'm old school, where a fight is one on one."

The last couple of years of his life was battling Agent Orange related cancer. He was a tough SOB and in constant pain, but you would never know it. Gunny's cancer had spread throughout his body and there was no longer anything the doctors could do for him. Thankfully, he made it to his eightieth birthday in 2015, and his daughter Jan, who had been staying with him and caring for him, organized a party for him.

A couple months after his birthday she had to put him in a home for veterans in Lebanon, Oregon. When she did this, she called to tell us that it could be any time now as her father was going downhill fast. Before my wife Malinda and I went to visit, Jan told us Gunny now had dementia and he probably would not remember us, but he loved it when someone came to visit as he would start telling stories.

We drove down on a late Saturday afternoon and checked into a local hotel down the street from the veteran's home. It was about 6:30 PM when we decided to drop by to see him, and all the veterans were eating dinner. We approached his table and Gunny looked up and looked shocked. He stated, "Ken, Malinda, wow, I thought I was seeing ghosts." We had a great visit. Malinda sang several songs to him and the other veterans. The entire visit Gunny had the biggest grin. He always got tears in his eyes when Malinda sang a song just for him.

The next day we came back right before lunch. Gunny remembered us again. We were so grateful and blessed. He requested that Malinda sing again. She surprised all the veterans by singing the military hymns. The pride on all of their faces and the tears running down their faces was such an emotional sight.

Military and veteran tradition is that when your branch hymn is played or sung, you stand at attention and sing along. Well, all of these veterans were unable to stand as they all were in wheelchairs.

Gunny however, when Malinda began singing the Marine Corps Hymn, refusing my help, slowly stood up. Once standing, he stood at attention. This old Marine whose body was shutting down, stood tall and was once again a proud Marine. He sang along with such pride and with tears running down his face. It was an awesome emotional moment.

Many, many times in Gunny's life, doctors have said Gunny wouldn't make it through this ordeal or that ordeal, but time and time again he proved them all wrong.

Semper Fi, Marine. I know you're reunited with your amazing wife, Shirley, your parents, your brothers and sisters, fellow Marines, and especially your older brother, your hero "Stubby" Brandon.

Gunny Brandon passed away in January of 2016 from cancer associated with exposure to Agent Orange.

JERRY PERO   Oregon Vietnam Memorial

Jerry and a couple of other Oregon Vietnam veterans were inspired by visiting the Dedication of the Vietnam Memorial 'The Wall' in Washington DC. in 1982. Jerry led the cause and recruited more Vietnam veterans and they all organized, fundraised, and built the Oregon Vietnam Memorial. It was dedicated in 1987.

This beautiful memorial honors Oregonians killed or missing in action during the Vietnam war. Every May, Jerry organized volunteers to power-wash the walls, pull weeds, trim, edge, and spread bark dust a couple of weeks before Memorial Day. For several years, we brought Milwaukie High students to help.

The memorial was Jerry's baby and his dedication to its upkeep was beyond impressive. Ever since 1987, he would go to the memorial once a week to clean the area himself.

Jerry attended the majority of our events since the beginning. He always took pictures with his impressive camera and put them all in a scrapbook, labeling everything, with a copy of the scrapbook always given to me.

He also came to Washington, D.C. with his close friends Ron and Shirley Cannon for my great uncle Frank Buckles' funeral at Arlington National Cemetery. Frank was America's last living WWI veteran whose story is in Volume I. Jerry took many pictures there also and gave me a scrapbook with all the pictures. I'm still incredibly grateful to Jerry.

Jerry refused to talk about his Vietnam experiences to anyone else including his wife, Karen. With the exception being only two other Vietnam Veterans, Ron Cannon, and Mike Goldade, no one knew about Jerry's time in Vietnam. Interestingly enough, both told me this about Jerry without knowing the other had shared with me also.

Jerry only told them that his Marines were overrun and wiped out. Jerry was spared because he was out on a night patrol and came back the next morning to the carnage and destruction. He told them he had to help with the bodies and clean up body parts of deceased Marines. That's all he told them. The Marine Corps kept this quiet, never talked about it, and buried the story. Jerry told Ron, "I'll never complain about anything in my life again."

I couldn't believe this, so Mike told me to search for the Red Beach ambush on the internet, and that I wouldn't find anything. I did and found nothing, so I called Major Mike Howard (A Marine Corps historian) and he told me, "This is an example that can be found in any war, and sadly we will never know the truth."

The only story Jerry told Ron was kind of a humorous one. Because Jerry was the tallest in his platoon, 6' 3" (190 cm), he always carried the radio. It was attached to a backpack frame and had a tall antenna. He tripped and fell feet first in a mud pit and was stuck up to his chest. Nobody saw it happen and when other Marines realized he was missing, Jerry was found and recused right away later only because the tall antenna was sticking up in the air.

Jerry was a great guy who I am proud helped build the Vietnam Memorial in Oregon. I have decided to use Jerry's Obituary written beautifully by his daughters Kari and Tami. Permission granted by Jerry's wife, Karen Pero.

> Jerry Lee Pero passed away peacefully on Oct 8th, 2020. Jerry is survived by his wife Karen Pero, his two daughters Kari Pero (Luke) and Tami Nichols (Josh), sister Judy Jackson (Rick), brother Jim Pero (Santa), many nieces and nephews and countless friends. Jerry was born in Salem, OR, December 16th, 1946, to parents William and Maxine Pero. Right after graduating from North Salem High, he decided to enlist in the Marines; it was 1966 and he was 19. He honorably served his tour of Vietnam from November 1966 until December 1967. By day he was a Remington Raider, and he stresses it was a manual Remington typewriter. By night he was the company's Radio Telephone Operator. In those days, anyone over 6ft tall could almost plan on slugging around a radio.
>
> He survived his tour of Vietnam without a scratch but lost many friends. He was in the Marines until 1968 but was a jarhead forever. This was the beginning of his lifetime of supporting veterans. On Nov 11th of 1982, Jerry and seventy other Oregonians celebrated the dedication of the National Vietnam Veterans Memorial in Washington, DC. After this awe-inspiring event, on the plane ride home, Ben Stanley said to Jerry, "we can do this", build an Oregon Vietnam Veterans Living memorial.
>
> Five Vietnam Veterans and the parents of another Oregonian who was killed in action bought in on the idea. After 5 years to the day, on Nov 11th, 1987, their vision was realized. A living memorial was dedicated for the fallen, not forgotten Vietnam Vets; a place for all to mourn, pay tribute and heal; a site of solace and life.
>
> He dedicated his life to fulfilling the dream of bringing the black granite of the Himalayas to be the Oregon reflection of the wall in Washington, DC. It was more than the names on the wall, it was for the human beings and the family and friends behind those names. Jerry was the driving force of the miraculous effort to

accomplish this in stone, pathways, landscaping, a bridge and a fountain. He spent most of his free time at the memorial maintaining her beauty, picking up the cigarette butts, making that granite shine, and just being there to support any veteran that needed someone. Jerry was a humanitarian, patriot, Vietnam vet, a soldier's soldier, generous, philanthropist, family historian, photographer, world traveler. He was humble, selfless, a great man with visions he always brought to life. He was never without his camera around his neck, "there will be two flashes" was the warning you got before you were immortalized in one of the hundreds of albums he created. If he met you once, you were a friend, and he was always there for anyone that needed it. There wasn't a "geedunk" (snack stand) that he didn't visit, and God forbid there was something healthy that would give you "scabies."

He served as vice president of the Vietnam Veterans of Oregon Memorial Fund's (VVOMF) board of directors during the construction years and served as president since the Memorial's dedication in 1987. From 1984-92, Jerry was on the Governor's advisory committee for the Oregon Department of Veterans' Affairs. From 2011-2013 he volunteered with Meals on Wheels, serving hundreds of meals to those in need until he was physically unable to drive.

What he could not fix in life, he secured with duct tape. We will remember his smile, his laugh, his crazy erratic dancing, his incessant picture taking, constant snacking. He was a husband, father, friend, neat guy, our "number one." We will honor Jerry's love for life by celebrating his in the most bodacious way. He made us all smile! And his smile will remain with us forever. Welcome home Jerry – WELCOME HOME!

Jerry Pero passed away in October of 2020 from Agent Orange related exposure.

ROBERT DELSI

Mescalero Apache
Purple Heart

Robert is a Mescalero Apache and Purple Heart Marine. He was one of 111 Native-American Veterans from 33 different tribes and eight different states I brought to Oregon in 2008. This was special because most had never been honored before off their reservations.

Robert and his wife Jossi were from Arizona and were both heavily involved honoring veterans not only in Arizona but around the U.S. They would ride their motorcycle with other Vietnam Veterans to Washington DC every Memorial Day.

During our Assembly of Honor in MHS's Gym, we would always have music and singers perform hits from WWII, Korean War, and the Vietnam War.

One year, we decided to do a rousing encore at the end being a 1960's hit 'Oh Happy Day'. It was an upbeat, positive, and fun Gospel song, and everyone loved it and even the majority of high school students joined in and sang. Afterwards, several performers asked if we noticed the one Native-American Veteran sobbing uncontrollably. I didn't think anything of it because many veterans cried during our Assembly of Honors.

We thought nothing about it until the next February, when the Delsi's invited us to their annual Ira Hayes Memorial Days on the Hilo River Reservation. Ira Hays was a Pima Native American and Marine who was one of the six flag raisers on Iwo Jima in the iconic photograph during World War II.

Robert and his wife Jossi were the major organizers of this impressive event which included a parade, Pow Wow, and banquet, honoring veterans and especially remembering Ira Hayes. I met Ira's brother there, and it was an honor.

Our first evening there in the hotel lobby, Robert pulls me aside and tells me he has something he needs to share. He said, "Last November at MHS we didn't get an opportunity to say goodbye or thank you in person because we had to rush to the airport to catch our plane home. Remember when you guys sang 'Oh Happy Day'?"

I replied, "Yes, that was fun."

Robert gets tears in his eyes and says, "Well, I just lost it and caused quite a commotion around me. I've never been able to talk about this until recently with my therapist, so bear with me if I get emotional. When you all sang that song, it was conformation from the creator that everything was going to be alright.

"My buddy and I were trapped in a small hole created by artillery fire in a rice patty. It was night, pouring down rain, The rest of our platoon had made it back to better cover in the trees, but we were both wounded and were stranded in the middle of this intense fire fight.

"I was scared to death and yelled let's pray. I just kept saying over and over 'Oh Happy Day, When Jesus walks.' I don't know why, but that's all that kept coming out. Next thing I remember is waking up in a hospital ship.

"The nurse comes in and greets me and says, 'Welcome back.' When she leaves, she turns on the radio. The song that was playing was 'Oh Happy Day.' I start crying because that was confirmation that I was going to be okay.

"The last time I heard that song was forty years ago, and then you guys sang it in the high school gym. Well, I've been dealing with some rough times with my PTSD lately and this again was conformation that everything was going to be okay. You have no idea how healing that experience was and has been for me, Ken. Thank you."

Wow, I was stunned and in awe. I knew this was something I needed to tell others about. That November of 2010, we put on a huge Tribute to Veterans. I decided to end the show with Robert's story and bring him up on stage to join everyone to sing it. It was very emotional.

Robert and his lovely wife Jossi have come up every year to talk to high school students, and Robert has become a very good, passionate speaker. He loves the Marine Corps and is always wearing something with a Marine Corps Eagle, Globe, and Anchor on it. He tells me every time he leaves to go back home, "Ken, speaking to the students every year is so healing for me. Every time I leave, I feel better. Thanks."

Every greeting or goodbye with Robert was with a hug. Robert's main way of healing was his hobby, where he creates colored beads and rock necklaces with a special meaning. Whenever he gave a necklace to a Marine Vietnam veteran, there would be the colors for the Vietnam War and an Eagle, Globe, and Anchor on it, and he would explain what every part of the necklace represented. He would step back and salute them. It was very impressive and always emotional. He was a great guy!

Robert Delsi passed away in March of 2018 from illness associated with exposure to Agent Orange.

JOHN STOFIEL

I met John as he attended many of the LHDs years ago. He has been heavily involved with Oregon's Marine Corps League for years.

"I was born in Oregon City on November 24, 1941, two weeks before Pearl Harbor," John always told everyone with pride. "I'm one of six brothers who served: four served during WWII, two as Marines, and two in the Army. Another brother, Tom, served during the Vietnam War in the Air Force.

"I was attending Benson High School and a counselor asked me not to come back to school. I was not a good person, skipped school a lot, so I dropped out as a junior at sixteen years of age.

"After I turned seventeen, I went downtown to the recruiting office to join the Air Force, but the recruiter told me I did not qualify. Walking down the long hall, I noticed a recruiter dressed in dress blues in the Marine's office. Man, he looked sharp and impressive. I joined but needed to get my parents' signature.

"My father always wanted me out of the house, so he forced my crying mother to sign the document. It was February 12, 1959, and two days later was sent to RTO San Diego.

"The very first moment I got off the bus and was ordered to stand on the yellow footsteps, I was in shock. All the yelling and screaming. All I could think of was, 'What the hell did I get myself into?' On the second day my DI (drill instructor) put his hands on my shoulders, and I knocked them off. I was triple teamed and taken down by three DIs.

"I just reacted, as I came from a very physically and verbally abusive home. I was used to defending myself and I had serious anger issues. I was then sent to a thirty-day motivational platoon, and after completing it was assigned a new platoon and lasted only two weeks this time and was sent back to the motivational platoon again.

"I was shocked that they didn't just kick me out, but they never gave up on me. It was demoralizing watching my first platoon graduate. That motivated me and soon my DI put me in charge as a platoon leader. After six months, I finally graduated from boot camp.

"After infantry training, I was stationed in Okinawa, and in 1960, we were sent to Laos. They were talking about making a landing there, but after three days, we were sent back to Okinawa.

"One of my big thrills was being in the Color Guard leading a big parade for President Eisenhower. I was close enough to really get a good look when he drove right by us.

"For some reason, the Marines thought I would make a good DI, so I spent three years in Bremerton, Washington for DI training. In 1965, I became a Drill Instructor and that was the best four years of my life.

"What was the best was taking boys from all walks of life, long-haired hippies, taking them from zeros and making them into hard charging Marines.

"I learned where the boots would sneak off to vent, so I would go hear what they had to say and they would pay for it the next day, laughing. After a while I needed a change, or I was afraid of doing something stupid and ending up in jail.

"I was given a new job for three months when I was promoted to Platoon Sergeant and ordered to Vietnam in March of '69. I was assigned to a platoon in the 1st Marine Division. The CO was happy to have me. He said to me, 'I love former DIs as you are better at keeping the men in line.' So, I told him, 'I'm not a DI anymore and I'm taking care of my men.'

"We patrolled and did security for an ammo dump south of Da Nang. I was shocked how bad morale and drugs had become. I decided to just throw away the drugs and try to help clean up some of my Marines. Twice I was almost killed by my own men because they were high on drugs.

"One night, a sergeant who is higher than a kite was shooting rounds into a friendly village. I walk towards him, and he starts shooting at me but hitting the dirt in front of my feet. Now, he's an expert shot, and I know he could put a round between my eyes, so I figure he is not going to really shoot me.

"It was surreal, I was walking in a haze. It was just me and him. I grabbed his rifle and beat the hell out of him. My company commander was watching the whole time. I got angry at him, yelling, 'You did nothing!' Two months later, I'm called in and told that I cannot be given any positive recognition for helping one of our own.

"The second time, a machine gunner didn't show up for inspection. I call him and he starts cussing me out. I could tell he was high on drugs. I walk across a bridge to him and with an M1, he fires a burst over my head. Luckily, I reached him while he is trying to put a new clip in and took him down. Two LTs were with me before I walked across that short bridge, but one ran into a bunker and the other hit the dirt.

"After that I was told they were sending me back to the states as they had learned I was on a hit list (Friendly Fire). It was twenty days early, and I try to tell them that they got some big problems that need to be dealt with. I'm yelled at, 'We don't have a drug problem or a race problem.' I angrily responded 'Bullshit, we do!'

"I'm ordered to the Marine Corps headquarters in Quantico, Virginia. Had to move my family. I get there, they don't know why I'm there and there is no job for me. I spent the next three weeks calling in everyday and sightseeing all the history in Washington DC area.

"I was then ordered to take a new pilot class with fifty of us and no getting out of it called Company Gunny NCO training. It is a standard class today, and helpful for Marines even today. Spent thirty days evaluating returning Vietnam veterans.

"But it all started getting too political, and I wanted out. I was transferred to on old Navy prison used for WWII Italian POWs in Norfolk, Virginia, and became the Corrections supervisor.

"I married my high school sweetheart and next-door neighbor, while in Bremerton, and we had two girls while in San Diego. My wife was pretty upset when I was ordered to Vietnam. She told me I came back a different person and just thought the whole world was screwed up. We had a third daughter while in Virginia. Our marriage lasted twenty-four years."

I asked him, "How were you treated when you came home."

"I flew into protected environments, military bases, no protests, but they did order us to wear civilians' clothes and not our uniforms.

"I had a good career, ups and downs, and I regret not staying in for thirty years instead of twenty. But I made that decision while standing in a hot and humid jungle during a downpour and realized I was back where I had started twenty years earlier as a private and nothing had changed.

"I said, 'I'm done.' I was then told, because I was just promoted to First Sergeant, I had two more years of commitment, and they would have to demote me. I told them on the spot, 'I want my kids to go to one school, live in the same house. Demote me back to 'Gunny.'"

John Stofiel is still living at the age of 80.

JAY LILLIE

Milwaukie HS Class of '58,
US Marine Corps

The principal during my high school years was Jay's father, Jerry Lillie. I did not meet Jay until our first Living History Days. Interviewing Jay was special for me as I learned some details about his father and some Milwaukie history also.

In the late 1920s, Jay's father Jerry was all-PIL (Portland Interscholastic League) in football, basketball, baseball, and track. He also shot a 76 at East Moreland Golf Club at the PIL Golf Championships. Jerry was a three-year letterman guard on the University of Oregon Football team. His college basketball career ended after his freshman year at the University of Oregon when his right shoulder was badly hurt while being towed on a sled behind a Model T during a snowstorm.

Jerry became a high school teacher and coached football, basketball, and track. At Grant High School in Portland, Oregon, he coached over 200 football players with only one assistant coach. Grant High School, under Jerry's coaching, won the first statewide football championship in 1943.

Art Jackson, one of Jerry's football players would earn the Medal of Honor at Peleliu during WWII (Art is in Volume I). Another player, Jerry's starting quarterback, was Japanese American and was interned at the Expo Center in Portland. Jay told me that his dad went down there and tried to get the authorities to let him out. But of course, he was unsuccessful.

Jerry was inducted into the PIL's Hall of Fame as first a player and then a coach after his retirement. Including all the schools Jerry Lillie worked at, he coached football for twenty-two years. He finished his career as the principal of Milwaukie High School for twenty-one years.

Jay Lillie, Colonel, USMC, retired, was born in 1940 in Portland, Oregon. The family moved around quite a bit until his father accepted a job at Milwaukie High School and moved the Lillie family into the Milwaukie High School attendance area.

Jay (MHS Class of '58) played varsity football and golf. Jay says, "I was short, slow, and not very good. I was a second stringer on both team sports, but we had fantastic teams. I caddied at Waverly Country Club as a teenager, got hooked on golf and became pretty good. My sophomore and junior year at Milwaukie, we were Golf State Champions. Five out of my seven teammates became professional golfers."

Jay continued, "Scholastically, I struggled due to my dyslexia. I couldn't read until the fifth grade. Dad got me a tutor and the first book I ever read was *Thirty Seconds Over Tokyo*. I struggled with reading in high school, and as graduation approached, I knew I was not ready for college.

"I had friends who were part of the Marine Reserves during high school. They were allowed to wear their dress blues to school and be a part of our annual 'Gold Star Assembly.' They looked impressive to me, so this and all the John Wayne WW II movies I watched influenced my decision to join the Marine Corps after my high school graduation.

"I went to boot camp in San Diego in the fall of 1958. After boot camp and basic infantry training, I returned to Portland as part of the Marine Corps Reserve unit at Swan Island from '59 to '65."

In the fall of 1959, Jay enrolled at the University of Oregon and made the freshman football team. The quarterback was Tom Smythe, later to be a highly successful Oregon high school football coach. Jay explained, "I never told my parents until a couple of days before our Freshman Civil War game at Multnomah Stadium against OSU that I was playing football.

"Too much time in the gym and too little studying contributed to my poor grades at U of O, so I transferred to Clark Junior College and then to Portland State University (PSU). I was a walk on to the football team at PSU, coached by the legendary Tom DeSylvia. My first year at PSU, I was the second-string quarterback and on all special teams. My last two years, I started at outside linebacker. I was on the golf team for three years as well at PSU!"

I replied to Jay, "Wow, you were a late developer just like me."

Jay laughs, "Yes! I majored in education and history to follow in my father's footsteps, but half-way through student teaching, I quit. It was not for me. I received my college degree in '65. At that time, the Marine Corps offered me the opportunity to go active duty and become an officer with an aviation specialty. Becoming a pilot sounded like an adventure to me and off I went to Officers' Candidate School in Quantico, Virginia."

I asked, "So, when were you sent to Vietnam?"

Jay responded, "In '66, the Marine Corps badly needed pilots. Usually, it takes eighteen months to earn your wings starting first with six months of the Basic for officers, then on to Flight School. Due to the increasing need for pilots, pilots were sent directly to flight training after Officer Candidate School.

"We were rushed through training, and I received my pilot's wings in fifteen months. After training, I was assigned to the Black Sheep Squadron flying A-4s in southern California. We did everything we could to get flight hours, often flying older planes that had been returned from Vietnam.

"After about a hundred hours of flight time in the A-4 aircraft, I was sent to Chu Lai, South Vietnam, in September of 1967. I was one of only two Lieutenants assigned to VMA-311's 'Tom Cats' squadron.

"We flew close air support for Marine Corps ground troops located near Chu Lai, covering about 150 miles of South Vietnam from the sea in the east, to the Laotian border in the west and the DMZ (demilitarized zone) to the north. We also attacked sections of the Ho Chi Min Trail in Laos."

Jay continued, "After a couple of months in country and dozens of missions, I became a section leader. This means I was in charge of the two-airplane flight, which included leading the takeoff, deciding how to attack the target, and communicating with the controlling agencies during the flight and the attack. After I was a two-plane section leader on missions for about four months, I became a division leader for a flight of four or more planes."

I, of course, asked, "Was it dangerous?"

Jay replied, "I often felt guilty because it was mostly pretty safe compared to being an infantry officer on the ground in Vietnam. We flew fast in the target areas and so were more difficult to be hit by enemy fire. We did still lose some aircraft and pilots to enemy fire and pilot mistakes."

Jay continued, "I flew daily missions, one to two per day, seven days a week. However, the tempo of operations dramatically increased in January of '68 when the north Vietnamese began the Tet Offensive. All hell broke loose as all major bases and towns throughout south Vietnam were attacked.

"For example, the 9th Marine Regiment at Khe Sanh was surrounded and it was feared it would be a massacre like the French disaster at Dien Bien Phu in '54. Hundreds of planes from all services flew in support of the Marines at Khe Sanh. There were so many planes in the air, it was an awesome sight, but dangerous.

"With so many aircraft, mid-air collisions were possible. I flew at least a dozen flights during this battle over Khe Sanh. Two of my squadron's A-4 aircraft were shot down. We were lucky in that one pilot ejected over Khe Sanh and landed within the perimeter, the other was picked up in the jungle by a helicopter and flown to Khe Sanh. Both pilots were returned to Chu Lai within forty-eight hours with only minor injuries.

"At the same time, we were supporting the battle for Hue City, a historic cultural and religious center of Vietnam. Originally, we were prohibited from bombing certain historical sites, which included Hue City and its Citadel.

"When the US forces learned that the Viet Cong and the North Vietnamese Army, who had occupied the town and the Citadel, were rounding up and executing the town leaders, including the mayor, business owners, teachers, doctors, and their families, many of these restrictions on artillery and bombing were lifted.

"The old walled city of Hue was called the Citadel. This massive old complex of buildings had a surrounding wall thirty feet thick, and the main entrance had huge double doors that were estimated to be four feet thick. On one of my missions, I was directed to fire five-inch Zuni rockets to blow out these entrance doors. I fired a total of eight rockets at the target and was told it was a successful breach."

Jay paused, and I assumed he was done, so I asked him when he was sent home.

He answered, "No, following the Tet Offensive, I was ordered to be a FAC (Forward Air Controller) attached to a Marine battalion on the ground. We went out on patrols on foot for five months. On one of our patrols in the mountains, we walked single file with six hundred Marines and the jungle canopy was so thick, helicopters couldn't see us to resupply.

"We started running out of water and food. We came to a blown-up area that was open, and I informed the commander it would be a good helicopter resupply point. Only water supplies were brought in, because the commander refused to stop marching long enough for both a food and water delivery. He allowed the troops to slow down to fill their canteens.

"Fortunately, the Corps had just started making freeze dried rations available as a choice in place of canned C rations. Many of us had chosen the freeze-dried rations and had some left We grabbed the water to use to make meals with the freeze-dried rations. That night we added the water to the packets and ate. The commander did not carry rations and refused to eat any of ours," Jay laughed.

"But we had a great surprise, included with the water drop was mail. That evening when we stopped, my friend, the other air controller, was in a hammock swinging, eating, and reading his mail.

He noticed I didn't receive any mail and said, 'Here Jay, read my mail.' I read aloud, 'Dear Tom, I had lunch with your father the other day, and he didn't know anything about what you were doing over there. Even I can't get any information from the Pentagon. Nobody tells me anything. Please stay safe. Signed, General Omar Bradley.'

"We're out in the middle of nowhere, so I read the second letter. The same, 'I had lunch with your father. Hope you are well and stay safe. Signed, Charles Lindbergh.'" Jay explained, "My friend's dad turned out to be the Vice-President of Pan American Airlines and a member of an exclusive New York City club."

Jay continued, "So the next day out in the middle of nowhere, we came upon a quickly abandoned North Vietnamese hospital. We spent the rest of the day sifting through what was left at the hospital for intelligence.

"The next morning, we had to climb down a ridge, in line, abreast; it took twelve hours crawling all the way to get to the bottom. We then waded across a shallow river. The water felt cold even though it was hot outside and over ninety percent humidity.

"We continued on, moving through very tall elephant grass. This was nerve-wracking as you couldn't see anything in front of you. The grass was over our heads, sharp enough to cut through our uniforms and had to be pushed aside with every step.

"Next, we crossed an abandoned rice paddy as it was getting dark. The mosquitoes were ferocious, and I had to wrap a towel around my face to sleep. Three weeks later dozens of the battalion came down with malaria, including the Commanding Officer, due to these mosquitoes.

"The next day we marched past a reservoir. It was a great opportunity to clean up, and take a bath, but that ended quickly as snipers began firing at us."

"Was anyone hit?" I asked.

Jay replied, "No, luckily. When we finally got back to base, I was ordered to clean up, given two meals, and ordered back out the next night. Crossing a moonlit rice paddy at night, a firefight started, and we were sitting ducks. The company about a thousand yards behind us was hit hard.

"They called in artillery support from a south Vietnamese unit that overshot their position the first time, fell too short the second time, and landed right on top of them the third time. It was a disaster, and every officer was killed. The highest-ranking survivor was a Staff Sergeant."

Jay stopped talking, so I asked, "When did you go back home?"

He responded, "Well, my original tour was from September of '67 to October of '68, thirteen months. I didn't feel right about going home then, so I extended my time in country for six more months to return to my squadron and fly more missions. I finally went home in May of '69.

"I got home just in time to play in PSU's Alumni Football Game! After my leave, I was sent to Texas to be a Navy and Marine Corps flight instructor. My goal was to be an airline pilot, but the airlines were downsizing. Many pilots rejoined the military or did not leave the military.

"In 1972, I was assigned to retrain as a helicopter pilot. I went to Camp Pendleton to fly Hueys. They were desperate for helicopter pilots as most did not want to go back to Vietnam. My assignment officer was grateful because I never complained about having to move to helicopters from jets. I was given a good job as the operations officer of a helicopter squadron, and I didn't even know how to fly one yet!

"While at Camp Pendleton, I played on the base tackle football team, and we won the West Coast Championship. I was thirty-two years old. I was sent back to Vietnam in November of '72. I was stationed on an LHA (helicopter support ship) off the coast of Vietnam.

"The war was winding down, and the peace agreement was signed in late January of '73. My unit was sent to Okinawa, Japan, to finish our overseas tour. In December of '73, I returned to the US. I had the opportunity to return to flying jets, and due to my experience in both jets and helicopters, was assigned to the new AV-8A Harrier.

"The Harrier was unique in that it could take off and land like a helicopter but fly like a jet. I flew the Harrier for fifteen years. I was able to be a Squadron commander, a Group commander, attend National War college, and fly with over twenty different squadrons.

"I remained in Corps until I retired in '91, returning to Milwaukie and buying my parents' home. It's great to be part of the same community that I grew up in. I am now over eighty and still enjoy life."

Jay Lillie is still living at the age of 81.

ED CONTRERAS   Father,
AARON CONTRERAS   Son, Iraq Helicopter Pilot KIA

Ed was born in Texas in November of 1945, and his family moved to San Jose California. He was a star halfback for his high school football team and graduated in '63. He has been married to Rosie, his high school sweetheart, for over fifty-five years.

I started by asking him why he joined the Marines.

"While working at a local clothing store, I would go for walks during my lunch break. One day, I noticed this impressive Marine Corps recruiting poster on a store window. The Marine on the poster was wearing Dress Blues, and they had the best-looking uniforms. So, I walked to the recruiting station and signed up. I was sent to Boot Camp in January of '64."
"When did you marry Rosie?"

"In March of '65, and then I was sent to Vietnam the same year and Rosie gave birth to our first son. I would not get to see him until I got back home a few weeks before his first birthday."

"What do you feel comfortable about talking about your experience in Vietnam?" I asked next.

47

"It's incredible how much I've blocked out. I do remember Operation Starlight was my first combat experience when I was with the 7th Marines attached to the 3rd Marine Division."

"Oh, I need to back up and tell you about the trip over by ship. The ship was the USS Alamo, and every night the only movies we were allowed to watch was every movie ever made about the Alamo. *The Man from the Alamo* was by far the dumbest of them all," he said laughing.

"Did you get seasick?" I asked.

"I usually got sick every time I went fishing out on the ocean in a smaller boat, but not on this trip. We even hit part of a Typhoon. It was so rough, even sailors got sick. But I didn't. We were confined to hammocks below. Hammocks were stacked and mine was the fourth highest, and I remember it swung wildly the whole storm.

"But, back to Vietnam. Whenever I try to remember, my anxiety comes back bad. I do remember trying to sleep in an old cemetery once and watching tracers during the night. There is one very vivid incident that I cannot get out of my mind.

"I was part of a helicopter support team, and we were in a fire fight out in jungle. After it was all over, we radioed for helicopters to come evacuate the wounded and KIA's. I helped pick up a body bag at one end and while loading it into the helicopter, I saw blood all over my hand and arm. It shocked me, and I dropped him. It haunts me to this day, and I have never forgiven myself."

There was a pause, so I asked, "Do you have any funny stories?"

"Oh, there are lots of those, but the one that stands out for me was when we were assigned to guard the perimeter of a LST (Landing Ship, Tank) that was unloading supplies. We were hit and immediately the LST closes its doors and pulls up the ramp.

48

"Well, the ship's captain was on shore and screaming at the ship in colorful cuss words to open the doors back up. There was no way that was going to happen. We all just laughed afterwards."

"When did you go home?"

"Just back from another operation, a Sergeant told me I was eligible for R&R in Australia, then come back to Vietnam or be transferred back to the states. It didn't take me long to make that decision," he said laughing

"Were you greeted with protestors?"

"Yes, they were around. We flew into El Toro, and they told us to wear our civilian clothes."

"You get out of the Marines, and you have five boys. Did you give up trying to have a girl?"

"Yes, five was enough. Rosie raised six boys, laughing. Two of my boys followed my footsteps and served in the Marine Corps."

"I would like to include your second son, Aaron, in your section. He played football for an old coaching friend of mine at Sherwood High School, and they were tough. Could you tell me about him?"

"Aaron was a team leader, All-League at running back and linebacker, state playoffs every year. Aaron played basketball, baseball, and was a student body officer. He wanted to fly, so he attended and graduated from Embry–Riddle Aeronautical University. He met his wife there also. The Marines wanted him to join and be a pilot. He flew all kinds of planes and Huey Helicopters.

"At thirty-one years of age, my son, Capt. Aaron Contreras, a father of three, was killed in action on April 1, 2003, when his helicopter went down while conducting combat operations in Iraq. In 2004, Sherwood High School renamed their football stadium The Aaron J. Contreras Memorial Stadium.

"Rosie and I were very moved when we went to Miramar air base. Many of the Marines who served with him and worked with him approached us and said, 'Captain Aaron Contreras was as fine a man we have ever known. He was highly respected and highly thought of.' It meant a lot to us."

"My wife Malinda and I have run into you a couple times at Willamette National Cemetery on Memorial Day Weekends. How often do you visit your son's grave?"

"Many times, a year. In fact, once a year, all of our sons and families will go there together. One lives in Washington and the other lives in California. His brothers always leave pizza, a hamburger, and a milkshake on his grave."

"Anything else you want remembered in your section?"

"Yes, my wife deserves a medal as she had to deal with me. She was so strong and helped me get through everything."

Ed Contreras is still living at the age of 76. He is an Agent Orange related cancer survivor.

JOHN HAYS SR.

I met John Sr. back in 1982 when my first wife and stepsons moved to Milwaukie. John Sr. lived next door with his son John Jr., and daughters Chris and Debbie. All three were my students at Milwaukie High School, and all were great kids. I also coached John Jr. in football. He was a hell of a quarterback and basketball player who went on to play football at Taft College.

John Sr. was a great guy, and still is. I reconnected with him after he read Volume I and called me. It was during our first phone conversation that he told me he was a Marine and served in Vietnam. He agreed to tell me his story for this Volume.

"I was born on the family farm in Enterprise, Oregon. Dad was the store manager for Safeway in the '20s and '30s. Mom was from Unity, Oregon and was a stay-at-home mom. I had one sister and three other brothers. I learned to work growing up on the farm. In high school I played football, basketball, track, and baseball."

"Why did you join the Marines?"

"Well, I really looked up to my older cousin, Robert Hays, who was a Marine during WWII and the Korean War. I joined mostly because of him, but I wanted to be in a branch that was elite like the Marines. Also, there is nothing much to do in Enterprise. On the night of high school graduation in '60, I took the bus to Seattle to join, and was flown to San Diego the next day.

"After boot camp, my MOS (Military Occupational Specialties) was Combat Engineering, and I was shipped to Okinawa. I was on the rifle team and competed and placed in several Far-East shooting contests. I was a good shot as I grew up on a farm and knew how to shoot a rifle."

John was another easy interview as he kept telling me his story with no pauses. "After four months, twenty Marines were picked and ordered to pack all gear and write our home address on a sea bag. I was one of the twenty. I was a little nervous as we were not told where we were going.

"First, we were sent to Japan and assigned to the 50th Sea Bees, then shipped to the Philippines, and finally on to Vietnam. We were the first Marines in Da Nang, and it was '61. We were there to build an airstrip. We laid down heavy rubber matting which was eventually paved over.

"At first, no ammo was issued to us, but we all did guard duty. We finally were issued ammo after being fired upon by snipers. It was intense there as the North Vietnamese and South Vietnamese were fighting. It was hard to tell who was who. We put trip wire out there which gave us a heads up. Even then somehow, they would sneak in at night and steal supplies.

"After we left Vietnam, we spent the next seventy-eight days on a destroyer, sailing back and forth in the South China Sea. It was hot and miserable. Everybody getting on everybody's nerves. At that time, I didn't realize how important our presence in the South China Sea was to our Allies. There was a lot of classified stuff happening all the time.

"I get sent back to Camp Pendleton and signed up for another year because I wanted to be an Embassy guard. I was sent to the DC area; the State Department Embassy School at Henderson Hall in Virginia. It was located right next to Arlington National Cemetery. We were taught how to do everything even how to eat," he said laughing.

"I was supposed to be sent to Russia, but it took two and half months to get my orders. So, in November of '62, I'm sent to our Embassy in Paris, France. Our job was to secure the buildings at night, and check all offices, and gave out citations to office workers who left anything, such as papers, on desks.

"While there I was picked to be assigned as a bodyguard for President Kennedy's trip to Mexico. I was in charge of guarding Jackie and the kids when they went sight-seeing. President Kennedy was a great guy, always checking on me and asking if I needed anything. After Mexico, I'm back in Paris, and started working with the C.I.A. to track down Americans who were smuggling drugs into France.

"I was picked to be on Honor Guard for the 20th Anniversary of D-Day at Normandy. It was quite an honor, lots of dignitaries, and the French President Charles de Gaulle.

"This next story I'm going to tell you, I truly thought I was going to die. I was flown down to Algeria by myself to close down our embassy as they were going through political upheaval after the armed insurrection and war against the French colonists.

"I had a diplomatic passport and someone from the American Embassy was supposed to greet me at the airport with the proper clearance papers. Well, he forgot. I was arrested at the airport and locked up in a closet room, stripped naked, and beaten badly from Friday afternoon until Monday morning. It was rough, I really thought I was going to die there.

"I was accused of being a spy and was there to assassinate President Ahmed Ben Bella. On Monday, someone at the embassy asked where I was and after some phone calls learned I was being detained at the airport. They raced down there and got me released. They told me, 'Keep this quiet, and man, you are lucky they didn't kill you.' It was quite a mess down there, and I was the last one to get on the plane to leave."

"Wow, that's something else. Did you do the job you were sent there to do?"

"Yes, we had to destroy almost everything, even melting down file cabinets.

"Then it was back to Paris for almost three years, played quarterback on the Marines football team, traveled, and played all over Europe. But I separated my shoulder and was sent to Camp Lejeune for surgery. I wanted to re-up, but the Marine discouraged me due to my injury.

"There is still a lot of stuff I can't talk about. I'll never forget having to raise the American flag early in the morning in front of thousands of protesters with only the fence separating us. The French police were amazing though, they always had our back. A police whistle would blow, then many police would attack the crowd with their batons, another whistle, and a second group of police would attack, and so on. The crowd would disperse quickly. They didn't mess around in France.

"But I'll never forget when I was working late at night at a desk at NATO in France. It was November 22, 1963, and I received a call telling me that President Kennedy had been shot and had died and that I must tell the American Ambassador immediately. This news really shook me up, but I walk down the long hallway and tell him the bad news and he responds angrily, 'That fucking Johnson(Vice President)!' You know there were lots of theories out there.

"Have I told you about my grandson, Staff Sergeant Anthony Massingale He is a Drill Instructor at Camp Pendleton. He taught classes and his class earned the highest scores in USMC history. He's also won the 'Dan Daily Award' (Dan Daily is one of seven Marines to receive the Medal of Honor Twice), 'The Band of Brothers Award,' and the 'Top DI of the quarter award.'"

"Any last thoughts on your time in the Marine Corps?"

"I really enjoyed being in the Marines. I never felt like I was alone and always kept my nose clean, you know, probably the small town up bringing, where everybody knows you. In Paris, the apartment we stayed in was five blocks from the Eifel Tower.

"We worked seven days on and seven days off, so I traveled all over Europe. Drove everywhere and stayed at Marine housing for free. It was amazing! Years later, I attended several Embassy guard reunions in the states."

During our interview, I learned that John Sr. was good friends with Bill Schonely, Marines, Korean War Era, Voice of the Portland Trail Blazers, story in Volume II, and also Harry Glickman, the founder of the Portland Trail Blazers.

John Hays is still living at the age of 79.

CHARLES PERSON   Freedom Rider

Several years ago, I talked to Charles over the phone, wanting to bring him to Oregon and join us in talking to high school students. While he was interested, it never worked out, and then the Covid years hit. Then, while in Atlanta with my wife for her Aunt's funeral in November of '21, I was able to visit Charles and his lovely wife and interview him.

Charles was the youngest Freedom Rider on the Congress of Racial Equality (CORE) Freedom Ride. At the time, he was a math and physics student wanting to become a scientist. As a freshman at Morehouse College, he became active in the civil rights movement by joining the Atlanta Committee on Appeal for Human Rights. He was also a member of on the CORE Freedom Ride, and wrote a book about his experiences called: *Buses Are a Comin': Memoir of a Freedom Rider.*

It was in his freshman year at Morehouse College in Atlanta, Georgia, when he and two other classmates were inspired by four A&T College students in Greensboro, North Carolina who sat at a segregated Woolworth's lunch counter and tried to order food.

55

Their plan was to avoid arrest by leaving the establishments when the owners called the police. However Charles felt the protests were not enough and he refused to leave. He was arrested and received a sixteen-day jail sentence, including ten days in solitary confinement.

Soon after, he was asked to apply for the first Freedom Ride being organized in Washington DC. He was accepted and began non-violent protest training. Then in May of '61, Charles, with nine other men and women, boarded two public buses headed for New Orleans, to test the Supreme Court's recent decision forbidding segregation in bus depots, restaurants, and restrooms.

The two buses were confronted violently by police and mobs of whites. One bus was met by a white mob in Anniston, Alabama. The mob attacked the bus with baseball bats and iron pipes. The local police were indifferent to the attack and arrived after. They then escorted the bus and abandoned them at the city limits. Again, the mob pulled riders off the bus and beat them with pipes, then set the bus on fire.

Future Congressman John Lewis, who was severely beaten, was among them. "An angry mob came out of nowhere, hundreds of people, with bricks and balls, chains," Lewis recalled. It drew international attention and became a pivotal moment in the civil rights movement.

Though he wasn't on the bus that caught on fire in Anniston, Alabama, Person didn't come out of the journey unscathed. He told me, 'I experienced nightmares some men only see in war. There were burning vehicles with the doors held shut while people burned inside. I saw mobs of people looking for people to lynch."

If you want to learn more about this historical event, I highly recommend reading his book *Buses Are a Comin': Memoir of a Freedom Rider*. It is unbelievable, shocking, disturbing, and inspiring.

I knew he was an Original Freedom Rider and a Vietnam veteran, and I had one huge question. "Why did you join the Military after you just got the hell beat out of you by the KKK?"

"That's a great question. I've never been asked that before. Well, being from Atlanta, Georgia, and being involved with the first Freedom Ride, my life was in danger. I had lied to my mother about where I was the whole time and when I came home, my distraught mother told me the only way to save my life was to join the military.

So, I went to the recruiting station first to join the Army. The Army was recruiting Blacks for potential West Point prospects, but as a black man, you could not get a Congressional appointment in Georgia. I had good grades in high school, so they had me take their test, and I the passed the test with flying colors.

"But I never went back. I was to be a Marine. My cousin, Morris Booker, was in the Marines, and he convinced me to join just weeks after the KKK in Birmingham, Alabama had almost beaten me to death. I reported for boot camp that July of '61.

"I was always spit and polish. I was the first to be promoted to Corporal. Twenty years and retired as a First Lieutenant. The Marines were good for me, and I was good for the Marines.

"I knew about their discipline and loved it. There were very few blacks as commissioned officers, and I felt I could be one. I wanted to fly, but my eyesight wasn't quite good enough.

"I was a good shot too! That kind of stuff was easy for me because my grandfather taught all the boys in the family how to shoot early. He said because he had a reason, but he never told us why. He had grew up the first generation out of slavery. And he used to say, 'Never again,' but he made sure all the boys in the family. We could shoot, and we could shoot well.

"The Marine Corps bootcamp was like typical Marine boot camp. My DI, he liked me because I could shoot. But when he found out I had the highest IQ in the platoon, he tried to force me out. He tried to do kind of things to try to make me quit, but he should have known I was not a quitter, because of my Freedom Ride experience. I was fearless now and as an NCO, I was always calm. Don't ask me why, I just was.

"So, after he realized he was not going to force me out, when we got close to the end of training, they messed with my rifle. I was shooting 48, 49s from the 500-yard line. You don't know that, but you are shooting at a 25 inch target from 500 yards and to put eight or nine in the black from 500 yards is good shooting."

"How were you treated in the Marines?"

"I had no problems, even in Vietnam. I had no problems, even with southern boys who hung confederate flags everywhere. I remember that many of the Marines hated the Puerto Ricans, especially when they spoke Spanish.

"I was the first in my family to go to Vietnam, my cousin was the second to go, and then my brother, Jimmy. We were all sent to Vietnam in a three-year period. My brother would never talk about it."

"Tell me about Vietnam."

"We were sent to Chu Lie in May of '65. It was a little fishing village. There was nothing there. We rebuilt the city, airfield, and the hospital. We had no interpreters, so they asked us who took foreign language classes in high school. I took French and three other Marines had taken French in high school also. The four of us were ordered the learn Vietnamese. We tried.

"The food was terrible. At first, we had 1950 sea rations from the Korean War. After about a month, we got new rations.

"I had a job. I was a peaceful warrior. I was an Electronic Technician. One job was to save lives repairing mine detectors. We never lost a man while I was there. My second job was to repair sniper scopes and the thermal images for the Marines' two-man sniper teams. I've always had mixed emotions about that.

"My first time going out in the jungle," Charles laughs, "I was so scared. I asked for a flamethrower because I felt I would be safer but was given a shotgun."

"Can you talk about your experiences?"

"Well Ken, this last May was the 60th anniversary of the first Freedom Ride. I wrote my book. Have been interviewed many times about it. All of the nightmares have returned. As for those Vietnam memories, I just can't talk about it yet."

"Tell me about your father."

"My dad, Hugh, served in the Army during WWII in the European Theater and loved to tell me how after the war, while stationed in Germany, German kids would ask him if it was true the black people had tails like a dog.

"When he came home, he was able to use his G.I. Bill for education only. Back then in the south, Blacks could not use the G.I. Bill for home loans. He worked two jobs, seventeen hours a day. He was a hard worker. Died at 66 years old.

"My mother, Ruby, married my father at eighteen, and I was born when he was overseas. She worked in a factory that assembled hand grenades during the war.

"I attended David T. Howard, where Dr. Martin Luther King and Vernon Jordon attended. I was small and fast, 5'6" 126 lbs. (167cm 57kg). At first, I was a pitcher and had a wicked curve ball. Started at catcher on the varsity baseball team. Batted over .400, and I could bunt well.

"We won the championship my senior year. My cousin was a hell of a pitcher and was drafted by Houston but joined the Army. He lost his hand in Vietnam, and it was reattached, but never the same. His baseball career was over. He did get a signing bonus though."

"What else can you tell me about Vietnam?"

"For several years, I have had serious health issues with my kidney all related to Agent Orange. The VA (Veterans Affairs) has been no help. My brother died of Agent Orange lung cancer and my cousin died of Agent Orange pancreatic cancer. Did you know that Aussies Vietnam veterans and South Korean Vietnam veterans are dying of Agent Orange Cancers too?

"My close friend and fellow Freedom Rider, Henry Thomas (Army, Vietnam, Medic, Purple Heart). We are the only living of the thirteen original Freedom Riders. Years ago, Henry went back to Vietnam and met with many Vietnamese people and former enemies. All forgave him and treated him with such great hospitality. He told me, "I've never been treated like that in Georgia."

"How were you treated when coming home?"

"When I got back to Atlanta, still in my uniform, I was refused service at a restaurant. Just wanted to order a hamburger. But I don't know if it was because I was wearing a uniform or being Black. Stationed in Texarkana, Texas, I was instructor to help the Vietnamese Refugees who had settled there. There was no animosity towards military or veterans there."

"Any last comments on being a Marine?"

"The Marine Corps, I loved it," laughing, "I was first stationed at Gitmo (Guantanamo Bay), during the Cuban Missile Crisis and ended my career, retired while stationed at Gitmo. There were a lot of great people in the Marines. I got an education and met many different people from all walks of life. I loved my jobs while serving."

Charles Person is still living at the age of 79.

LOREN CORPUZ — Marines Vietnam Era

Loren and his amazing wife Rebecca Corpuz have never missed any of our events and have become good friends. For many years, Rebecca has baked pies and sold them to help raise money for Remembering America's Heroes (RAH) annual Living History Days. They both are always very supportive and I'm very grateful.

Loren plays every Military anthem with his trumpet at every veteran related event. It's always a beautiful touch that all the veterans really appreciate. I recently asked him when he started playing the bugle.

"I played a little in school but didn't play for years until the family of a good friend of mine, a Vietnam veteran, committed suicide, and they asked me to play at his funeral. The priest told them he could not have a military funeral because he committed a sin by taking his life. I've been playing ever since."

In 2019, I surprised Loren with a special gift at our annual Welcoming Dinner for the out-of-state veterans. The previous summer, he told me that his uncle was a WWI veteran, who was in the Marine Corps and was wounded at Belleau Wood. His uncle had committed suicide at 75 as a result of his PTSD. Loren told me, "He told my mom that he missed their mother too much."

The surprise was that years ago, a former student-athlete of mine who had served in the Marine Corps, was stationed at the American Embassy in France gave me a small glass jar filled with dirt from Belleau Wood.

"So, I had a plaque made with his uncle's name on it "Harry Harper, US Marine Corps, WWI, Belleau Wood, Purple Heart, LEST WE FORGET." During the program, I presented Loren the jar filled with dirt from Belleau Wood battlefield with the plaque. It was an emotional moment.

Loren grew up in Yakama and was born July 5, 1943. "I played football and baseball and boxed. Everyone thought I was a good boxer, but I was no Sugar Ray Leonard. My dad, Max Sr., was a good boxer, but my mom hated it. She wouldn't let Max Jr. box, so I never told her I boxed," he told me laughing.

"I graduated in '61 and tried college and working but didn't like it. My older brother Max Jr. joined the Marines in '55, and I had no choice but to join the Marines. All my family were Marines, but I always wanted to be a Marine because my Uncle Al Lane was also a Marine. He fought in WWII and the Korean War. He was a Chosin Few. He really inspired me.

"Max called our mother and told her to tell me 'Not to join the Marines because it's not easy. That made me mad, so I joined the Marines. I reported for boot camp in January of '63. Right away I asked myself, 'What did I get myself into?'"

"Were the DI's still physical with the boots then?"

"Oh, yes. I was slammed against the wall a couple of times. I saw some guys getting hit because they didn't like following orders.

"After boot camp and then infantry training, I earned high scores and was sent to Army Mechanic School at Fort Sill, Oklahoma, for wheel and track school. I worked on tanks and self-propelled howitzers.

"I was then stationed at 29 Palms (Marine Corps Air Ground Combat Center) for the rest of my service and was expecting to be sent to Vietnam, but never was. I was processed and had to fill out insurance forms. I was lucky, but I was not opposed to going. I got out in '69 but was put into the reserves because of the war still going on.

"When flying home, we were told not to wear our uniforms, but to wear our civies. But the airline tickets were cheaper when wearing a uniform, so, I wore my uniform home and was greeted by protesters yelling 'baby killers!' and spit at. I was pissed, and thank God someone yelled to me, 'Don't touch them.'"

Loren is still living at the age of 78, and his brother Max is still living at the age of 83.

VIC GANUELAS SR.   Yakama

Vic and his lovely wife, Christine, have attended several of our events going back to the '90s.

I was born on November 3, 1937, in Toppenish, Washington. My dad, Steve, was a farmer, and my mom, Blanch, was a homemaker. Mine was a broken family, and I left my parents' home at fourteen. Worked in the fields to make money. I stayed with friends and relatives and attended Toppenish High School my freshman and sophomore years.

"The principal wanted to expel me, so I moved in with an aunt in Torrance, California for my junior and senior years. She offered me a place to stay, but I'm required to get a job to help out and go to school too.

"I was able to play basketball for North High School. My senior year during Christmas break, I came back to visit, but I had no money to go back to California. I dropped out and would have been the Class of '55. I talked my cousin into to joining the Marines.

"I served mostly the Cold War era. After serving in the Marines, I joined the active reserves. Joining the Marines was the best thing that ever happened to me, and I enjoyed it the majority of my time. The only disappointing experience was when they asked us to take a test to be promoted to Sergeant. Only four of us passed."

Vic shakes his head and looks away with a disappointed look on his face. "But I did get my GED (Graduate Equivalency Degree) in the Marines though.

"I've tried to help our Vietnam veterans who experienced the horrors of combat. I've always felt bad for them. In 1990, the Yakama Nation, led by Secretary Joe Jay Pinkham, created an all-Native Healing Camp for Native Veterans. It was named Camp Chaparral and built on sacred ground. The camp provides a unique and positive experience which includes our traditional healing ways."

I can help support our combat veterans but can never relate to what they all went through. We were able to get my good friend, Vietnam veteran Steve Kinsey, to the camp. He was struggling so bad he even contemplated killing himself and went so far as to putting a loaded pistol in his mouth. This really helped Steve. He is a changed man.

One week of help and therapy with Native traditional ways helped him more than the VA could! We also wanted to teach the VA how to treat Native American veterans, and we believe this can help all veterans. Steve came to Milwaukie High School with us years ago, and it was very healing for him. He told me, "Those Milwaukie students put on quite a program."

One of the Yakama Warriors' great memories was meeting and spending time visiting Frank Buckles (America's Last WWI veteran, Volume I), who took pictures with him, and they made him an honorary Yakama Warrior and presented him with a Yakama Warriors pin.

I told him, "Do you know that Uncle Frank put that pin on his jacket and wore it all the time? He received hundreds of gifts, pins, and challenge coins, but told me the Yakama Warrior pin meant the most to him."

Vic continued, "Ken, you must have a guardian spirit watching over you. No words can describe my admiration for what you've done for our veterans."

I told him, "Sir, recognizing and honoring veterans has been one of the great blessings of my life. I'm so grateful to you all."

"Anything else you would like to tell me?" I asked.

"My wife Christine and I have been married since 1959 and have five children, three boys, two girls. One son is named Vic Jr. and I didn't want a Junior, but my wife overruled me. Vic Jr. was in the Army; a Grenada veteran, and he has some issues from that experience. He went to the recruiting station to sign up for Marines, but they were not there, and the Army talked him into joining."

Vic Ganuelas Sr. is still living at the age of 84.

RENE GARCIA   Purple Heart

I first met Rene when he attended our 1998 Living History Day at Milwaukie High School. He stood out as a dashing, sharp looking gentleman, wearing all black. He had on beautiful black cowboy boots, black slacks, and a black dress shirt with a Marine Corps tie, and to top it off he wore an impressive looking black cowboy hat. Walking up to me to shake my hand, with a huge grin, he said, "So you're Ken Buckles. Thanks for all you do for all us veterans. It means a lot to us."

Rene attended all of our LHDs at Milwaukie, and I lost track of him when he retired from the VA and moved. I tracked him down in January of 2020. I called him and asked if I could interview him and include him the book. He responded, "Of course."

Meeting him in person became out of the question because of the quarantine from the Covid virus spreading around the world. So in April, I called and asked when the best time would be to call to set an appointment to interview him over the phone. "Let's do it now," he quickly responded with a firm tone.

"I was born in Asherton, Texas, and as a child my parents moved to San Antonio, where I attended a Catholic School. In the fifth grade, they moved me up a grade saying I was too smart. I was not happy about it.

"I dropped out of high school at sixteen years of age. Told my father I wanted to go out to California to visit relatives and find work. But I never told him or anyone else, I was going to join the Marines."

"How did you pull that off at sixteen?"

66

"My older brother had passed away, so I forged all my documents with his name, Raoul. It worked for three weeks of boot camp. I didn't know they did background checks.

"Boy, were they pissed. They threatened to lock me up and it scared the hell out of me. At the airport, as I got out of the Marine Corps car, one of the sergeants yelled at me, 'If we find out you tell anyone what you did, we'll come back to get you and put you in front of a firing squad.' I flew home and went back to high school. My dad picked me up at the airport and never said one word."

"So, why the Marines?"

"My grandfather served with the Marines during WWI, and my father served in the Marines during WWII and the Korean War."

"Wow, where did they serve?"

"I have no idea. They never talked about it, and I was instructed to never bring it up. After a few days, my dad told me, 'You know the Marines own you now, and will come get you when you graduate from high school?' I told him I changed my mind about being a Marine. He said I had no choice, and he started making me get up at 5:00 AM every morning to run and do PT (physical training).

"I graduated in '66 and called the Marine Corps recruiting office, and the next day, they sent two Marines to pick me up. As I got into the car, I asked where are you taking me? The Sergeant yelled, 'Get in the car and shut up! It's none of your business!' They drove me to Lubbock, Texas for a physical, which I passed, and then flew to California for boot camp."

"So, how did that go because you had to start over, right?"

"Yes, and it was hell the first few weeks. My Drill Instructor was all over me, 'Why did you run away from Boot Camp after three weeks? Are you a quitter? Are you a pussy?' Then he started in on me, 'You are liar, aren't you?' and, 'Did you lie about your age?' I did so many 'no Sir, yes Sirs,' I couldn't win," he said laughing.

"How soon were you sent to Vietnam?"

"I was sent to recon training with the 2nd Force Recon in North Carolina for basic and then six more weeks of training after that. We did so much jumping, running, and ground troop training. What's funny is I was so naïve, I actually thought recon was going to be an easy relaxing assignment.

"It was scary. We were not allowed to talk, go to the PX, and no bars. But we became a very tight knit group. The last night before we shipped out, we were allowed to go to the E-Club and drink. I was drunk after two beers."

"You were sent to Vietnam in '67. Is there anything you would like readers to know about your experience?"

"NO!" he quickly responded with a raised voice. "And I'll tell you why.

"When I came back home, I had a rough time. Lots of drinking and fighting, trying to keep jobs. Once as a bouncer someone attacked me from behind, and I went crazy. I thought he was the enemy, and I was trying to kill him. The bartender told me to get out of there as the police were on their way.

"I was told the next day that the guy I beat up was in the hospital with a broken jaw, broken ribs, and a broken arm. And the police were looking for me, so I never went back.

"Another time, I was driving home after work and some guy cuts me off and flipped me off. He turned into a gas station, and I followed him. This big guy gets out of his car and starts walking to me. He sees a Marine sticker on my car and a disabled veteran on my license plate. He yells, 'Oh, you're one of those stupid Jarheads?'

"Trying to keep my cool, I said, 'Hey, I was doing sixty. Why you so impatient?' He kept coming towards me and yells, 'Bring it on!' and then takes a big swing at me. I ducked and punched him in the solar plex. He went down and was having a hard time breathing. I stood over him and called him a big pussy. One of the gas station workers told me to leave as they had called the police.

"There are more stories, but you get the point. Anyway, I started going to the VA in Vancouver, Washington for help and was put into a support group with several other Vietnam veterans. I had never told anybody anything before and only feel safe opening up to my fellow veterans.

"Once we all decided to go swimming at the Lewis River after a session. One of our buddies gets up on a large rock and yells, 'I can't take it anymore, goodbye.' He pulls out a handgun and shoots himself in the head. I yelled out, "Call a medevac now!" not even thinking that they don't exist. I ran for over mile down this dirt road in my flip flops till I found a home. I frantically begged to use their phone to call for help. It didn't matter as my buddy died instantly."

Rene did not pause while talking. It was if he had planned to get this all off his chest with me. All I said was "I'm so sorry."

He kept talking "I don't remember how soon, but shortly after that, we all gathered at one of the other veterans in our group's home. We were sitting out on his patio drinking beer. He worked for the VA helping other veterans and his wife was a nurse at the VA. Three times he tells us, 'I can't do this anymore.' We get upset with him and try to calm him down.

"It seemed to work, but about twenty minutes later, he gets up and says, 'I'll be right back, gotta use the bathroom.' After about twenty to thirty minutes, I get up to check on him. I knock on the door several times and yell out his name, but no response. I tell his wife that I'm going to kick the door in. He had hung himself. What a shock."

"Damn, Mr. Garcia, I'm so sorry." I asked him if he knew about my fathers' suicide and that it was the driving force to honor all you veterans?

"I didn't know," he responded, after which I began telling him a very quick version of my father's death.

Rene interrupted me towards the end, "Sorry, but there's more.

"Not long after that, I reconnected with my captain. He saved my life. His helicopter he was flying was shot down and he was badly wounded and was paralyzed from the waist down. I used to go to his house for a few drinks to catch up. I helped put him to bed. I called him on a regular basis just to check on him.

"He was pressured by the VA to talk to another veteran about PTSD, but because he didn't personally know any of them, Captain declined. They threatened him if he didn't follow up. Days later, I called to check on him, he had hung himself on his wedding anniversary.

"I was devastated and went out to my car and grabbed my 45. My father came outside and sat next to me on the porch and said, 'Is the enemy attacking?' 'No,' I snapped back. 'Then why in the hell the gun?' I told him, 'Can't do it anymore.'

He said, 'Son, I don't want to know what you went through. I've had to deal with my memories too, and it's been really tough. I even thought about ending it all many times in the past, but what saved me was my mother's advice. She told me, 'Whenever you have bad thoughts start saying, 'Our Father who art in Heaven,' and trust in the Lord.'

"My dad and my grandmother's words saved my life."

"I'm so sorry Mr. Garcia, I don't know what to say. I feel as if I picked a painful scab off you. Please forgive me."

"Ken, I'm doing better these days. You know I worked for the VA and retired from there. I still have my moments, but my horses helped me a lot. I do woodworking every day, staying busy helps. My uncle was a pilot in Vietnam and was shot down. We call each other and help each other when needed. So, that's it. No more to say."

Rene Garcia is still living at the age of 74.

MIKE GOLDADE

I have known Mike for over twenty years as he attended a lot of our LHDs and other events. I was able to sit down with Mike after seeing him for about six years. We were finally able to reconnect at the Oregon Vietnam Veterans Memorial's first meeting since the Covid outbreak.

"Please tell me about your mother and father."

"My mother, Marlene was a stay-at-home mom and was heavily involved with our neighborhood's stay-at-home mothers, organizing all kinds of events. My dad, Arthur, was a Navy WWII veteran who started out as a boiler maker and then served as a boiler tender on two different destroyers. They sailed from New York to England, protecting ship transports from German U-Boats in the Atlantic."

"Did he ever talk about any of those experiences?"

"No, he only talked about the horrible storms in the Atlantic."

"So where were you born?"

"I was born on April 15, 1949, in Eugene, Oregon, but we moved, and I grew up in West Linn. I played two years of football, basketball, and three years of baseball. Oh, my grandfather, John, and his brother Steve (Chief of West Linn Police for twenty-five years) helped the community to build West Linn High School's first grandstands. That football field was always a muddy pit."

"I remember that field well. It was in horrible shape every October whenever it rained a lot."

"I did not graduate with my class in '67 due to illness in my sophomore year and again in my junior year. I was four credits short in the spring of '67. For whatever reason, I was unable to do any 'make up' classes or test my way through. I was told that I could walk at graduation and then attend summer school to earn the necessary credits.

"But a buddy of mine, Mike Garrett, had graduated early in California and was living with his dad, Major Don Garrett, in my neighborhood. He talked me into joining the Marines with him. His dad was a Korean War Marine and Ex-POW.

"Mike told me that his father had been tortured with hot knives stuck in his neck. Anyway, I never did get my high school diploma. I earned my GED while in the Corps in '69 and eventually my Bachelor's in social science in '84 from Portland State.

"Anyway, we reported to bootcamp in September and while still in training in January of '68, the Tet Offensive starts. In February of '68, the 27th Marines are sent to Da Nang. As we were landing, I could see the explosions out in the countryside. I remember getting off the plane and the smell and the heat. And right next to the airfield was a dump, and it was horrible.

"We were stationed about fifteen to twenty miles out of Da Nang. I was a M60 machine gunner. We had day and night patrols from February through April. Only some firefights, found lots of boobytraps though. In May, the Marines decided to start downsizing, and I was sent the 27th back home."

"Wow, you got to go home quicker than most."

"Not me, I'm transferred to 2nd Battalion, 5th Marines. The 5th Marines were hit hard during Tet, not much left when I got there, they were at about half strength. We did lots of day and night patrols.

"I'm at Hotel 2/5 (Hotel Company 2nd Battalion, 5th Marine Regiment) and volunteer for what was called Combined Action Patrols and had to complete a three-week school for this. In Quan Tri Providence, in small units out in the field, we would go into villages in a last gasp effort to win the hearts and minds of the local Vietnamese. We were called Roving CAPs (Combined Action Platoons doing counterinsurgency) and would bring medical supplies and more to the villagers, just trying to build relationships.

"The most memorable incident was the two times we were assigned to a security detail to escort some corpsmen into a leper camp or village. Apparently, the VC were afraid to go near people with leprosy.

"In November, monsoon season begins, and we could not go out much. It is bad. I get a skin disease all over my upper body. It hurts and I can only wear a T-shirt. The doctor who treats me is a WWII veteran, and after three weeks, he sends me home. I left on December 19, 1968. First, I get treatment in Guam for a week, then flown to Washington for a month at the Naval Hospital in Bremerton."

"How were you treated when you came back home?"

73

"Luckily, I never landed in a public airport, so I avoided protesters. Of course, I didn't like what was happening to other veterans. In fact, I was going to enroll at Portland State, but after the Violent anti-war protests on the campus, I changed my mind. I just didn't want to be around that, so I attended Clackamas Community College instead. Just kept to myself, kept my head down, just took care of business.

"I went to McIver Park for Vortex (inspired by the concert at Woodstock) to see what it was all about. Because the American Legion was having their National Reunion in Portland in August, the Governor of Oregon, Tom McCall, helped organize with state funds to attract the protesters to Vortex. And it worked. There were no problems in downtown Portland. I had nothing to do with the drugs and alcohol though," Mike laughs.

I responded, "I remember our Milwaukie High School head football coach, Erv Garrison, told the team during daily doubles, 'If we find out that anyone of you goes to Vortex, you will be dismissed from the team.'" We both laughed. "Anyway, I met Jerry Pero through a neighbor, after we both learned we were Vietnam Veterans. Seventy-nine of us went to the dedication of the Vietnam Memorial Wall in Washington D.C. On plane back home we all talked about building a Memorial in Oregon.

"Two days after the D.C. trip, Jerry asked me to help him. We formed a Non-profit in 1983. Robert Hunter, who was in the Army, was our first president. Doug Bomarito was our second President. Jerry Pero was our third President until he passed away in October 2020. We did a fundraising walk in downtown Portland and even Senator Ron Wyden joined us. Can't believe I'm the last original board member that is active."

"Any last comments, Mike?"

"I have no regrets at all as it led to us building this wonderful memorial."

Mike Goldade is still living at the age of 71.

GEORGE WINSLOW

I've known George for many years as he attended many of our Living History Days and traveled with us to many high schools around Oregon. The charter bus trips were a great time with all of the veterans and their spouses. "It sure was great when all us veterans got together years ago, especially the out-of-town trips," George said.

At every event, George was prepared and shared a lot of pictures from his time in Vietnam. Before I could even ask a question, he started talking.

"Ken, I joined the Marines three days after President Kennedy was assassinated. He really inspired me. I was nineteen years old. I was a '62 graduate of Grant High School in Portland. I was working at the old downtown Meier & Frank Store. Every summer I worked at my sister's and brother in law's ranch in Eastern Washington.

"My dad, Arthur 'Bud' Winslow, worked with the Army Corps of Engineers and helped build the Bonneville Dam. My mother, Wilamine, was a stay-at-home mom.

"I quit working at Meier & Frank and went to work at the ranch in the spring of '63 through the summer of '63. I never planned on staying, and I always felt like an intruder."

"Why did you join the Marines?"

"I picked the Marines because a good friend, Barry Seietz, joined and served with the 9th in Vietnam. I also read the book *Battle Cry* and watched the old black and white movie version. I was gung-ho to be a Marine. So, in November of 1963, I joined the Marines.

"After boot camp at MCRD in San Diego (Marine Corps Recruit Depot), I was sent to infantry training at Camp Pendleton. Man, that was harder than boot camp. My MOS was heavy artillery training, and I spent my first year at 29 Palms. We learned that the top brass knew we were all going to be sent to Vietnam, but we were never told.

"But I'm sent to Kodiak Naval Air Station in Alaska for one year. While there, I became good friends with Bob Ringler. He earned the Silver Star posthumously; he was twenty years old when killed in action in Vietnam."

I asked him if when he went to the Wall dedication if he saw his name.

"Yes, and I've got a picture of it too. After Kodiak, I was rotated to Camp Lejeune, then in the summer of '66 to Guantanamo Bay, Cuba.

"I'm sent back to Camp Lejeune, and I'm a happy short timer. I'm assigned help out at the rifle range. You have to qualify once a year in Marines. I was a Corporal and worked the Charlie Range up and down the line checking on Marines.

"Then I receive new orders assigned to 3rd Battery, and we're going to Vietnam. I was sent to the 3rd to be in a M55 8-inch Self-Propelled Howitzer, with walls so thin a bullet can go through it. I had the capability to fire nuclear rounds. Thirty of us were sent to nuclear school for a week. The FBI even went to Eastern Washington to ask farmers about me.

"On the day I left for Vietnam, my cousin, Joe Rivers, an Air Force officer, stationed at Travis Air Base, spent the day with me, and we said goodbye at the airport. We both had tears in our eyes. I thought he is the last relative I might ever see again. I was twenty-two when I was sent to Vietnam, and I could read the writing on the wall.

"We went to Chu Lai and checked in with the Battery. We were at Nuc mon 2nd Platoon Firebase supporting the Marine infantry. It seemed like we were shooting all the time, every night. Then, every morning we had to clean the gun. It was tough dirty work, and no sleeping in," George laughs.

"I sever the tip of my thumb while working on the gun. A Corpsman just sewed it up. One of my toes becomes infected, and I'm sent to Chu Lia Air Base for the infection, and here I am next to wounded Marines. I felt really guilty being there as many of these wounded Marines were pretty shot up, and here I am with only an infected toe."

"Ken, have you heard of Priest Capodanno? He was a Navy Chaplain assigned to the Marines."

"No, I haven't."

"He was well loved by us Marines. He talked to me for a while and all of the wounded too. And two days later, he delivers to me two big boxes of cookies from a grade school in the states. Asked me to write a thank you letter."

After talking to George, I did some research on Chaplain Capodanno and learned that his battalion was taking casualties and about to be overrun. The chaplain, unarmed, ran to the wounded and dying Marines, helping and comforting them and giving last rites. He was first wounded in the hand, arms and legs and refused medical evacuation. He then ran on to the battlefield where he was killed. He was trying to help a seriously wounded Navy corpsman and two wounded Marines only a few yards from an enemy machine gun.

Returning to George: "I was sent back and soon after, the whole 1st Marine Division is moved to Da Nang. We moved our howitzers at night on LSTs and sailed to Da Nang to Hoi An Firebase.

"There was lots of artillery there. We shot all the time. All around us was NVA (North Vietnamese Army) and the grunts had to go on ambush patrols daily. One was ambushed and lost over half their men.

"In August, we start getting rocket attacks on three separate occasions. My Staff Sergeant was Oliver Jones, twelve years in the Marine Corps, and this was his second tour. I was Jones' assistant. We worked all night on repairing a blown engine. Jones decides to get some sleep in our tent about fifteen yards away. Parked between our howitzer and our tent is a two-and-a-half-ton truck.

"Later we heard Chinese made rockets coming in and the tent gets a direct hit. The truck shields the shrapnel from us, but Sergeant Jones is killed." George pauses and gets tears in his eyes and looks away. He turns back to me and says, "I still have survivor's guilt."

"Sorry to hear that." And then after a long pause I ask, "Could you tell me about coming back home."

"Coming home, we landed at night at El Toro MCAS (Marine Corps Air Station) and was lucky, no protesters, but I was very mad about that happening.

"Back home, I went to get my taxes done at H&R Block. The tax person asked in a sarcastic tone, 'Why didn't you pay any taxes in '67?' I told him, 'I was in Vietnam.' He responded with a very condescending, 'Ohh.'

"In 1982, Jerry Pero organized a group of Oregon Vietnam veterans to go to the dedication of the Vietnam Memorial Wall in Washington D.C. A total of seventy-nine of us went. It was a trip of a lifetime. The camaraderie was awesome. Just being around thousands of other Vietnam veterans was very special. After that, our group from Oregon was inspired and organized to fundraise and build Oregon's Vietnam memorial up at Washington Park next to the Zoo."

George then reminded me that he had worked with my father. "I worked for Pacific Northwest Bell Telephone for thirty-one years and worked on a CWA (Communication's Workers of America) committee with your father. We sat side by side at many meetings and neither of us knew we were Marines. I also had met the two fellow employees, Hug Hughes and Jim Orrell (Both WWII veterans). They worked with your father at the Milwaukie Barn."

"I forgot about that! My dad was best friends with both of them and all three worked together for many years."

"My only regret was I should have stayed in the Marines. But I passed the physical and joined the Air Force Reserve at forty years of age. I served in the Air Force Reserve from 1985 to 2004."

"How have you dealt with the memories?"

"Well, physically my hearing was damaged as those Howitzers are extremely loud. I've used hearing aids for a while now. I finally turned to the VA for help. For years I've dealt with my PTSD at the VA's Vet Center. We have group meetings that have been very helpful.

"But when we pulled out of Afghanistan it triggered angry memories of 1975. I was angry all over again.

"Ken, I want you to know, I savor every day of my life, because I always think about those who never made it back home. I'm blessed."

George Winslow is still living at the age of 77.

ARMY

> I am an American Soldier.
> I am a warrior and a member of a team.
> I serve the people of the United States, and live the Army Values.
> I will always place the mission first.
> I will never accept defeat.
> I will never quit.
> I will never leave a fallen comrade.
> I am disciplined, physically and mentally tough,
> trained and proficient in my warrior tasks and drills.
> I always maintain my arms, my equipment and myself.
> I am an expert, and I am a professional.
> I stand ready to deploy, engage, and destroy, the enemies of the
> United States of America in close combat.
> I am a guardian of freedom and the American way of life.
> I am an American Soldier.
>
> ~Soldier's Creed

MAJ GEN RAYMOND F. REES   Oregon National Guard
Adjutant General for Oregon

Even with his very busy schedule, Major General Rees attended a Living History Day and was a keynote speaker at the first Oregon Military Hall of Fame induction ceremony in 2007. After he and his wife moved back to Oregon, with the help of his good friend Lt. Gen. Russell Davis, Gen Rees was a keynote speaker for us again in 2019 at the Night of Honor Dinner with over three hundred veterans. I knew that he was a Vietnam veteran, and I'm grateful he agreed to be interviewed for this section.

"I was born September 29, 1944, in Pendleton, in eastern Oregon. My family lived on a farm near Helix, Oregon. It was a very small town. I attended Griswold High School, graduating in the Class of 1962. Enrollment at the high school was around 40 students, and my graduating class was just seven students.

"My Dad, Raymond Emmet Rees, was a farmer and served as a county commissioner. He married his high school sweetheart, Lorna Gemmell, my mom. She was so smart, she skipped a grade, went to college, and was a teacher for many years.

"An interesting side note, she had five brothers who served during WWII. The oldest was a counter-intelligence investigator for the FBI. One served in the Army Air Corps, B-24s in the South Pacific, another two served as Marines in the Central Pacific. I know one of them fought on Peleliu. The Baby brother was in the Glider Infantry just as the war ended."

I asked, "Did attending a small high school hurt you academically while attending West Point?"

"No!" It was a firm and immediate response. "Attending such a small high school was really a blessing because the classroom sizes were all so small, you got lots of individual attention. It really prepared me for college. Also, because it was so small, I played football, basketball, track, participated in school plays, and even played in the junior high band."

"How did West Point happen?"

"Back then I had to take a Civil Service exam as well as the SAT, etc. It was a very competitive process. I received a West Point appointment from Congressman Al Ullman."

"I know that it is mandatory to be involved in sports at West Point. What did you do?" I asked.

"Yes, that's correct. For those cadets not competing for Army's Division I sports, the rest were required to compete in the intramural sports and that included mandatory practices with upper class coaches.

"It was all extremely competitive. I ran intramural cross country and orienteering, which was map and compass competitive running. I was also on the water polo team and ran the 880-yard race during track season.

"The entire four years there was very demanding and challenging. It was a very broad education with heavy emphasis on math and engineering. There were a wide variety of fields to go into. It was a fantastic education. I know many who after their military service obligation became doctors, lawyers, engineers, and many had master's degrees in wide ranging fields.

"I graduated with the Class of '66 and was commissioned as a Second Lieutenant and then completed Airborne and Ranger training. We all figured we were going to Vietnam as the summer of '65 was the beginning of the buildup. Many of our instructors had been over there as advisors.

"I chose a Cavalry career for my field and was assigned as a platoon leader with the 2nd Squadron, 2nd Armored Cavalry Regiment assigned to West Germany. We conducted patrols along the West German and East German border. I was then sent to Panama for jungle warfare training in November of 1968.

"From there I was assigned to Vietnam to a Reconnaissance squadron with 101st Airborne, which had a great history, and pride, a real Esprit de Corps. I was fortunate to go there. The 1st Cavalry was so successful as an airmobile division that the 101st was converted into that same model. My unit was 2nd Squadron, 17th Cavalry.

"We operated with I Corps in South Vietnam. Our operations were from the South China Sea to Laos to the DMZ," laughing that it was called the DMZ. "Typically, our AERO scouts (aeronautics) would find the enemy. Our squadron would then air assault our ground recon platoons in the area. I commanded Troop D, The ground recon troop of the squadron."

"How were you treated returning home?" I asked.

"I never experienced anything as I was lucky. We continued to serve at military bases such as Fort Bragg and Fort Knox. But I was very aware it was happening. It really perturbed me." Major General Rees' tone of voice changed to one of disgust.

"First of all, I have the utmost respect for the individual soldier, I don't care if he was a volunteer or drafted. Back then they were just discharged into civilian life, society, and most were not prepared for it.

"While in law school, I just kept it all to myself. It was not worth going down that road. I just kept my opinions to myself. But I stifled my feelings over the years. I still have strong emotions."

General Rees sounded upset while telling me this, "Being called 'baby killers.' That's the furthest from the truth. The sacrifices so many made, especially those who perished, that it speaks ill of our society. I knew many, many great guys, top notch, which did not deserve such treatment."

After Vietnam, General Rees served with distinction with several impressive assignments. He even earned a Juris Doctor degree at the University of Oregon Law School in 1976, graduated from the US Army Command and General Staff College and the US Army War College.

Through his career as The Adjutant General for State of Oregon National Guard for seventeen years is how I met him. In all my years of meeting any veteran, men and women who served under General Rees one hundred percent of them had nothing but praise, respect, and admiration. Even veterans who never served under him respected General Rees.

General Rees finished his amazing career as the Deputy Assistant Secretary of the Army (Manpower Reserve Affairs) for Training, Readiness and Mobilization. He retired for good in 2019 and moved back to Eastern Oregon with his wife, Mary Len. "It was easy moving back to eastern Oregon. First, my great-grandfather homesteaded there. I'm a fourth generation and I'm very loyal to the area. I love it here."

"Please tell me about your good friend Lieutenant General Russell Davis whose story is in the Air Force section."

"In many respects, Russ was a pioneer, he took advantage of every opportunity, and his capabilities were so great. He served at the highest levels and never shirked from any responsibilities. He always exceeded expectations. We met at an Annual Winter meeting in DC when he was the Air Guard Commander for Washington DC. He always greeted us at the airport every time we came there. We became close friends and our wives too."

Two days after interviewing General Rees, he called me and told me, "I'd like to include remembering five of my men who were killed in action during the war. I've made it a point to remember them during my career and life and I will remember them for the rest of my life.

"We all owe a debt of gratitude to those who sacrificed their lives while serving our country. When I was in command of Delta Troop, 2nd Squadron, 17th Calvary for the 101st Airborne, I lost five men who were a microcosm of the US. They came from around the country, different ethnicities, and backgrounds."

"Four of them were killed in a firefight on the Laotian border engaged with NVA regulars. Staff Sergeant Raymond Torres was a regular and Mexican American from the Rio Grande Valley in Texas, Specialist Joseph Stockbauer from Missouri was planning on becoming a priest.

"He was opposed to the war but joined and chose to be a front-line medic. He was German American. PFC William Bobo, he was a big, strong, and young black man from Ohio. Pfc Santos Rivera, Porto Rican and a native of New York City. They bravely performed their duty sacrificing their lives regardless of being a draftee or a volunteer.

"Then we lost Staff Sergeant Harry Yingling. He was Pennsylvania Dutch and what we called a Shake 'n Bake NCO, or a 90-Day Wonder. He was willing to lead and received accelerated promotion. His service in Vietnam was very short. He was killed by a trail watcher. They were North Vietnamese who were the warning system for the NVA. Harry volunteered to walk point and was ambushed."

"Did you look up their names on the Wall in D.C?"

After a short pause and with emotion in his answer he said, "Yes."

On May 27, 2022, General Rees joined us with other veterans to speak to the almost two thousand students at Hermiston High School in Eastern Oregon. He gave a powerful speech where he told the students all about his five men. He ended his speech with, "For me personally, every day is Memorial Day. I remember my men every day. Please remember them on this Memorial Day also."

Major General Raymond Frederick Rees is settled, but still active in life on his 2,200-acre wheat and barley farm at the age of 77.

TERRY PIESTEWA   Hopi

Joining us in 2008 was Terry and Percy Piestewa and their daughter Lori's children, Brandon and Carla. Lori Piestewa was a member of the Hopi tribe. She was the first Native American woman to die in combat while serving in the US military and the first woman in the US military killed in the Iraq War. She was honored by the state of Arizona by naming the second highest peak in her honor. Her death also led to a joint prayer gathering between members of the Hopi and Navajo, which have had a centuries-old feud over tribal land.

Lori was also best friends with Jessica Lynch, who became well known for being rescued by US Special Forces while a POW. During our Assembly of Honor, we honored Lori's sacrifice and recognized her children and parents up on the stage. It was a very emotional moment.

In November of 2007, I was reaching out to Native-American veterans and several of them were close friends of the Piestewa's and gave me their phone number. I called them and invited them all to Oregon. It was at Jesuit High School that I heard Terry speak of his experience of serving in Vietnam to over seven hundred students in the auditorium session.

When it was Terry's turn to speak, he approached the podium on the stage and immediately started to cry uncontrollably. You could hear a pin drop.

Terry regained his composure and said, "I'm from the Hopi Tribe, and we are a peaceful people. We don't have a warrior culture in our history." Terry started crying again and then said as he cried, "We're not taught how to kill, there is no word in our language for killing. I cannot forgive myself for what I was a part of in Vietnam."

He started crying again and said, "I'm sorry, I just can't talk about this." He started sobbing uncontrollably and his wife, Percy, walked over to him and put her arm around him and walked him back to his seat.

Sadly, Terry started having health issues for several years as a result of Agent Orange cancer. He passed away in 2017. I recently call Percy and invited her to Oregon again, and she said she would be honored. She told me that her daughter's children were all grown up now. Brandon was a freshman in college and Carla was graduating from high school in a few days.

Percy came back to Oregon in November 2018 and again in 2019 and spoke to students at four different high schools. Her talks were very emotional and powerful. She is committed to keeping her daughter Lori's legacy alive. Her grandson, Brandon, came and spoke to students. He is an impressive young man and quite the motivator also.

At every speaking event, Terry and Percy spoke of healing others by bringing people together. Terry taught me to see people without exclusions or judgments. I will miss Terry's smile and kind words he had of everyone.

Terry Piestewa passed away in 2017 from illness associated with exposure to Agent Orange.

WALTER 'JOE BEAR' RUNNING CRANE — Blackfeet

I met Walter when he attended our Living History Day at MHS for the first time in 2009. His brother, Bruce, Marines, pressured him into coming, but because it was just too emotional for him it took us nine years to get him to come back. My first impression of Walter was he was very humble and a gentleman.

He had many, many rough years dealing with PTSD, but has overcome a lot of it by going back to the Old Ways of the Blackfeet (sweat lodges and sun dances). Bruce told me after he came home from Vietnam, for months he would climb up a tree with his rifle because he only felt safe up in that tree.

In Volume I, I spoke about the Blackfeet Veterans Honor Guard's impressive involvement at America's Last WWI veteran, Frank Buckles' Funeral at Arlington National Cemetery in March of 2011. Afterwards, at Frank's Gap View Farmhouse, Walter gave me a pipe that he had hand carved. This is considered quite an honor. Walter then had us all sit on the floor, and we all participated in a Blackfeet Pipe Ceremony. It was very moving and an incredible memory. Thank you so much, Walter.

It took the last five years of Bruce and myself trying to get Walter to share his story. He never said no, but kept saying, "I'll get back to you." Please understand that me being a former coach and because he never said no, I would not give up on him. I'm very grateful I was able to interview him.

In January of 2022, Walter called me early in the morning, I was still sleeping, and my wife answers the phone. Walter tells her, "I'm ready to talk to Ken now!" She wakes me and says, "Walter's on the phone, and he sounds upset and says he is ready to talk to you."

I jumped out of bed, grabbed a pen and my notebook, and said "Hey Walter." Walter just started talking fast and gets on a roll. I just started writing as fast as I can. He already had the list of questions from me.

"I was born on March 26, 1949," laughing, "my grandmother would always answer that question with, 'I was born when it really snowed hard.' She was born in the 1800s during a bad snowstorm. We believed she lived to be a one hundred sixteen and some claimed it was one hundred thirty-six and she still had her teeth.

"My Dad, William Sr., was a tribal councilman. Mom's name was Helen Sinclair Running Crane. All four of my brothers, many cousins, nephews, and nieces, have served in the military, and I currently have a granddaughter in the Navy," he stated with pride.

"That's amazing, I respond. "Yes, you should be very proud of your military service."

"I was not a good student, and I skipped school and drank a lot. But I was good horse rider. I won a lot of Indian Horse relays and several of the tradition horse races as a jockey." He laughs and says, "I was a baa'd ass rider. Being a country kid, I was around horses all the time. But I got in lots of fights. So, I was sent to a boarding school in Oklahoma and was still in high school when I was drafted at eighteen."

"Forty-two Blackfeet from Glacier County were drafted and almost all were sent to Vietnam compared to only four white draftees were sent.

"I'm sent to Boot camp at Fort Lewis, then on to Fort Ord. One night, I got in after 3:00 AM and they thought I went AOL. So, I had KP duty for two weeks peeling potatoes. At the end of graduation, when we were still in parade rest, we are all told, 'Congratulations, you are all going to Vietnam.' We got twenty-one days of leave to say our goodbyes.

"In October '68, we're sent to Vietnam. We were flying very high and drop down fast as tracers were firing at our plane. When I get off of the plane, we were greeted with a big sign 'Welcome to Vietnam, The Fun Capital of the world, Life expectancy three seconds.' Walter pauses.

"That's horrible" I say.

"Yeah, that scared the hell out of me, but it kicked me into survivor mode.

"One day, while in a long line at our base camp for a hot dog. This soldier covered all over with dirt keeps starting at me, holding his rifle with his finger on the trigger. We kept moving forward and around a building, I turn around and he's followed me, still staring at me. Then he yells, 'Hey ain't you Joe Bear Running Crane? Don't you know who I am? I'm 'Hot Dog' Marceau, your cousin.'

"We visited while eating a hotdog and drinking a coke and met again that evening at the NCO club to drink a beer. This story is funny: all of a sudden, this rock band comes in and gets up on the stage and gets ready to play. I yell, 'What the hell! They're all Vietnamese! How can they be a rock band?'

"Then the lead singer says in a deep voice, 'Hello, I'm Johnny Cash.' Wow, they were great. The next morning, I wake up and my cousin was gone, but he made it back home.

"Later, I was sitting outside writing a letter home, when we are told, 'Get your shit together, you're going on a suicide mission.' The helicopters were landing one or two at a time to pick us up, get on and take off. On my helicopter there were two priests giving us last rites.

"That evening we set up perimeter and bunkers, they sent four of us in four different directions. We are walking on a well-used trail, and we hear gunfire from the north of us. The NVA are coming at us fast. I jump behind the bunker and fire off a couple hundred rounds. I see a NVA aiming an RPG (rocket-propelled grenade) at my Lieutenant. He fired but missed. I opened up on him and took him out.

"After the fire fight is over, I try to sleep a little in the early morning. It's amazing how even the snap of a twig can cause you to immediately crawl into the bunker. Then the NVA start firing at us again. Everything was too high, but there's lots of damage.

"We would go on patrols and back to the base. Once we came across several shallow graves of NVA. One of our guys, a crazy red neck, pulls a dead Vietnamese out of a shallow grave and cuts off his Chinese Belt Buckle. Back at the base he shows us his collection."

"How did you earn the Silver Star?"

"My brothers and I will never forget the 5th of June in '69. We walked into one thousand strong NVA. A couple a days before C Company was wiped out, one soldier played dead, even while a NVA soldier took his ring off his finger.

"We were surrounded, and we circle up. It was chaos. It was the longest day of our lives. I burned a 60mm machine gun barrel or maybe two. When the barrel of the machine gun got hot, I switched barrels. I used up all the ammo and had to have my brothers cover me while I ran, flipped, dodged, and grabbed ammo, a barrel, a grenade launcher, and any parts of a machine gun I could muster. I even grabbed weapons from our dead.

"Everybody is scared, some are crying. I see an NVA crawling towards me in a ditch. I took him out and just kept firing and fought like hell till I was hit.

"I pray for my brothers in arms every day. They are all heroes. I'll never forget you. Love you all for saving my life. Thank you all. Brothers. Fifty-two years is a long time! Remember all those that made the ultimate sacrifice for the good old US of A.

"The Medevacs are coming in and out now. One of my buddies, a black guy, Owens, gets shot in between his thumb and index finger. He starts screaming and runs and gets on a helicopter and won't get off. They just take off. I'm pissed, because we need all the help we can get.

"This battle lasts from around eight in the morning until dark. It's a long exhausting day. We are getting wiped out. There is a break in the fighting, but we know the NVA is gonna come back at night to finish the job. Thank God twenty-four soldiers from our Firebase volunteered to join and save us.

"I'm so hungry and I need some coffee real bad. Everything was quiet, so I dig a small deep hole in the dirt and take out the cup from my ruck sack. You know what C-4 is? If you take a really small piece of C-4 and put in the bottom of a hole, light it, and in thirty seconds you have boiling water. I poured in three instant coffee packets and a lot of sugar. God, it tasted good.

"Right after my first sip. I got hit in the back and knocked forward on my face. I can't breathe, and I can hear my blood gushing out, I can only move my arms and head. Then I hear, 'Chief's been hit.' Every Native veteran I know gets nicknamed Chief. A couple of guys grab me and drag me back into the jungle where my Lieutenant is. There are three freshly dug holes like graves and they put me in one. My breathing was slowing down, and I was fading in and out, but the two guys kept slapping me and yelling, 'Don't go to sleep.'

"I thought I was dying. I'm put in an underground bunker, and I heard someone say, 'He's not going to make it.' Just then a Native soldier, a Sioux, came in to check on me. He's angry and yells, 'I'm going to waste those mother fuckers! I'm taking no prisoners for what they did to you.' He was crying. He lit up a cigarette and starting praying, had me take two puffs, no pipes. When we finish, he says, 'You are going to go home.' I never saw him again. I missed my R&R because of that firefight.

"I'm told I'm being transferred again to Pleiku in the Central Highlands. I try to get up but can't. Two guys pick up my stretcher and put me on the helicopter. After landing, a doctor greets us at the helicopter and demands a scalpel immediately.

"A nurse runs back with one and gives it to him. He orders everyone to hold down my feet, my legs, my arms. He cuts an X in my wound. I'm screaming, crying for him to stop. Couldn't breathe, they wheel me into surgery and put a mask on my face with cold air. It felt like Montana air.

"The next morning, I wake up coughing up blood. A nurse is at my side and starts crying, "I almost lost you during the night. You're going to make it.

"A few days later, the nurse brings in the bed pan because I need to go to the bathroom, but it's about twenty yards away. I tell her, 'No way I'm using that. I'm going to walk.' I could only take two steps at a time, rest, pain, but I refuse to give up. 'Don't bother me,' I keep saying to her." Laughing, "It takes me three hours to go and back to my bed.

"The doc tells me I will take six months to recover and will not be able to do anything while healing. I'll prove him wrong. The next day I take a few steps, next day a few more, and I do that every day. I'm slowly getting stronger and stronger. I'm flown to Okinawa for recuperation, and we flew over Mt Fuji. I look out and we fly right by the summit. It was big.

"As we get close to Okinawa, we hit an air pocket. My straps are not tight, and I'm lifted off my stretcher but held down from hitting the ceiling of the plane. Afterwards, the pilot apologizes, 'I'm so sorry, we dropped over three thousand feet.' When we land, there are Okinawans at the fence yelling at us, 'Yankees, go home, we don't want you here.'

"One day, while in my pajamas, I wanted a beer. I walked a quarter mile, and it took me most of the day. At the PX, I got some large clothes and put them over my pajamas. It was staring to get dark when I walked into the Canteen. 'Bartender, Give me a Budweiser.' He responds, 'Where are you coming from? I can't serve you. I see your pajamas sticking out.'

"Well, I ain't leaving until I get a beer. I just kept arguing with him to give me an ice-cold beer. Two guys at the bar ask if I could join them. They buy me a beer. I'm served a forty ouncer with a straw. I wake up in my bed the next morning and I don't remember anything.

"The nurses come in to clean our wounds. Guy next to me starts crying, 'Please don't clean me today.' They would wash and clean open wounds. It hurt bad."

"I bought my dad a reel-to-reel tape recorder and ordered me a tailor-made suit, but I never got the suit. When I got on the bus to take us to our freedom bird, I forgot my dad's recorder. I came home in July of '69 and was taken to Madigan Medical Center Hospital at Fort Lewis, Washington. Once there, I asked for two weeks leave to visit my parents, but I'm given thirty days convalescent leave with pay."

"Did you ever run into protesters?"

"Hell yes," Walter says with a tone of anger in his voice.

"While walking in the Seattle airport and wearing my kaki uniform, I'm hit in the back with a couple of rotten eggs and screamed baby killer by a group of people. I couldn't understand it. Why? What did I do to deserve this. I was so angry.

"I had to call my cousin who is the only one in our family who has a phone, and he has to drive to my folks' home to tell them when I was landing at Great Falls. They met me at the airport. On the plane to Great Falls, I sit next to a guy with a service dog. He introduces himself to me and asks me why I'm so skinny.

"I tell him, 'Well, I was over a 140 lbs., now I'm 98.' Then he whispers to me, 'Don't tell anyone, I'm a millionaire,' and then tells the airline stewardess to get me a drink and keep them coming. By the time we landed, I was wasted.

"But it was great being back home especially since it was the same time as the North American Indian Days on the Rez (reservation) at Browning, Montana.

"Going back, I only had enough money to take the train to Spokane, about halfway to Fort Lewis. It's about midnight, and I'm in civilian clothes, and I didn't know what to do. So, I walked to the bus station, but all I had on me was just a couple of cigarettes, and no money for a pay phone.

"I went into the restroom and changed clothes and put on my uniform because I believed I had better chance of getting a ride. In the restroom, this big guy is looking at me, and says, 'Are you Joe Bear? I'm David Wells?' I said, 'Of course I remember you.' He was also Blackfeet from Browning. We smoked a cigarette, and he says "Don't you Blackfeet ever have any money? (Native humor) I'll give you a ride to the freeway.'

"It's so hot, and I'm sweating. Soon, a policeman stops me walking on the freeway, 'You can't do that. Stay right here and just stick your thumb out.' Very soon a VW bug stops and he's going to Seattle. After I get in, he says, 'There is a cooler in the back, grab yourself a beer.'

"But halfway to Seattle, his VW breaks down, so I start hitchhiking again. A farmer stops and picks me up, and after a drive, I see a sign to Yakama. 'Hey, let me off here. I got a sister who lives there, they'll help me.' It's sixty miles away, it's hot, and I need water. Luckily, another farmer picks me up and drives me to Yakama.

"I just started walking around the town, into taverns, bars, stores, asking anyone if they knew where my sister lived. After it gets dark, I walk into the police station, 'I'm lost and need help.' Because I'm wearing my uniform, the captain orders another officer, 'Drive this soldier around until he finds his relatives.'

"It's about 1:00 AM in the morning, I'm sleepy, and I can't remember anything. The officer keeps asking me question after question. Finally, I remember after he asks, 'Do they live in the farm housing area?' That's it! They live in a neighborhood of small houses for the farm workers.

"We drive there, and I surprise them while they are all getting ready to go to work. 'We heard about you in Vietnam,' says my brother-in-law. He likes to cuss a lot. He yells at my sister who is still in bed, 'Get your fucking ass out here.

"We all catch up while eating breakfast, and then I slept all afternoon. The next day, using a pay phone, I call Fort Lewis to ask for more money to get back and some more days of leave. I can't believe it; they give me another thirty days and send $2000 in travelers checks. I took everyone out to dinner and the drive-in movie.

"I report back at Madigan Hospital, Fort Lewis, and they finally took the drain tubes out of my side. They couldn't believe how much I had recovered. I get new orders, but first another thirty days leave at home.

"Back at home, I get drunk, get into a fight with a cop, cut my head, and thrown into the drunk tank. The next day at the arraignment, I tell the cop 'I'm sorry, but I have orders to report back.' The Judge says, 'You have twenty-four hours to get out of town.' The charges were dropped.

"I didn't want to leave, but my mom made me. She had my uniform dry cleaned and said, 'I'll see you in a couple of months.' My new orders, I'm sent to Fort Riley, Kansas. We had PT every morning with a five-mile run.

"One morning, we're all out in formation doing calisthenics when I see a black soldier walking towards us down the street. It's Owens. I start running towards him. He ran off, and I couldn't find him. I wanted to kill that SOB. He left me and my brothers for dead. I got an Article 15 (non-judicial punishment) for that stunt.

"I had PTSD real bad, every day. My folks would drive into town and be gone most of the day. We lived out in the country. I was so paranoid that I would load my rifle, walk out a ways and climb a tree, smoke cigarettes, and just watch all day. I didn't want to talk or see anyone.

"For months, my family would take turns hitting me with a broom stick to wake me up from a bad dream. Many times, my older brother, Clayton, would straddle my body and keep slapping me until I woke. Once, I attacked my sister, hit her, and grabbed her by her throat. I woke up while I was choking her.

"I drank heavily for years and eventually, I wanted help, badly. I went to the Blackfeet sweat lodges to volunteer with building and cleaning. Soon, I went back to the old Blackfeet ways, sun dancing, sweat lodge, prayers, smoking pipes in traditional ways.

"This takes all the negative bad stuff out of you. First you offer tobacco, then start putting rocks in, twenty-eight rocks, the size of a basketball, into sweat lodge. This is called a 'Buffalo or Warriors Sweat.' Fifty-four small rocks are used for people who have health issues.

"Ken, do you know how long it took me to make the homemade pipe I gave you? One month with lots of prayers during the process. You can take that pipe and hold it to your chest and pray. It has tremendous power and positive energy."

"Thank you so much, Walter. This took us a few years, but I'm very grateful to you."

"Ken, I'm sorry it took me this long to finally do this interview. I kept saying I'll get back to you, but just couldn't do it. I had more crazy experiences, but it's just too tough talking about it all."

Walter Running Crane is an Agent Orange related cancer survivor still living at the age of 73.

CHARLIE GONZALES   Yakama
                             Tunnel Rat

I met Charlie when he agreed to attend our Living History Days in November of 2019. For years, Loren and Rebecca Corpuz of the Yakama Warriors tried to get him to come with them as they believed the experience would be healing for him. He was very quiet and stayed to himself for most of the days. I assumed he was not having a very good time. I tried talking with him a couple of times and he was not very talkative.

On the final evening back at the LaQuinta Inn & Suites, everyone was saying goodbyes with many hugs and tears. Charlie approached me and said he needed to get something off his chest which had been haunting him since his Vietnam years. He looked very shook up and emotional. I asked Chris Spence, Army, Special Forces, Horse Soldier, Afghanistan, if he would join us. Charlie was fine with Chris joining us.

With tears in his eyes, he started talking. "We were crossing a rice paddy in the middle of the night when a sniper starts shooting at us. We saw exactly where the tracers were coming from, and we fired back and the shooting from the sniper stopped. At the end of the rice paddy was a small shack, hootch. I ordered my guys to enter through the front after I entered from the back door and gave them the signal.

"I entered very slowly and quietly and standing right behind the front door was a small boy about six or seven years old. He was holding a hand grenade behind his back. I reacted and opened fire killing the little boy."

Charlie was really having a hard time now; he was crying, and his voice was quivering. He pauses and then says, "I cannot forgive myself and am haunted by that memory every day."

I said, "I'm so sorry," but then Chris Spence gave his thoughts, and I was deeply impressed.

"Charlie, your training kicked in. You reacted, and because of your actions, you probably saved your life and your buddies' lives. In Afghanistan, we were put in tough situations many times because the Taliban would use women and children as human shields. Tragically, war is hell, and the civilians pay a terrible price. I hope you can find a little comfort knowing that your actions were because of your training and not a decision. Five men are alive because of you."

I am so grateful for Chris being there and providing such wisdom.

In July of 2021, Malinda and I drove up to the Yakama Reservation to interview Charlie. Rebecca set it all up. We met at the Yakama Veterans Center, and Charlie and I went into an office for some privacy.

I started it off, "Thanks so much Charlie for agreeing to be interviewed."

Charlie looks at me perplexed. "What are you talking about? I don't know anything about this."

I responded, "Didn't Rebecca set this all up?"

"I don't remember" he said.

Rebecca had told me that Charlie was starting to get forgetful these days, and I can relate myself. So, I tell him about the other books, and that I would be honored to include him in the next one as he is a Vietnam veteran.

He looked shocked and very uncomfortable, so I told him, "Well, most of the questions are real easy, and I already have one of your Vietnam experiences that you told me two years ago." He didn't remember telling me that either. So, I decided to go for it. "Where were you born?"

"I was born in Sidney, Montana, but we lived all over Washington, Idaho, and Montana as my father picked crops in the fields. We traveled to the work. My mom was born in Texas, and they both had the last name with a 'Z' and an 'S'. He laughed. They had five children, three boys all born in Montana and two girls born in Washington. One of my brothers was found shot dead in his pickup on Boise Cascade property. The murderer was arrested back east and ended up serving a life prison term in a federal prison.

"As kids, we also worked in the fields, and at thirteen, I worked full-time in the hops fields. I also played basketball and baseball in high school. I graduated from Wapato High School in '64 and just worked for a year. I decided to enroll in community college but screwed around too much and after the second term, I joined the Army. I was told because my grades were not good, and I was screwing around too much, my draft number was moved up.

"I took the bus to Seattle and joined my platoon. We were nicknamed F Troop after the comedy TV show because we were always late and getting into trouble. The only time we were on time was for graduation, and we beat everyone else.

"At Fort Lewis in '66, my MOS was 11 D Bravo Infantry. I was then sent to Fort Polk, Louisiana for leadership school. My duffle bag was lost and had to wear my dress uniform every day for two weeks. The barracks were being remodeled so we lived in tents, opened the sides during the day, one heater, oil, and we stole oil from other tents.

"I was promoted to platoon sergeant, me, and Herbert Louks went head-to-head for the award 'Head Soldier of the Cycle.' He won. Sadly, he was killed in Vietnam. In Vietnam, we left our hut to dig deep pits for protecting ammo, two sandbags deep, seven high. He was the only guy in the hut when it took a direct hit with motor fire." Charlie became emotional with tears after telling me this.

"I was flown to Vietnam in '66 on Braniff Airlines, great looking stewardesses, lights out on landing because of snipers. Later, I was asked if I would volunteer to be a tunnel rat and I turned it down.

"A friend volunteered and he went into the first tunnel we came upon. The tunnel collapsed and I went it to dig him out. He was already gone. I volunteered from then on because I felt guilty about my friend.

"We were out in the boonies (jungle) for two months. We were so tired of sleeping in water and getting sick all the time. Shit, the only way out of there is to find a booby trap. I was walking when I hit a wire. The blast threw me forward in the air and I landed standing, like a standing broad jump. I could see my elbow sticking out of my arm, and blood all over my right leg.

"My first Purple Heart and it was '66. I remember back at the M.A.S.H. unit, a nurse, a large black woman, came in with a razor and said this is going to hurt. She then scraped the dry blood and scabs off my legs. Yes, it hurt like hell. I was medevaced to Cu Chi and then was moved to Vung Tau, an R&R place. Surgery was done there and then daily therapy for my leg.

"I got to go see a Bob Hope USO show, with Raquel Welch and Ann-Margaret. It was great and amazingly, there were no attacks during the show.

"My second Purple Heart is embarrassing. We were all walking on a trail when a sniper started firing at us. We all dove into the tall elephant grass. I landed on a block with a large metal fishhook looking pole in it. It was the same leg that was wounded from before. A buddy tried to pull it out, of course I screamed. The medic had to numb me up to remove it.

"Flying back to the states, I learned that my brother was being flown to Vietnam at the same time. And yep, we were greeted by protesters yelling 'Baby Killers' and spitting on us. I had bought a six pack of rum in Guam during a layover. I tripped getting off the plane and dropped the rum breaking every bottle. I was so pissed I got down on the ground to lick it up and cut my tongue.

"The MPs would not allow us to sleep in the airport because protesters would try to harass us. I was sent back to Fort Lewis and my new job was to teach the skills required to be a tunnel rat at the Field Training Exercises.

"There was the stateside manual and the combat manual in Vietnam. I did not use the stateside manual. I told them if I had followed the stateside manual, I wouldn't be here to teach and that the combat manual was the only way to survive."

"How did you handle the memories, PTSD ?"

"I just buried it, but it builds up, and I'd get too emotional, so I just kept burying it. There was stuff that was done, and I can't take it back. I just don't talk about it.

"First time I went into a spider hole I was scared, but the adrenalin just kicks in. You are never supposed to jump feet first into a spider hole as they might be booby trapped.

!Well, once I did that and landed on a 'Bouncing Betty' (land mine which is propelled a meter or two into the air before exploding) that did not go off because my foot landed on a root from a tree that was sticking out. My foot missed the trip wire by about an inch. I learned my lesson and I was very lucky.

"We used a flashlight with a red lens. Red improved your vision in the dark. and also it minimized your light profile. Red was great because it's difficult to see it from a distance, and you could sneak up on someone. Also the Viet Cong only used white lights and candles. You know that you never hold the flashlight in front of your body in a tunnel? That's where the first gun shots are fired, at the light."

"Any funny stories?"

Charlie smiled and said, "To many funny stories. Once I was so hungry I asked a Vietnamese guy if I could have a piece of his jerky. He gave me some and it tasted kind of sour.

"I asked, 'What is this? What kind of meat?' He answered 'monkey.' Another time we were served a small bowl of rice and the rice was moving. It had a lot of tiny worms in it. We were told to just eat it. It's protein.

"Because I had type O positive blood, I gave my blood often, but mostly because they would give you a free shot of whiskey. One day I gave blood three times and could barely walk back because I was so lightheaded," Charlie laughed.

"Once we were burning shit and we threw too many chemicals on it to burn. It exploded and shit flew everywhere. We got in trouble for that stunt. We were always stealing beer too.

"When I surprised my parents back home, I was used to cussing in every sentence. I walked into the kitchen and yelled 'Hey mother fuckers, I'm home!' My mom was in the kitchen with several women friends.

"I apologized and then went straight to a restaurant and lounge and asked if I could work for a meal and some drinks. I washed dishes and peeled potatoes for the next three days. Ate and drank too much. On the fourth day, I went to see my girlfriend, boy was she pissed."

"Wow, nowadays kids beg their parents for money for beer and food. No one could do what you did. I'm impressed."

"I learned this as a kid. I asked my dad for a baseball glove, and he told me to work, save my money and buy your own baseball glove."

On March 26, 2022, I spoke, and my wife Malinda sang at the Yakama Warriors Memorial with Military Honors for Charlie in Toppenish. This was our second Native American funeral and memorial service, and they are very impressive and moving. The Yakama Warriors did a great job in honoring Charlie.

I wanted to include Charlie's obituary from the Yakima Herald-Republic website because I want everyone to know that not only did Charlie give service to his country by going to Vietnam, but he also kept doing it when he came back home:

> Our Easter Bunny & Santa Claus made his last call on March 10, 2022. Charles (Charlie) Julian Gonzalez was born to the late Julian and Maria Gonzalez in Sidney, Montana on September 28, 1945. Charlie graduated from Wapato High School in 1964 and graduated from Central Washington University in 1973 with his B.A. degree in Recreation, Art-Minor, and P.E. Minor. Charlie was a proud veteran and served in the United States Army in 1966-1968 at Fort Lewis Washington; Fort Park, LA; and Vietnam. He trained as an Infantry man, 81MM mortars, and on the job training as a Tunnel Rat in Vietnam. Charlie was proud of his countless Military Medals Awarded which included 2 Purple Hearts, Army Commendation Medal, National Defense Service Medal, Bronze Star, Vietnam Service Medal with Bronze Star Attachment, Republic of Vietnam Campaign Ribbon with Device Combat Infantry Badge, Expert Medal for M16 rifle and .45 caliber pistols, Sharpshooter Medal for M14 rifle, Sharpshooter Medal for 81MM mortars, plus numerous Leadership Training Awards and Recognition Awards from the Department of The United States Army. Charlie worked with the following Recreation Programs in various positions such as the Wapato Community Center as director, Yakima Recreation Department as recreation leader, Quinault Indian Nation

Recreation Department as director, and Yakama Indian Nation Recreation Program as recreation leader. Charlie also worked as a laborer in the hops, lettuce, tomatoes, corn, watermelons, apples, and potatoes. He was also employed with retail, logging with Smith-Greene Logging in Warm Springs, Oregon for 11 years, and Jeld-Wen Corporation in Yakima & White Swan for 4 years. Charles was an avid sports person. He started the Wapato Men's Softball League around the 1970s. He coached men & women's softball teams, men & women's basketball teams, numerous youth teams in softball, baseball, basketball, and tee-ball. He traveled the Northwest playing in numerous tournaments as well. Charlie was an active member until his illness with the following Referee/Umpires Associations: Yakima Valley Basketball Officials Association for 34 years, Grays Harbor Referees Basketball Association for 3 years, Central One Basketball Officials Association for 16 years, Washington AAU Referee Association 34 years, and National Indian Activities Association for 15 years, Central One Baseball Umpires Association for 16 years, Central One Softball Umpires Association for 16 years, Washington ASA Umpires Association for 37 years, Yakima Valley Umpires Association-Softball for 23 years, and Yakima Valley Umpires Association-Baseball for 28 years. Charlie received individual awards from YVUA, YVBOA, CWBO, WIAA, 2004 Jimmie Silver Memorial Award, 2005 30+ year Service Award for Basketball, 2006 WIAA Meritorious Service Award, and in 2007 YVUA Above & Beyond Service Award. During basketball season he would referee numerous All-Indian National Tournaments in Toppenish, Yakima, Spokane, Warm Springs, Oregon; Los Angeles, California; Fargo, North Dakota; Fort Washakie, Wyoming; Billings, Montana; Fort Hall, Idaho; as well as districts, regional, state playoffs for the W.I.A.A. During baseball season he did W.I.A.A. high school games and playoffs in baseball & softball, Senior Legion Baseball, Junior Legion Baseball, Senior Babe Ruth Baseball, Junior Babe Ruth Baseball, Babe Ruth 12U to 16U league and tournaments including playoff games; ASA 18U, 16U, 14U, 12U, 10U league and playoff games for fast pitch softball; Yakima Recreation League slow pitch games and tournaments for men, women, and co-ed. While living in Oregon he did numerous tournaments for softball & baseball little league at the league sub-district, district, state, and regional levels. He was selected to do the Softball 12U National at Alpenrose in Oregon but could not attend do to work commitments after moving back to Washington during the summer of 1999. Charlie loved his Seattle Seahawks, Seattle Mariners, and Washington Huskies. He loved to make his hot sauce and barter when he would travel to referee or umpire. Cooking and gardening every hot pepper and vegetable you could imagine while never allowing a single weed to grow were some of his other favorite hobbies. You would frequently find him at the casino or scratching scratch tickets somewhere. You could also always find him at some of his other favorite local spots such as the Wapato American Legion 133, Thursday at Wapato Filipino Community Hall, and St Jack's for his snacks and movies. He enjoyed watching WWE, cutting out coupons for all the best deals, and he was active with Yakama Warriors Association and enjoyed every second. Charlie was a busy man, never would he stay in just one spot and always was ready to lend a hand. Perfectionist in everything he did, from gift wrapping to folding laundry. Charlie always had this saying "when I die, I'll probably be in the 3-second key or in the baseball field somewhere."

Charlie Gonzales passed away in March of 2022 from cancer associated with exposure to Agent Orange.

MEL GARTEN   WWII
                                        Korean War

I met Mel for lunch several years ago at The Stafford Retirement Home he was living in. Mel was among the most decorated combat veterans as a veteran of WWII, Korea, and Vietnam.

He told me he enlisted in April 1942, after graduating from the City College of New York. He said he ran to the draft board the day Pearl Harbor was attacked, hoping to volunteer with the Marines. He was rejected because he was blind in his right eye from birth, so he memorized the eye chart and joined the Army.

He had a difficult time getting into the infantry division because the Army wanted him in the finance department. He told me, "I wanted to see action." He was eventually able to get his wish and was shipped off to Europe.

In WWII he was wounded three times and received a Silver Star for taking over for a machine gunner who was killed after his gun jammed. There he received three Bronze Stars and participated in the paratroop raid to liberate Los Banos prison camp in the Philippines that freed over four thousand prisoners, including Frank Buckles, America's Last WWI veteran. He also received three Purple Hearts, a Presidential Unit Citation, and a Combat Infantry Badge.

In Korea, Mel was recommended for the Medal of Honor, but in the end, he was awarded the Distinguished Service Cross. His citation reads:

> Captain Garten distinguished himself by extraordinary heroism in action against enemy aggressor forces near Surang-ni, Korea, on 30 October 1952. On that date, observing that assault elements of Companies F and G were pinned down by withering fire on a dominant hill feature, Captain Garten voluntarily proceeded alone up the rugged slope and, reaching the besieged troops, found that key personnel had been wounded and the unit was without command. Dominating the critical situation through sheer force of his heroic example, he rallied approximately eight men, assigned four light machine guns, distributed grenades and, employing the principle of fire and maneuver, stormed enemy trenches and bunkers with such tenacity that the foe was completely routed and the objective secured. Quickly readying defensive positions against imminent counterattack, he directed and coordinated a holding action until reinforcements arrived.

In Vietnam, he told me, "The Army put me in command of the 327th where I was seriously wounded just north of Tuy Hoa when the jeep I was in hit a mine." I learned later that Mel was so beloved by his men that when he was hurt, they took heroic measures to rush him to aid.

"After I lost my leg and ten months recuperating at Walter Reed Hospital, I returned to duty as post commander at Fort Bragg. I retired in '68 and started teaching political science at the University of Tampa in Florida."

Mel is one of the few men to see combat in three wars, something only a little more than three hundred men in U.S. military history can say they have done.

When I spoke with Mel he had just lost his wife, Ruth, of seventy years and he gave her credit for all of his successes in his military career. "She did it all. She raised our children, ran the house, handled most of the responsibilities. We moved forty times during my career. She was amazing. I couldn't have done any of it without her.

"Five times Ruth received telegrams stating I was wounded, and the last time I lost my leg and almost died. She was at my bed side every time. I miss her a lot."

MEL GARTEN passed away at the age of 93 in May of 2015.

RALPH COLIN　　　　　　　　Bronze Star
　　　　　　　　　　　　　　　Purple Heart

Ralph was best friends with Antonio Mendez, Army, WWII, Silver Star. He told me, "I met Tony at an event for veterans many years ago." Antonio had a 9th Infantry Division patch on the hat he was wearing, and Ralph said to him, "Nice patch, 9th Infantry." Tony responded, "How'd you know it was the 9th Infantry? You weren't even born when we were active." Ralph says, "I was in the 9th in Vietnam."

They became close friends and when they came to Oregon to talk to students, they both requested to be together in the same classroom. Ralph loved to tell his "Carnitas story."

"We were out in the jungle in North Vietnam (Vietcong territory) up the Mekong Delta. We traveled with what we called Tango Boats. They were old WWII small LSTs. We were told that this was supposedly the first time the Navy and the Army had worked together since the Revolutionary War," Ralph laughed after telling that part of the story.

"We followed the Vietcong into Cambodia, and we were told we weren't there, and even today we're told we weren't in Cambodia. But we were there alright. It was very intense and dangerous. There's about ninety of us, and we have around-the-clock guarding all of us in a big circle.

"Now, I don't know how this ever happened, but we get a mail delivery, and I get a package from my mom. I opened it up, and it's homemade carnitas (Mexican slow cooked pulled pork)." Ralph cracks up and says, "Mexican moms don't send cookies or candy, just homemade Mexican food."

"Well, the carnitas are all covered with mold, so I scraped off the mold. A buddy offers to test it and says it tastes great. So, several of us eat all of it and it was great. Out in the middle of the jungle in Vietnam, and I'm eating my mom's home cooked carnitas. It was the best tasting food I ever ate.

"That reminds me, we would use C-4 (plastic explosives) to heat canned food. It worked great, and then we could eat a hot meal out in the jungle."

I asked him one time, "What did you do to survive every day?"

"When I first got there, another guy told me, "Just follow me. Do what I do or what I tell you to do. Don't pick up things like food or plates, they might be booby-trapped. Don't go the easy way. Just because there is a bridge, and you don't want to get your boots wet. Walk in the water because the bridge might be booby-trapped. And they usually were.

"I also learned teamwork. I trusted the guys I was with. One time, I put a M16 rifle up to a new guy's chest. He was threating the lives of us by not being a team. I told him, 'You either do what we tell you or you're not going to be here anymore. You either change or they'll take you out in a body bag.'

"That same day he came up to me and said he would straighten out. He also asked if I would have really shot him. I looked at my buddy then looked back at him, "At that moment, yes, but right now, no. Everybody else is willing to die for you. And you have to do the same."

Ralph's last visit to Oregon was in 2018. He was so very friendly and had a wonderful sense of humor. Every school we visited; the students loved him.

Ralph Colin passed away in March of 2021 from cancer associated with exposure to Agent Orange.

JOE MENDOZA   Army

I first met Joe in Orange County, California at an event with UMVA (United Mexican American Veterans Association). He was a quiet friendly man, and I don't remember him speaking much at all.

He first came to Oregon to join us in 2016. UMVA has been telling him he needed to go; telling him it would be good for him. He didn't talk much at all then either, but he's been coming back ever since. I've always assigned him to be in a classroom with his buddy Richard Garza, also a Vietnam veteran.

I spoke to him over the phone. "So, when were you born and where?" Joe not only answered my question, but just kept talking.

"I was born on October 27, 1952, in Southern California. Was named after my Uncle Joe, Army, Korea War, who was killed in action at the Chosin Reservoir.

"I was drafted right out of high school and reported to boot camp. I was infantry, and we were told we would never be sent to Vietnam because they were drawing down the troops. But right after graduating from basics, we were sent to Vietnam as replacements in November of '71. The goal was for the South Vietnamese Army to take over. I was there until April of '72."

"My job was going on patrols for observation purposes only, to see if the village was friendly. We had no contact with the NVA. Right before we arrived, patrols used to be search and destroy missions. Everything was all so confusing, and I've never seen such disorganization before. Everybody wanted out. Soldiers refusing orders, calling in sick every day, and just taking advantage of the situation. Drugs and drinking were out of control.

"I started to hang around with the guys who would go out on patrol. We didn't want to associate with the cowards. It was crazy, very sad and depressing. We were not a team. I really believed we would all be united and have each other's back, and have a bond just like the WWII and Korean War veterans I knew and talked about being a band of brothers. It was a bad, horrible experience."

"How were you treated when you came back home?"

"I didn't think serving in the Army could get any worse, until I came back home. We were greeted by angry protestors, they screamed, 'Baby killers!' at us and they spit at us too. I knew this was already happening to returning soldiers, but I was not prepared for how much it hurt. I was just doing my job and grew believing it was honorable. All just for wearing my uniform. Why is our country turning against us?"

Joe's tone of voice sounded very sad with bitterness still in it.

"Many Vietnam veterans turned to alcohol and drugs, and we were labeled as losers. It was very sad and depressing. Eventually all this led to PTSD being discovered as real.

"Then the years of us fighting for help; the cancers that were discovered led to Agent Orange Cancers. My Agent Orange lung cancer is currently in remission. But it took years to get help from the VA. Nobody believed us.

"I saw all the dead areas, no life, dead vegetation, when in Vietnam. It was so unbelievable, I even asked what happened there. They told me it was sprayed with poisons. I have several Vietnam veterans friends who died from cancer because they could never get help from the VA. It's just horrible."

Joe kept talking. "Well, after years of non-stop pressure from my wife Karen, I finally got help and was diagnosed with PTSD in 2014. For years I would have all these bad dreams, and she would say I had it, and I would say I don't. I didn't experience combat. But the dreams became worse, she was scared, and then I started hitting her in my sleep. I agreed to go see a therapist. It was so helpful.

"I knew about your program up in Oregon because UMVA sent veterans up every year and tried to get me to go, but I told them, I don't need it, I'm OK. Let the others go. But after counseling, I decided to go and see for myself.

"I was amazed. It was the first time in my life as a veteran, I felt appreciated, honored, and accepted. I really appreciate all you have done for us veterans. The experience absolutely helped me in my healing process. And I'll keep coming as long as you keep doing this, Ken."

Joe and Karen have been married for twenty-one years. His first wife, Lorraine, passed from lung cancer in '98. They had two adult children, a boy, and a girl.

Joe Mendoza is still living at the age of 69.

RICHARD GARZA

Richard has been coming up to Oregon with the United Mexican American veterans to speak to high school students for many years. He would wear his uniform to every school and always looked sharp. I could always count on him, and the feedback was that he did a great job.

Sadly, Richard suffered a depilating stroke in 2022 and is currently rehabilitating. He is working hard and has a tough road ahead, but after learning what a completive athlete he was back in the day; I'm betting on Richard.

Linda, Richard's wife, interviewed him for me.

"I was born on January 26, 1946, in Los Angeles to my parents Andres and Juanita Garza. I was the youngest of nine children, three girls and six boys. Three of my brothers also served in the military.

"Played football and baseball my freshman and sophomore years and basketball all four years. Switched to cross country and track for my junior and senior years." Linda told me with pride, "He ran the mile in 4:23, which was a school record that stood for twenty-five years."

"After graduating from Santiago High School in Garden Grove, California in '65, I attended Santa Ana Jr. College and ran cross country and track." "He set the school record in Cross Country by running the four-mile course in 19:18, and was awarded the Most Valuable Cross Country award," Linda said.

"I was offered an athletic scholarship to Long Beach State University but was drafted." "Five months after we married, he was drafted August of '68," Linda added.

"So, I'm sent to Vietnam in February of '69, and when I first steeped out of the plane, I thought it was the hottest place on earth. I'm assigned to the 9th Infantry Division in the Mekong Delta. My unit was the 6th Battalion 31st Infantry, and I was there for a whole year.

"We went on many ambush patrols by truck, boat, or helicopter into the jungle. Of course we walked from a base camp into the jungle. I had many jobs, I carried the radio, sometimes a M60 machine gun, and I would walk point for many months.

"On May 4, 1969, I was walking point with a platoon sized patrol when in the middle of a clearing, I saw a VC hiding behind a banana tree. Seconds later I noticed another VC running. I motioned with my hand for the rest of the platoon to stop. Both had AK 47s. I shot at the one behind the banana tree. I shot twice and he fell. Then I hit the ground and so did the rest of my platoon.

"There were other VC and more of them opened fire on us. I preceded to fire back, knowing they could not pinpoint my precise position with so much firing from them.

"The rest of my platoon were not firing because they did not know where I was. Armed with my rifle and two grenades, I continued to fire while still on the ground and then threw a grenade in their direction, and they stopped firing. Then I took another grenade and threw it at them, and they scattered.

"After I threw the first grenade, Lt. Dicks yelled, 'Medic! Garza stepped on a booby-trap.' Then I threw the second the LT. yelled again, 'Garza stepped on a another one.'"

"The medic, a Native American, bravely came to check on me as I was still on the ground. Then several members of the platoon came beside me and fired on the tree line. Minutes later the VC retaliated by firing a couple of mortars. We scattered.

"After the mortars stopped, we went back to the area to check it out. We located a corpse and took his weapon and ammo supplies. We did ambush patrols all night, but no action took place. When we returned to base, Lt. Colonel Gerald J. Carlson, Battalion Commander, congratulated me and looked at the AK-47 that I took from the dead VC.

"All my GI buddies congratulated me, and Lt. Dicks said he was putting me in for a Silver Star, but he was transferred, and it never happened.

"A buddy of mine, Steve Cox, brought his six string Spanish-made acoustical Aria guitar to Vietnam with him. I played it many times. Steve would play it and sing many folk songs from the '60s when we were back in the company area. The music helped us all cope with the traumatic times we faced.

"But Steve was badly wounded when a booby-trap grenade went off. He was evacuated by helicopter and then to Japan and back to the states. His guitar was kept by the radio operator Sam Quintana until he was wounded. Then a soldier from Hawaii claimed it. When he need to borrow fifty dollars to go on R&R, I loaned him the money.

"But he had a nervous breakdown and we never saw him again. So I took the guitar home with me. Thirty-four years later, I tracked down Steve who was living in southern Oregon. We got together and I reunited him with his guitar."

Linda told me about what it was like when Richard returned home. She said, "Coming home after his flight landed at Los Angeles Airport, he called. I had been waiting by the phone all day and it was late at night. But I got a flat tire on the way and a stranger helped me fix it. When I got here, Richard was standing under a light, all alone, looking tired and worn out."

"On the ride home, he said, 'No one would make eye contact with me on the plane, probably because I was wearing my uniform. They just ignored me, and I felt very unappreciated and sad.'

"After his cousin, Ralphie, died from Agent Orange cancer, the PTSD really started. Ralphie came back with an Agent Orange rash all over his body that internalized, he was always sick. Richard had nightmares and fought the war in his sleep. He was always very restless, waving his arms and struggled in his sleep," Linda told me.

"Richard does not like fireworks at all because his first 4th of July back from Vietnam, a stranger fired a bottle rocket which hit Richard in the chest. This led to severe depression and lots of flashbacks. His toughest challenge was on his UPS (United Postal Service) route, which would take him thru 'Little Saigon' in Westminster. The signs would bring flashbacks. He would isolate himself in his room as soon as he got back from work. Finally, he was diagnosed with PTSD.

"But Richard made lasting friendships with fellow Vietnam veterans Samuel Zuintana and Larry Daubs. They had many reunions over the years. Then in 2002, he had throat cancer that was Agent Orange related. Then again in 2004, prostate cancer, and then a bad stroke in 2020, also Agent Orange related," Linda said.

Richard Garza is still living at the age of 76 with his wife of fifty-four years, Linda.

RON CANNON   Purple Heart

Ron and his wife Shirley are such great people and have devoted their lives to veterans. They have been heavily involved and supportive of any event for all veterans, but especially Vietnam veterans. Ron has attended the majority of our events since the beginning, most with his good friend Jerry Pero.

Ron, Shirley, and Jerry Pero traveled to Washington D.C. in 2011 to attend the funeral of Frank Buckles (America's last WWI veteran) at Arlington National Cemetery. They took many beautiful pictures and gave copies to me. It sure meant a lot to me that they would travel so far to be supportive. That was such a beautiful gesture. I cannot tell them how thankful I am for doing it.

In 1987, Ron joined several of his Vietnam veteran buddies to help support Oregon's Vietnam Memorial through financial and physical maintenance. He has also served as the Vice President of Vietnam Veterans of Oregon Memorial Fund, Inc. for over 30 years.

He was only in Vietnam three weeks as he stepped on a land mine and lost a leg. At the beginning of every classroom session, Ron would walk into the classroom, sit down in the front, take off his prosthesis and toss it to a student who looked like he didn't want to be there. He would laugh and say, "Wake up, you need to pay attention to what we have to say."

At first the students sat in stunned silence, but when Ron started laughing, the rest of the class laughed. He told me, "Everyone pays attention after that." He has a great sense of humor.

On March 14, 2022, my beautiful wife Malinda and I met with Ron and his lovely wife, Shirley, at Backstop Bar and Grill in Canby. The owner Ken Arrigotti asked me if I could interview any Vietnam veterans there as he wanted to meet them and shake their hand. As a small gesture of gratitude, he would buy our lunches.

Ron came well prepared with copies of a lot of paperwork he said I could use. Before we even looked at the menu, he started talking about Vietnam.

I called, "Time out, let's start at the beginning. When were you born?"

"September 28, 1947, in Portland, OR. My dad, Maynard, was exempt from serving during WWII because he was working with the Corps of Engineers on the building of the Bonneville Dam on the Columbia River.

"He felt so guilty, he joined the Coast Guard Reserves and told me, 'I patrolled the docks of Portland, shot rats, and protected the ladies.' He was really into Dixie Land Jazz and dancing.

"My mom, Violet, worked for the State of Oregon until she had a bad stroke in '66.

"I graduated from David Douglas High School in '65, and I was not a good student. I must have had ADHD; school was not my thing. I wouldn't have made it if it were not for the Dean of Boys, Richard Miller, a WWII veteran who served in the 41st Sunset Division. He later became the Adjutant General for the State of Oregon.

"I ran into Major General Miller years later at the dedication of the new Oregon Department of Veterans Affairs building. He yells, "I know that face! Hey Cannonball!'

"There was a trade school in Texas (Career Academy of Broadcasting), and I started taking classes in the fall of '66. After graduating in '67, I started working at KVAN radio station as I wanted to be a disc jockey in Portland. I'm nineteen years old, and in '67, I get my draft notice. My dad appeals it, saying he needs me to help take care of my mom. But you know how that went over.

"My dad drove me to the induction center in downtown Portland and there was a huge crowd of protesters. I cut through the protesters who were chanting, 'Hell no, we won't go!' I'm scared and during the physical, they take my blood and I faint," Ron laughs.

"At Portland's processing center, I met Ron Van Avery and we just hit it off and became best friends. We were buddies all through training including while we served in Vietnam. Van was twenty-three and married with four children. Our platoon nicknamed him 'Old Man' and he was like a father to us all. He talked about his family and the future all the time. He loved to sing 'Daddy's Home' all the time and he couldn't carry a note," laughing again. "But we were inseparable.

"When I received a 'Dear John letter' from my girlfriend back home, Ron helped me deal with it.

"On April 21, 1968, we went on a foot patrol, 'out in the bush' which was a ways from our home base at Chu Lai. It was hot and muggy. We hiked up to Hill 56 to establish a perimeter observation post, but we come upon Concertina razor wire, sharp blades which can slice deep and cause fatal injuries, across the trail. We were on that same hill only the week before and the wire was not across the trail then.

"Our Lieutenant is a real asshole. I was in the lead squad. We radioed back to the Lt. and explained the situation. But the Lt. tells us to move up the hill! We radio the Lt. again and caution that we 'strongly advise' against moving forward. Again our Lt. orders everyone to move forward.

"Within moments after reaching the top of the hill, the Lieutenant steps on a Bouncing Betty and is killed instantly. Van is behind him and gets hit in the face. His face is blown off. Behind Van was Jim Rudd who is killed instantly. Man, Jim was such a beautiful man," Ron says shaking his head, and becomes emotional again.

"I'm standing still, close to a fox hole, and Specialist David Tunnell tells everyone to stay in place and watch for more landmines. A Dustoff (helicopter ambulance) is called in and the lead pilot saw only five or six of us that appeared to not be injured and called for a full extraction of our unit.

"As the third Dustoff settled into the LZ (landing zone), Tunnell told me to head up the hill toward him and pointed out a trip wire glistening in the sun between our locations about twenty feet from my position.

"I take one step and then *BOOM*. I'm blown about fifteen feet in the air and into a tree. I hit the ground hard but feel no pain. Most of my left leg was shredded and my right leg mid-calf down is gone. I'm bleeding profusely.

"A buddy, Johnny Winn, came to my position to administer lifesaving care. Winn and Tunnell continued first aid measures then placed me on the Dustoff chopper. Tunnell is holding my hand and keeps moistening my lips with water. The whole time he rubs my face and keeps saying, 'Stay with me' over and over." Ron gets very emotional for a moment.

"I'm pumped up with adrenaline, shock, and morphine. The helicopter was jammed packed with wounded. I still remember the helicopter taking off, tipping nose down during takeoff to get out of there fast. I feel the wind from the chopper blades hitting my face. I look out and see this beautiful blue sky with puffs of bright white clouds." Ron and Shirley both get emotional.

Choking up Ron says, "I see a giant hand reach out through a cloud to me. It's a message. I'm going home. I'm at peace and feel no pain.

"I wake up in 2nd Surgical Hospital in Chu Lai. The nurses had pumped thirty-three units of blood into me, and after some time in the operating room, the doctor discontinued the initial operation as he felt that my body could not stand much more trauma. I discovered later that I was not expected to survive. I was told they fought hard for my life.

"Back home, my dad was awakened in the middle of the night by a knocking on the front door. He opens the front door and a Western Union currier hands him a telegram.

"My best friend had his face blown off by a Bouncing Betty. He didn't make it." Ron pauses and gets emotional again. "All this information was kept from me, but I'm trying to find out about my buddy. The doctors felt I would give up and not survive the shock of learning that Van didn't make it. The Army even told my parents not to tell me until I got home. But I put one and one together and became very depressed.

"We land at Travis Air Force base in California. I'm on a stretcher and they lay me on the tarmac. I see the California mountains and say to a Major standing next to me, 'That's the most beautiful sight I've ever seen.' The Major looks at those barren, brown hills, then back at me like I'm crazy.

"Years later I meet General Patrick Brady after I invited him to be our featured Memorial Day speaker at the Oregon Vietnam Veterans Memorial. He was a Dustoff pilot who earned the Medal of Honor just a month before me arriving in Vietnam. General Brady had another commitment and was unable to accept, but so I thanked him, then on behalf of all those that he and his crews saved for their bravery, skill, and heroic actions to save so many lives.

"General Brady asks me, 'When were you over there?' I answer, 'March of '68 to April of '68.' 'Where were you?' the General asks. 'I was up north with I Corps, the 5th of the 46th, 198th Brigade.' General Brady asks, 'Were you injured?' I respond, 'Yes.' 'What was the date?' 'April 21, 1968.'

"The General says, 'I remember that. I was on stand-by and activated for full extraction at a mine field.' I respond, 'I was on the fifth and final dust-off (liftoff) from the LZ.' Gen Brady, 'I was there, and I flew that chopper.

"What are the odds? I thanked him over and over and tell him, 'I'm so grateful. General Patrick Brady, you were my golden ticket."

I then asked, "How did you deal with it all, PTSD?"

Ron turns and looks at Shirley, "She has been my angel. She has had my back all these years. I don't know why, but it did not hit me hard until 2003. I went into major depression. I was working as the Oregon Director with the United States Department of Labor for Veterans Employment & Training.

"My assistant Tonja Pardo, who was promoted to Director when I retired in 2010, would watch me during the day and Shirley at night. I was so depressed. One day, Tonja asks, 'Are you going to call the VA or am I?' I couldn't talk, and we have a stare down. After over a minute she raises her voice, 'I'm calling them.'

"I meet with Dr. David Collier, and he starts asking me questions like, 'So your father passed away, and you and your brothers had to sell the family farm?' I told him, 'Yes, it's depressing.' And he says, 'So let's talk about Vietnam.' I immediately respond in a raised voice, "I don't have PTSD from Vietnam, I was only there three weeks.'

"Dr Collier keeps asking questions, 'So you were blown up and lost a leg after stepping on a mine?' I answer, 'Yes.' He says, 'You lost a couple of friends over there? You felt like you were unable to protect them?' I say, 'Yes.' He says, 'You felt you were not there for them?' I again say, 'Yes.' He asks, 'You have survivor's guilt?' I say, 'Yes.' 'You have PTSD!' Dr. Collier tells me in a raised voice.

"I learned that Tonja had told Dr. Collier everything, but I'm very grateful to her. The counseling at the Vet Center has been very helpful.

"After a few years, it became my goal to meet up with all who saved me. I realize that the doctors and nurse of the 2nd Surgical Hospital fought hard to save my life. I felt compelled to find them and thank them personally.

"I found out the doctor, Dr. Robert First, who saved me was still working in a private practice in Concord, Massachusetts. I called and told the receptionist my story. Jerry and Karen Pero and Shirley went with me. It was in November of '99."

"The receptionist and nurses gave me the last appointment of the day and did not tell the doctor. He walks in wearing his white coat into my waiting room, Jerry, Karen, and Shirley are standing in the back with cameras. He doesn't recognize me. I present him with a copy of my prognosis report from '68 with the notation of 'Survival not expected'. I ask, 'Can I have a second opinion?' We laugh, cry, and hug several times. Both Ron and Shirley get tears in their eyes. Robert was one of the top orthopedic surgeons in the world.

"He tells me that I was not supposed to make it, and that they felt that I lost too much blood, and my body was in too much shock and trauma to complete the initial operation. Also, the heel of my boot was lodged inside my left thigh and could not be removed right away. And I had lots of shrapnel in me.

"Dr. First felt guilty because he could never give complete and quality care to his patients during initial surgeries because there were just too many wounded being rushed through the operating suites and not enough time to properly treat them.

"After that, we attended the big event 'Delta to the DMZ' in Washington D.C. when the Women's Vietnam Veterans Memorial was dedicated in November 1993. Jerry and Karen Pero went with us, and we made signs that said, 'Looking for nurses who worked at 2nd Surgical Hospital in April of '68.' I also brought a copy of my medical paperwork.

"After a while, a lady approaches me says, 'I was there in '68. I hand her the paperwork and she starts crying. 'This is my handwriting' she says. We hug and cry. A little later we find another nurse.

"For hours, the three of us dance together and hold hands." Shirley laughs and says, "It's a good thing our marriage was strong." Pam (Beck) Brann and Lieutenant Colonel Pat (Gruber) Sowder were the nurses. Ron shows me a picture of him and both nurses at the dance. The joy and happiness of all three just jumps out of the photograph.

"After the dance that night, late at night, Jerry and I walk down to the Vietnam Nurses Memorial with a fifth of Jack Daniels to toast the nurses. We cry and toast them many times," Ron gets emotional again and then laughs. "Good thing we were walking from our hotel," laughing again.

Ron raises his voice, "Ken, these nurses would not let me die. Did you know these nurses would crawl in bed and cuddle with a badly wounded soldier who was going to die at any moment? They would softly stroke their hair and let them know they were loved. They would lie with them till the end." We all have tears in our eyes now.

"And all of those Dustoff pilots who went into harm's way time and time again. Whenever I hear the whop-whop of one of those birds, I stop and tear up. That was a lifeline for Vietnam veterans. They were there when we needed them.

"I tracked down Ron Van Avery's adult children in Portland in June 1998. I met his son Brian and daughter Debbie. Debbie was two years old, and Brian was four years old when their father was killed in Vietnam. They were thirty-two and thirty-four when I met them. I showed them my scrapbook with all of my pictures and answered questions with lots of tears and laughs. Very healing for us all."

Every April, Ron goes up to Oregon's Vietnam Memorial to pay his respect to Ron Van Avery. There is a granite bench with the words etched in it that says, 'So long as we are not forgotten, we do not die. And this garden is a place of life.' Ron always toasts his buddy with a bottle of Jack Daniels.

Ron Cannon is still living at the age of 75.

MIKE BRESHEARS

Mike and his wife Irene are two fantastic people. Both have been heavily involved with veteran related causes and especially Vietnam veteran causes ever since seeing our Traveling Vietnam War Wall in 1986.

Upon returning from Vietnam in '68, Mike said, "I didn't have anyone spit on me or say anything bad, but the army was very unappreciative. There were threats from the military that if I said anything, I was going to be in a lot of trouble. I felt intimidated. I put everything on the line only to come back feeling like a criminal by the VA and by the Army." Mike would have nothing to do with veterans. But the Wall changed his thinking.

Mike's father, Herb, was a WWII Navy veteran who attended the first few LHDs at Milwaukie High, and Mike came with him. Mike also helped organize a big parade in the small town of Canby in '95 to honor the 50th Anniversary of WWII.

He also sold Ackerman Middle School administration and staff to invite WWII veterans to the very first Living History Day at the school to honor the 50th Anniversary of WWII.

With the help of his wife Irene, Mike's most impressive feat was the fundraising and building of the Vietnam Era Veterans Memorial in Canby. It took eleven years of fundraising. He went to organizations for help, but donation money was slow. They weren't getting donations from large companies, but from mainly small groups and organizations around Canby.

It was a community affair raising. Mike even set up a table at our local Cutsforth's Thriftway where local residents were donating to his cause. In the end he was able to get the funding to secure a helicopter from the Department of Defense.

The memorial features a one of the most recognized helicopter types in the world, a Bell UH-1, better known as the 'Huey'. It sits aloft in the air on a pedestal made to look like it is approaching a landing pad with a giant Red Cross symbol. Next to the pad is and a bronze statue called 'A Hero's Prayer', depicting a wounded soldier carried by another soldier with a Vietnamese girl holding the wounded soldier's hand.

The wounded soldier being carried represents Army Spec. Warren E. Newton of Canby, who was eighteen on January 9, 1968, when he went missing in action. The soldier carrying Newton represents Marine Pfc. Gary W. Martini of Portland, who was awarded the Medal of Honor for rescuing two other Marines during a firefight that killed him at age eighteen on April 21, 1967.

The memorial that Mike and Irene helped to become a reality, stands as a testament to the goodwill of Canby residents in its continuing support of veterans. If you ever come to Canby, Oregon, you must see that actual full-sized Huey helicopter, which was donated by the Department of Defense, suspended high above the landing pad. Thank you, Mike and Irene!

Mike Breshears is still living at the age of 75.

NORMAN HAUGK

Norm was very loyal and supportive of our mission at high schools for many years, but I never heard his story. I'm so grateful to him for talking with me, as well as the many other Vietnam veterans who have been sharing their personal experiences.

"I was born in Portland and attended Portland Public Schools graduating from Cleveland High School in 1963."

"Were you involved in any extracurricular activities?"

"I threw the discus on the track team, and my proudest accomplishment was running a mile in seven minutes and fourteen seconds on a route with many hills." As he said this I could hear the pride in his tone of voice.

"I enrolled at PSU in '64, but I was a little too wild though and my grades were not good. I was into drag racing on public highways like 99E and lost my driver's license after receiving my thirteenth speeding ticket," He said laughing.

"Did you cruise also?"

"Oh yes, lot of fun back in those days. At that time, I started working full time at the Oregonian newspaper and lost my student deferment and was drafted in '65, so I decided to just enlist in the Army for three years.

"Starting in May of '66, I spent eight weeks of Basic Training at Fort Ord and then eight weeks of individual training. I was then sent to Fort Sam Houston in San Antonio for Medical Field Training.

"Because my scores were always over ninety, I was put in Administration. After eight weeks of that, there were one hundred and thirteen of us, which was thirteen over what they needed for billet. We thought we could relax and went out drinking that night.

"We got in trouble and the thirteen of us were sent to Vietnam first. I was assigned the 277th Combat Support Battalion at the Replacement Depot in Long Bien. Found out later that it never existed. The first six days I worked four hours on and then four hours off on guard duty or KP (Kitchen Patrol). I was so scared hearing our B-52s bombing.

"Then I was assigned to the 1st Infantry at in Di An. We flew in a commercial airline and walked through an airport busy with many Vietnamese people. We were not issued rifles yet and were loaded on a bus with bars over the windows and two armed guards.

"The road we traveled on was full of traffic and would stop from time to time as a Vietnamese person would stop their car, get out, take a pee or a crap on the side of the road. They acted like it was no big deal.

"It was something else. We arrived around two in the morning. It was so dark you couldn't even see your hand in front of your face. That first night I couldn't sleep, heard every little noise. When I was issued a rifle, I was told to not 'Lock 'n Load' while sleeping because us new guys could not be trusted. I was a new grunt in country and was so scared that I never took my boots off for a week.

"The heat was so tough on me; I used a blanket to cover my face. We were taught all the dangers of trap and insurgency. I spent my first night sleeping outside the perimeter, laying on the ground, being silent, wide awake all night. We always carried lots of ammunition.

"But I do have a somewhat humorous story. We finally were given half of a Sunday off, so a bunch of us walked to village close by to get a beer. After we drank a few beers, my buddies grabbed me and shoved me into a room and locked the door. There was a naked Vietnamese woman laying on a bed.

"I turned around and started pounding and pounding on that door, cussing them out and yelling, 'I'm engaged to a woman back home. I was not that kind of guy. After I don't know how long, I turned around and saw that she was the most beautiful woman I'd ever seen. I succumbed; I took advantage of her."

"Wait a minute, you want this in your section?" I said in a surprised voice. "Does your wife know about this?"

"Yes, It's okay. I told my wife everything before we got married, and we've been married fifty-seven years. This will shock you, but it's the truth. It cost $1.67 for sex and if you wanted to be with her all night, it was $9. And the 67 cents because it was 1967. I was two hours late back to camp and was ordered two hours extra duty every day for weeks.

"Soon after that, I don't remember how long, I was reassigned to Medical Headquarters with Company A in the Dispensary on December 24 for only two days. My buddy, Ron Reneau, and I were the only ones there and just drank on Christmas Eve and Christmas Day. It was the shittiest Christmas ever. After Christmas, I was offered to be one of four company clerks and that was my job for the next six weeks."

"You sure got bounced around a lot," I added.

"It didn't end. Because I had good grades and said I was smart, I was assigned 52nd Infantry 3rd Division Battalion Clerk, Security and Intelligence Medical Operations at Battalion headquarters. My job was keeping records, updating records, and preparing the casualties report every day. On the intelligence side, I would prepare reports on the locations of the NVC. It was difficult because they were constantly on the move. We tried our best at anticipating their next move."

"What was the casualty report work?"

"Everyone was issued a Field Medical Card with all their information on them. The soldier received half of the card and we had the other half. Every single day I received the Soldier's half filled out with how they were wounded or killed in action."

"Was that hard to do emotionally?"

"Shockingly, I became numb to it all as I typed up reports. They were just a name. But the guilt overwhelmed me at the first Milwaukie High School Living History Day I attended. Attending the Gold Star assembly, suddenly every name I typed on those reports became human."

Norm's voice became very emotional telling me that and he paused.

"Junction City was the name of an operation and Shenandoah II. There were sixty-seven KIAs from one company. I had to type up the letter that was sent to the mothers, fathers, and spouses. Watching the movie, *We were Soldiers* was painful for me. Seeing the part of the movie when the taxi driver delivers the telegram to the widows, I cry every time. I've seen that movie over thirty times."

I said, "Yes, that is a powerful movie. I actually tried to get them to come to Milwaukie. They all wanted to, but it was always the same week as their reunions."

"I want to share this experience also; I witnessed three different interrogations of the enemy, and we all used the word "gook" all the time. But this was the first time I saw them as human beings. We were taught that they were second class citizens. I never used that word again.

"With my new assignment, I only faced danger three times. Once I was brushing my teeth when eight rounds came into the building very close to where I was. I dropped to the floor. The second time, I was ordered to drive an officer into Saigon. That was something because 1st Division was not allowed into Saigon then.

"On my drive back to base, I took a wrong turn and was driving into the Kill Zone. I backtracked and made it back before dark. The third time, I was driving to the PX for beer and cigarettes and came to a stop. A hand grenade rolled out from under the seat and the cotter pin was three quarter the way out. For about five seconds, I was scared shitless and slowly pushed the pin back in.

"I'm very glad I served in Vietnam, and I promised myself when I got home, I would not waste any day I lived as I owe those all those men and women who were killed in action. I still get tears in my eyes when I hear 'Taps.'"

"Is there anything else you would like to share about your Vietnam experience?"

"I remember going on R&R in Bangkok and how beautiful it was. It was so clean and smelled great. Lot of areas in Vietnam smelled so bad, like a garbage can. Lots of rats. I had a big candy bar next to my cot and the next day it was half eaten. I accused my buddies only to learn, rats had been helping themselves. I opened my footlocker, and it was full of maggots. Took it outside and burned it.

"Oh, Our M16s would jam on the first shot, and someone figured out that if you took the first round out of the chamber and left the other nineteen rounds in the clip, it solved the problem.

"I do have a funny story for you though. Remember the half card from soldiers I would get every day. Well, many of them had on them 0303 which is the clap (gonorrhea). Every detail, how, why, time, location, and how many times they had intercourse." Norm laughed about telling me that.

"I came home in December of '67. We had to surrender our rifles and many of us were waiting for the bus when a chaplain approaches us, circles us up, and prays for our safe trip home. When that plane lifted off from the ground, we were all very happy.

'I remember taking my first hot shower for over an hour. In Vietnam, you got your body wet, turned off the water, soaped up, turned water back on and rinsed. If you worked late there was no water. Just walking to the latrine in the heat, I would be soaked from sweat by the time I got back to work."

'Were you greeted with protestors when you returned?"

"No, I arrived in Portland at 5:00 AM, took a bus downtown, ran into a former co-worker from the Oregonian. He gave me a ride home. I surprised my mother. I didn't tell her anything. It was very a moving and emotional homecoming. Within two months I married my girlfriend, Ginny, married fifty-one years, three children. And, I went back to school and averaged a 3.65 GPA."

"That's awesome, any last thoughts on Vietnam?"

"I have made it a goal to find the names on The Wall of as many soldiers who I typed up their information for the telegrams sent home to loved ones. I have found all those sixty-seven killed on that one day. Every name I touch, I always cry, can't help it. I'll never forget them."

Norman Haugk is still living at the age of 77.

TERRY LOW

Terry is the president of the 1st Cavalry Division Oregon Chapter and their chapter always stood out as they wore their distinctive Black Cavalry hats, and they looked sharp. He agreed to be interviewed for this book, but not to talk about any bad stuff by simply stating, "I'd rather not."

Terry was born in Portland and graduated from Washington High School in '66. He wrestled for two years and then got a job. He kept working until he was drafted in April of '68. He decided to enlist.

"My MOS was as Artillery Surveillance with the 4th Armored Division, which was the spearhead of Patton's 3rd Army during WWII. I spent ten months in Germany. I was assigned to the 1st Air Cav and was sent to Vietnam in October of '69. I was first assigned to the Air Warning Control Center for a short time, then transferred to be a Radio Operator on the Cambodian border with Special Forces.

"Humping with a radio on your back was not fun. That assignment wasn't very long either. I was then assigned as an Artillery Liaison with the 1st Battalion, 7th Cavalry, Custer's own, and the same unit that was at Battle at Ia Drang Valley. Did you watch the movie *We were Soldiers*? I did that job for over seven months.

"Several of us went back to Vietnam a couple of years ago, and we went back to the place where we served. The jungle was completely gone. It was a huge rubber plantation. There many rubber trees and cashew trees also.

"The trip was very healing for me as I was filled with a lot of hate even towards the South Vietnamese soldiers. I felt many of them did not want to fight, but my hate for them disappeared because of that trip."

When my wife Malinda and I started the Vietnam Veteran Apology Cause in the summer of 2019, I emailed a personal apology to all of the Vietnam veterans I knew. I received many heartfelt emails and phone calls of gratitude from them. They all started sharing their personal experiences being confronted from protesters when they returned home.

A local news station, KPTV, wanted to do a story on our Apology Cause and asked if they could interview a veteran. I called Terry and asked if he was interested. "No. It's too painful to talk about." Was the answer I got from him.

A few days later, KPTV called me again and asked if they could call Terry. I told them no, but that I would call him one more time. I asked Terry to please consider the interview again, because felt it is very important that Americans know about the injustice the veterans had when then returned home. He said, "Ok, I think about."

The next day he called me back and said, "Ken, just thinking about it is triggering my PTSD bad. I had a hard time sleeping last night. The answer is still no."

Well, it was the month of September, and KPTV decided to wait to run the piece close to Veterans Day and asked me to try to ask other Vietnam veterans. Every one of them I called declined.

Several weeks later, Terry calls me. "Ken, I have been thinking about it a lot, and I'm ready to tell my story." After he sat down with KPTV for the story Terry told me what he had said and kept telling me more.

"While I was in Vietnam, my parents received a phone call telling them that I was Missing In Action (MIA). My mother sat by the phone for days waiting to hear any news. Nothing came. We learned years later that the VC had infiltrated some of our bases and were sending personal information back to the States to protest organizers. They were calling the parents and telling them that they were glad their baby-killing son was dead.

"About two weeks after we came back from Cambodia to our base, I was ordered to a MARS station (Military Auxiliary Radio System) with short range radios and ordered to call home immediately. After several attempts, none of the calls went through, I was ordered to write a letter home right now. My parents never received the letter and didn't learn I was alive till I got back home."

"Tell me about coming home," I said, changing the subject because I could see Terry didn't want to talk about the subject further.

"We were required to be in for thirteen months, around six months active, and then we could get out. I was in 150 days, but then they extended it to 180 days. After that I was ordered to grab my ruck sack, and told I was going home. A helicopter took us to the 1st Air Cav Base.

"Every day, names are called out for plane assignments. After five days, I checked with a Segreant why I was not called and couldn't find out why. He tells me to put in for a flight to Hong Kong for a delay in route. It gets turned down, and I'm told just go back to my unit and come back in twenty-five days.

"Well, I'm pissed, I'm not going back. I catch a ride on a jeep to Saigon to our major bases at Long Binh. I was not assigned to anything, nobody cared about me, and nobody turned me in. So, I drank beer at the NCO club every night. I even tried smoking dope for the first time. I stayed in a hotel in Saigon and had a great time."

"So how did you get back home?"

"I finally got flown to Okinawa and sat next to a young soldier who was going to be a lifer. He had a girlfriend in Okinawa and offered to show me around, but I had to report to the office. An Air Force officer tells me to get back on the plane. My new friend says, 'Just come with me we can drink and party.'

"After a couple of days, I go back to the base and the officer yells at me, 'What in the hell have you been doing? The next flight is at twenty hundred. You better be on it.' We got in late in Oakland, and missed the protestors, thank God."

"Is there anything else you want to say?" There was a long pause.

"I decided I have something I want to share. It took us three days to build our bunker where I would work twelve to eighteen hours a day. It was right next to the Tactical Operation Center close to the Cambodian border.

"The first night we were attacked by ground. They had no weapons and only wore underwear. They carried bombs and our bunker was one of the targets. They blew up the bunker close to us by mistake. My best friend, Phil Salgado was badly wounded and medevaced out before I could see him. We could not find out if he made it or not. We were not allowed that information.

"But I don't know how they made the mistake as our bunker had two guards posted in front, and we were about sixty feet away from the center. It was the only time I did not have my rifle with me, I had accidently left it outside. After the explosion and firefight, a bunker was found outside the perimeter with NVA clothes and a map. The map had everything on it. I was just lucky.

"We were attacked again the next night. I was at the tent where the cooks were serving coffee and started walking back to our bunker when someone yells, 'We got movement'. I was wearing a dark colored T-shirt, my fatigue bottoms, bare feet, no hat, it's pitch black, and I'm Chinese American. I stop walking as a M16 is pointed inches from my face. Lucky for me it was not a new guy as he realized I wasn't a 'gook.'

"Anyway, I couldn't stop thinking about my buddy, Phil. Was he alive or not? About a year after I got home, I went to the library, got a Eugene, Oregon phone book, found his parents number and called them. Phil was living with his parents. We visited each other three times.

"The fourth time I called, his parents said he was gone. It wasn't until 2010 that I found him in Spokane, Washington. I called his office number, Phil answers and is silent for the longest time.

"He finally says, 'I guess it was meant to be, you tracking me down again. I just retired, had cleaned out my office, and my phone rang. I wasn't going to answer it.'

"I told him, 'The 1st Air Cav is having a National Reunion in Portland, Oregon in 2012 and I would love for you to attend. He agreed, but never showed up. On the third day of the reunion, I called him, and he apologized and said, 'I just couldn't do it. But my brother is having a concert in Happy Valley, Oregon this summer and I'm coming down for that."

Phil's younger brother is the well-known and successful Blues musician Curtis Salgado. "Well, me and several of my 1st Air Cav buddies go to the concert, but Phil never shows. So, during the first set, I hand a note to one of the stage guys basically writing that his brother and I were good friends in Vietnam. During the first break, I get in the line for buying CDs with an autograph.

"My note is handed to Curtis, he reads it, stands up and starts looking around and sees me. He points to me and waves to come up front. We talked for the rest of his break. Curtis was so happy to meet me.
"Later that summer, I attended another concert, and I had a picture of Phil in Cambodia blown up and gave it to Curtis. I've gone to many of his concerts in the years since."

"I do have one funny story for you. It's funny now, but at the time I wasn't very happy about it. In Saigon, I went to a steam bath house. My buddies told me you could negotiate for sex with the women.

"So, I start talking with this older lady who greets me, and after finishing I am escorted inside. I guess she misunderstood me. She puts me in a steam box, shuts the door and leaves me in it for a half hour. To this day, I can never go in a steam bath."

Terry Low is still living at the age of 73.

AL BLAIN SR.

I first met Al Sr. in 1980, when I taught PE at Redland Elementary in Oregon City. I coached his son Al Jr. in three sports. He was a great kid who was very friendly and respectful. After getting to know his father and his mother, Sue, I learned why. I saw them as great parents and Al Sr. always had a smile and a positive attitude.

"In 1982, I was hired at Milwaukie High School and lost track of them until Al Jr.'s senior year in high school. He was awarded the Scholar Athlete of the Year, representing the entire league and then went on to be a starting defensive back playing for some great Portland State football teams.

"On our first Living History Day, Al Sr. showed up with two other gentlemen, all dressed in Revolutionary War Continental Army uniforms. The three of them loved teaching young people about our veterans. I recognized him and we had a great visit.

As I started to walk away, Al Sr. stated, "You know, I'm a Vietnam veteran. I was in the Army." Al Sr. came to many of our Living History Days and always dressed as a Continental soldier.

"I was born raised on our family farm in Conway, South Carolina, 14 miles from Myrtle Beach. My parents bought the farm using my mother's dowery, and they had fourteen children. I graduated from Whittemore High School in 1963. It was an all-black school as schools were still segregated. In my senior yearbook, I was the only graduate who's only goal was to be a farmer.

"In high school I was a boxer, and I thought I was good. My sparring partner was Johnny Goss who fought both at the amateur and professional levels. "Johnny had an exhibition fight with Muhammad Ali, and he sparred with Joe Frazier.

"After high school, I worked on the farm, did yard work for money, drove delivery trucks up into North Carolina and down into Georgia. I owe my strong work ethics to my parents.

"I had to get up early to do farm chores, go to school, boxing practice, and back home for more chores. We grew cotton, tobacco, peanuts, and watermelons. My father always preached to us, 'You move up in life. Don't drop down. Make something of yourself.'"

As I started to ask my next question, Al Sr. interrupted me, "You know we're talking about the '50s and early '60s out in the country in South Carolina, right? My father had to work full time at a lumber mill, so we had quarantined income.

"And almost every year, the local KKK would burn down some or a lot of our crops. It was their way of letting us know that they were always in power. The town's sheriff, police officers, and most of the business owners were in the Klan.

"I learned how to shoot a gun as a child and always carried it with me and still do now, except now it's legal. I had to get out of there, or I would be dead or in prison. I just couldn't handle all the 'whites only' or 'colored only' signs. There was always two bathrooms for whites and only one for blacks. We had to step off the sidewalk, into the street to let whites pass."

"Why did you come to Oregon?"

"In the seventh grade, I read *The Oregon Trail* for a book report. The required length was one and a half pages." Al Sr. laughed, "mine was seven pages. I got an A+ and the teacher wrote on the back, 'You owe it to yourself a visit to Oregon someday.'

"So, Sue, my sweetheart from seventh grade, and I drove to Oregon. We were coming down Highway 84, came around a corner and there was Mt. Hood. In a loud excited voice, I said, "Oh my God, this is heaven. This is home. We've been here ever since.

"After the war started, I was drafted into the infantry and because of my experience driving trucks. I was made a heavy equipment operator, driving not only trucks, but bulldozers and graders. I was sent to Vietnam in '67 with the 815th Engineer Battalion, B Company. We were shipped over with all of the heavy equipment."

"Now I have to ask the question I've asked the WWII and Korean War veterans. Did you get seasick?"

"No, I never did, but most did, and the worst was when we got hit by a storm. It was scary. Big tremendous waves. The whole ship would shake. Everyone was praying. Yes indeed. You could see the sides of the ship bend back and forth from down below. I also got my first sunburn. It was very hot, and we spent a lot of time up top with shirts off. I got blisters.

"Finally, we pulled into Cameron Bay and had to climb down rope netting into landing craft just like they did in WWII. Then they let us out into chest high deep water to walk up to the beach. Our very first night, Charlie hit us with shells, and we had to hunker down.

"We convoyed to Pleiku in Central Vietnam in the mountains where I witnessed my first fatality while being shelled. Finally, we made it and took over from the 25th Infantry Division who then moved out.

"Our jobs were to build roads and landing strips. Part of our assignments were to go out and look for Charlie.

"Many times, we had to go support the 4th Division about ten miles from Pleiku. Sadly, the 4th was having drug problems and had some instances where their coordination with air strikes was bad. One time we came to help, and it was bad."

Al Sr. paused and seemed very shook up, and I knew it might have been friendly fire with us hitting our own because of coordinating mistakes. I decided to move on.

"Other times we had to pull guard duty, two weeks at a time for the Air Force across town. We watched Charlie, right in front of us ride bikes, three-wheels, and even water buffalos, all were carrying mortars and rockets. They knew we were ordered to not shoot unless fired upon. Every night we got hit with those mortars and rockets. We were told the reason why is because this was the first war shown every night on TV. We were very angry.

"Once, when I was driving the grader out of town to work on a runway, there were lots of bicycles and three-wheel traffic on this dirt road. A Vietnamese man riding his bike next to me pulls out a rifle and aims it at me.

"Thankfully, I see this and duck before he can shoot me. After his shot goes off, I quickly fire back emptying a clip and a half. I have no idea how many I hit. The grader was still moving forward when the blade of the grader hit a mine. The shrapnel from the explosion hit the blade and bounced away from me. The blade was destroyed, but I able to drive back to base.

"I wrote my wife a letter and wrote what happened and she wrote back, 'Bunny, you take better care of yourself over there.' Bunny was my nickname since childhood."

Al Sr. paused and then said in very serious voice, "I've got a painful experience that needs to be told. While I'm in Vietnam fighting for America, my sister Feena Bell was attending Claflin College, an all-black college in Orangeburg, South Carolina. Many black students protested a local segregated bowling alley and within two days it got ugly with the police.

"The mayor of Orangeburg tells everyone, 'We don't want all those niggers coming into town.' The Governor activates the National Guard and orders troops and the local police to the campus, private property by the way. The college kids build a bonfire towards the entrance. Someone starts throwing rocks at the police and the police open fire. Three students were killed and twenty-eight wounded mostly in the back while running away.

"When I got a letter from home telling me what happened, I was so angry I wrote a letter to President Johnson and in that letter, I said as soon as I get off the plane back in the USA, I'm going to kill the first white person I see.

"I was already getting really tired of dealing with racist crap in Vietnam. Anyway, President Johnson wrote me back and included eight pages of information on what he was doing about racism in the States."

"That's amazing. Do you still have the letter from Johnson?"

"No, my sister does, I don't want it. My name was turned into the FBI. They must have thought I was a Black Panther and for the next seven years we would hear clicks during phone conversations. I strongly believe our phone was tapped and then one day the clicks just stopped."

Getting back to Vietnam, I asked, "How did you deal with the memories of Vietnam?"

"I owe a lot to my wife. I had to have constant noise and could not handle the quiet. I could only fall asleep with noise. If it was quiet, the hair on my arms would stand up.

"Sue saved my life once. I had driven up to Connecticut to pick her up from college, and we stopped at a 'colored's only' beach around Atlantic City. As we started driving back to South Carolina, a car cut me off, so I followed him to a gas station.

"I get out of my car and the owner of the gas station yells at me, 'Hey nigger, what the hell are you doing driving so fast?' As I walked toward the car of the guy who cut me off, I see an Army sticker on his bumper.

"I asked him, 'Were you in the Army?' He responded, 'I still am, a PFC.' 'Well, I'm a Sargent. Be careful who you cut off!' He said, 'Yes Sir.' The gas station owner gets really angry now, calling me names and telling the private he doesn't have to listen to a nigger. I tell him to shut up, or I'm going to get my gun out my car and shoot him.

"He still keeps calling me names, so I run to my car, open the driver's side door, and grab for my gun under the seat. It's not there. Sue had taken it and would not give it back. I was going to kill him. We headed down the road and the local police followed us for a few miles, but never stopped us."

Al Sr. immediately changed the subject. "So now I have a heck of a humorous story for you. Coming back after a two-week duty, a care package from my wife was waiting for me. There were all kinds of goodies, a cake, and some Kodak film. I shared it all with my buddies. It was late, and I wanted to go to bed, so I tell my friend, a tall Native American named Buck to pull down all of the netting.

"Well, in the middle of the night I'm awakened by a large rat biting my finger. I was so angry at Buck, he forgot to pull down the netting, and I wanted to beat the hell out of him. For fourteen days in a row, I was given a shot in the navel. I chewed Buck out really good.

"Another humorous story is that we all got all kinds of skin rashes, jock rot, feet, etc. But I got a rash on my penis, and it looked like tiny warts. Don't worry about putting that in your book. It don't bother me. It's the truth.

"The doctor told me I needed to be circumcised as it would allow the medicine to work. The night after the operation, my penis swells to about ten times its normal size. There are seven other soldiers in the tent with me and all had the same operation, and their penises were swollen too.

"Another thing, because Charlie liked to attack at night, I told everyone we needed a plan if we get attacked. If anyone comes through the door, I'm going to shoot. Well, in the middle of the night, we are awoken to some noise outside our tent. We all stand up, buck naked aiming our rifles at the tent flap. Nothing happened until we all looked at each other and started laughing.

"I'd like to end this with by saying, 'My country sent me to Vietnam, and my Heavenly Father brought me back home.' Ken, True Love won't look at anything but love. Love conquers all."

Al Blain Sr. is still living at the age of 77.

---- ⋆ ★ ⋆ ----

DAVID BRANHAM

David dropped out of Milwaukie High School at the end of his junior year, and that summer he joined the Army after they told him he could finish his senior year while in the Army.

"They kind of lied to me."

I asked, "So why did you drop out?"

"Well, it's kind of a long story. My parents divorced when I was a kid. My mother remarried, and my stepfather did not like me or want me around. I left at sixteen and moved into an abandoned house in Milwaukie. The lady that owned the house eventually found out but allowed me to live in the basement. I worked two different jobs all through high school. My father signed for me even though he had no legal right. My mother didn't even care."

"So how did you end up in Vietnam?"

"That's a hell of story. Boot camp was at Fort Lewis, and I wanted to drive heavy equipment, so I was sent to Kentucky driving mostly APCs (Armored Personnel Carrier), but I wanted to drive tanks. After that training, I was told I would not be sent to Vietnam and was going to be stationed in Germany. I was very happy about that.

"Back home on leave, I get a call from my sister who tells me Daniel Mambretti was killed in action in Vietnam. Daniel was a good friend, great guy, very popular, outgoing, everyone at Milwaukie loved him. My sister's boyfriend was Daniel's best friend and they both joined together to be paratroopers.

"I was so angry at hearing the news, I requested to be sent to Vietnam not Germany to avenge the death of my friend. I was reassigned to infantry; I never drove the entire time over there. We were all put in Bravo Company the same unit of Lt. Calley of the My Lai Massacre. Everyone was new.

"One month in Vietnam, a buddy of mine was killed in action. We were out in the field and there was a huge explosion down the road. A truck was hit and one of the men was blown out of the truck and landed in a rice patty. He was upright on his knees screaming for help and then fell over dead. The bottom half of his body was gone. That was my first experience, and everyone was scared and shook up."

"Damn, I'm so sorry David." David didn't respond and he just started talking again.

"We protected a tiny LZ (Landing Zone), and some locals warned us that we would be over run that night, so we stayed up all night and moved out in the morning. We humped all over for three weeks in the jungle and had several firefights. After one of them, we came upon some dead NVA soldiers and one nurse. With them was a Red Chinese soldier in full uniform with all kinds of papers on him. Our company received a medal for that."

"I've heard talk that there were Red Chinese soldiers involved, but you are the first veteran I've met who saw it firsthand."

"We were sent out again to protect another LZ. At one end was a large U-shaped tree line. Behind the trees was a battalion of NVA, and we were hit bad. Most of my platoon was wiped out. Our Captain was hit in the chest and instantly killed, seven were badly wounded, missing limbs. Four were killed. Several collapsed from battle exhaustion or combat fatigue. A good buddy of mine, Jerald DeLong from Wisconsin, was killed on October 12th, 1970. I zipped up his body bag and it was difficult.

"I came out without even a scratch. I was then an assigned to another platoon. Because I had been in the jungle the longest, I was ordered to a seven-man snake squad to go out at night to find villages. The Lt. ordered me point, and we found a VC soldier, and I was ordered to guard her as we returned to base.

"She was in front of me, and she tripped on purpose on a booby trap. The blast was set up to explode towards anyone walking towards the village. I caught the back end of the blast, was thrown into the air and landed upright on my knees. I got up and started to run but fell. There was lots of blood on my legs. I was evacuated to a M.A.S.H. unit and then an evacuation hospital.

"I was out for three days and when I came to, the nurse told me, 'You lost so much blood, you were actually dead for twenty minutes till we brought you back.' My entire body, arms, and legs were strapped down. I was hit on the back of my legs, and there was shrapnel lodged against my sciatic nerve, and they left it there for the time being.

"When I finally woke up again, I asked if I was home and if I still had my legs. The nurse standing by my side said, "No, you are still in Vietnam and yes, you still have both legs." They did many tests. I had no movement or feelings in my legs. The doctor said, "You are paralyzed from the waist down. You have a fifty-fifty chance of ever walking again. You can go to Germany or stay here. If you go to Germany, your odds of losing your legs is higher.

"I stayed and went through several surgeries. If it wasn't for a nurse, Sandy, she was an angel, I wouldn't be here today. Every night, she would roll me over and give me massages. She gave her heart and soul to me. She pushed my bed down the hallway to the payphones to call home. Those nurses are amazing.

"My father was told by the Red Cross that I was killed in action. He answers the phone and I say, 'Hi Dad.' Dad angerly yells back, 'Who is this?' I told him, 'David, your son.' He yells back, 'No, my son is dead.' My father who was a WWII, Purple Heart veteran yelled even louder, 'Are you some communist?' It took some talking, and I got him to ask me some personal questions that only he and I would know, till he finally believed me."

David continued, "Dad called my mom and my wife. Over a week later, I receive a letter from my wife. I asked Sandy to read it. 'Dear David, Due to the fact that you are an invalid, I want to end our marriage.' Sandy starts crying uncontrollably. I was more concerned about Sandy than the letter.

"'I'm so sorry about the Dear John letter." David laughs and says, "She was just the first of three wives. The other two left me because of my drinking and anger issues.

"So, my legs were all wired up, and I had lost the majority of my muscles on the back of my legs. I was sent to the Cameron Bay Hospital for rehab. Soon, I was able to move my toes and walk on crutches using my left leg, my right leg was in the worst shape. Man, they pushed me hard.

"After completing rehab, I was sent back to my platoon using crutches and a walking cane sometimes. My CO (Commanding Officer) yelled at me, 'What in the hell am I supposed to do with you?' I was assigned to guard a radar base on Hill 103 with a sandbag hootch. High profile guests would visit us.

"One of the soldiers I became friends with was a backup singer for Elvis Presley and every night he would sing for us. Man, he had a beautiful voice.

"After a few months, this base was closed down, but I had improved my ability to walk. Back at the main base, a Lt. asked me to drive a jeep to the rear and pick up supplies, but a Captain ordered me to stay as he wanted to go and spend the night there. On his way back, the captain was almost hit from a grenade that a soldier, high on drugs, had fired at the jeep. He was arrested and charged with attempted murder."

"Wow," I said. "Did he serve prison time?"

"Twelve years in Leavenworth. The grenade was meant for me as he hated me because I would never do drugs with him. His name was Ron Mason.

"After that, I was assigned guard duty in a tree fort. Every thousand yards was another tree fort. It was in the rear and well protected. The new guys would love to talk with me, but got very upset when I showed them my scars.

"Our company was hit real hard, and every available body was ordered out. The first night we went out on a snake again and set up claymore mines. Later that night we heard the explosions. We went out the next day and found three dead NVA in uniforms.

"We also took out a gun on top of a hill and found a family and wife's pictures on one of the dead. There was a letter that we had a Vietnamese boy to read for us. The soldier was coming home for good in less than two weeks. That really bothered me. It made him human. A couple days later, I noticed three ulcers on my leg, and they were bleeding. I was flown out on the next chopper.

"After a while, I was starting to crack up, and I spoke to the Chaplin about recommending some R&R. He immediately said, 'No, you're going home.' We flew in at night and were unloaded from the plane on the tarmac and into a bus to avoid the protesters.

"My sister screamed so loud when I snuck into the back door of the kitchen. The lights were out, but she saw my medals shinning in the dark. My dad got out of his chair in the living room and gave me the biggest hug. The next morning, he drives me to Mac's Pit, a restaurant in Milwaukie, no longer there, where my mother is working as a waitress.

"When my mom sees me, she drops a tray of glasses. That was the most reaction I ever received from her. We hugged. My Dad then drives me to Eastman's Car lot in Milwaukie. He's friends with the owner and the owner offers me a beautiful 1960 Chevy for $200.

"While I'm staying at my father's home, this little snot-nosed girl next door sets off some fireworks in the front yard. I dove for cover and ripped my uniform. I would pay her back though as we've been married over forty years. I met her when I was a bartender, and she, Anita, was the sister of a friend. We went on one date, and then a year later went on a second date.

"Back at Fort Lewis, my legs were starting to hurt, and I had to use crutches again. I was put in a dorm by myself and was late to morning revelry. The CO gave me an Article 15 and cut $50 off of my pay. I was late again the next day, so bought an alarm clock, but it didn't work. Late again, another article 15 and $50 cut in pay.

"Next, I asked a sergeant who promised to wake me up but forgot. The CO was so angry at me he gives me new orders back to Vietnam. I took a swing at him and missed and drove home AWOL (Absent Without Official Leave).

"I went to see a doctor, and he said I was not in good shape; my nerves were shot. Even visited Senator Packwood who told me, 'I can only help you after you report back. I went back and was put in the brig. I asked to see a General.

"Later, my attorney made the meeting happen and when we got to his office, the General said, 'I know this man, he served with honor in Vietnam. This order back to Vietnam is a gross example of incompetence of leadership here. Give him an Honorable Discharge.'

"I was a mess; turned to heavy drinking. Got married for the second time, divorced less than a year later because she told me I was half a man. Married a third time, divorced three months after that, but found out she was pregnant. I never got to see my daughter.

"I couldn't afford the alimony and child support and got behind, in court my ex's attorney would drop all charges if I signed adoption papers over to her and her new husband.

"It was 1977 and my dad died from alcoholism and bad PTSD. I got so drunk and, driving down the freeway, pulled into a rest stop, got on my knees, and started praying to God. I cried for about an hour.

"back in my car wouldn't start back up. I thought it had enough gas. I fell asleep and, in the morning, called a friend to bring me some gas. I never had an urge to drink or smoke again.

"I kept bartending though. Then one night, a lady asked if she could see me. I answered, 'Yes, at Church tomorrow. Three weeks later she comes to church, and we've been married ever since."

"And was she was the snot-nosed little girl?" I asked. David laughs and says, "Yes, she was." I then ask, "How did you deal with your PTSD?"

"I had anger issues for years. The VA put me into the psych ward for two weeks. The doctor then sent me to Roseburg, Virginia and put me through some tests. My doctor diagnosed me 100% disabled and the worst case of PTSD he had seen. I went through twenty-one days of therapy and had to come back many times when the anger returned.

"In '91, it got so bad, I couldn't work or help raise my family. I was sent to a PTSD hospital in American Lake for three months. I was diagnosed with 190% PTSD.

"My nightmares were bad, and they taught me how to control them. Life started getting better. My wife stood by me the entire time. She would not let me give up."

I then reminded him, "At Milwaukie High School in 2004, during our Assembly of Honor, we gave you a real diploma, and you wore a maroon graduation cap and gown."

"Yes, it was one of the greatest moments of my life. My whole family was there. It was such an emotional moment, and I was the first Vietnam veteran in Oregon to receive his diploma from their high school.

"It was also the first time I was welcomed home. I was so nervous, but it was very special and gave me a lot of healing. I still get tears in my eyes just thinking about it."

David Branham is still living at the age of 70.

LARRY BUSSEY

I talked over the phone with Reverend Larry Bussey a couple of times when he was helping my wife Malinda organize a memorial service for Malinda's aunt, Mary Alice, who had recently passed away. I asked him if I could interview him about his military and Vietnam war experiences.

He agreed, and I planned on interviewing him over the phone. However, we were able to meet in person in Atlanta for lunch two days before the funeral.

"Okay, let's start when you were born and tell me about your parents."

"I was born June 7, 1949, in Atlanta, Georgia. My mother, Irma Jean, was a nurse in the WACs (The Women's Army Corps) during the Korean War. My father, Freddie was a WWII and Korean War Marine. After the war, he and my mother met while both were stationed in Germany.

"Because of the Korean War and both were career military, they decided it would be best for my grandparents to raise me. I first learned that my mother was not my sister when I was eight years old. I was devastated and it took some time to accept it. I moved in with my parents when I was twelve years old.

"After my freshman year at Morris Brown College, I majored in education and psychology by the way, I decided to take a semester off, get a job, and buy a car. Well, I was drafted, went down to the old Sears building, and was greeted by a large poster of Uncle Sam saying, 'I Want You!' I was put in the line for the Army.

"I had never been out of Atlanta, never been on an airplane. I had no choice. I was put in Infantry and reported to Fort Benning in Georgia. After boot camp sent to Fort Polk, Louisiana for AIT (Advanced Individual Training), jungle training, hand to hand, sniper, tunnel (rat), and reconnaissance training, then to Ranger schooling. I was scared to jump; I hated it. Especially the night jumps. But I made it.

"Our last night, we ate steak and lobster. The next day, we flew to Vietnam on a charter plane. I was there from '70 to '72. The weather was crazy. One minute the sun is out, then the next raining hard, then sunny again.

"I went in the Army with two other high school classmates. We were all sent to Vietnam. I was the only one who came back home. "

Their names are on The Wall. One of my buddies stepped on a mine and heard the click. They tried to weigh it down with sandbags but no luck. He stepped off the mine to save everyone.

"I was 5'9" and 130 lbs. (175 cm 59 kg) soaking wet. The very first time I went down into a tunnel, I came face to face with Charlie. I froze. He says to me in English, 'Brother, this is not your fight,' turned and walked away. I was so scared, I said 'Lord, thank you for saving me, whatever you want me to do, I'll do it.' I started praying every night, the 23rd Psalm and the Lord's Prayer.

"Soon after, during some R&R while I was eating in a restaurant, a rocket hit part of the restaurant. I was lucky again. I took this all as a sign, I'm supposed to do God's work someday.

"We were two per foxhole and put up front, increasing the odds we would get hit first. To this day, I don't know why we were there and what for.

"Leaving Vietnam, as we ran up the ramp into the C-130 and strapped in and took off, our barracks were hit. For me, this was a third sign from God. We flew to Germany, then a charter plane to Seattle. In my duffel bag were three Claymore mines, a M19 mortar, and a RL (Rocket Launcher). I was young and foolish. Customs went through my bag and let me keep the rocket launcher as a souvenir."

"How were you treated coming back home."

"I made the mistake of wearing my uniform, and at the Seattle airport was greeted with, 'That's a son-of-a-bitch who killed babies. You have the nerve to walk through an airport!' Back in Atlanta, even in uniform, I could not get a taxicab ride. But back then in the south, it was difficult to get a cab as a black man.

"I was an Atlanta Police officer from '75 to '88, then transferred to the Fulton County Police. One night, I knock on an apartment door and a Vietnamese lady answers. I yell, 'What are you doing in my country?'

Her husband came to the door, and I left. It was an apartment filled with Vietnamese. I asked if I could not do that area again, as I did not like them, but I didn't know why. It took me some time, but now I have some close friends who are Vietnamese American.

"As a detective, I had to go into two different crack homes with babies living in the most horrible conditions imaginable. I broke down, quit my job, and started drinking again." Reverend Bussey told me what he saw, and it was too disgusting to write about. "I was walking in the pouring down rain and thunder and crying. I heard a voice telling me, 'It's time to preach.' I've been called by God to preach.

"Everything I experienced in Vietnam prepared me for preaching. Reverend Bussey has been preaching ever since and is currently the Associate Minister for Jackson Memorial Baptist Church in Atlanta.

Larry Bussey is still living at the age of 73.

MARK DERRY — Medic

I met Mark years ago at a Canby Rotary luncheon where I was a guest speaker and have run into him several times as we both live in Canby. He is heavily involved with Rotary especially the International Rotary Youth Exchange program. Mark finally agreed to be interviewed after I requested many times.

"I was born in Glendale, California, in September of 1950. The day after graduating from high school, my dad, Kermit, tells me the rent starts now. My dad Kermit was in the Army Air Corps in WW II. My maternal uncle Miles Wollam, served under General MacArthur in Japan after WW II. My father and uncle Miles were classmates in high school.

"My maternal grandfather, Harold Wollam, was a Navy submariner and served in both WW I and WW II. My step uncle, Robert Ordway, was an infantryman and was in the landings of North Africa, Sicily, Normandy, and fought in the Battle of the Bulge. He was my mentor helping in choosing the Army when I enlisted at age seventeen in September 1968.

"With no real interest in going to college, nor having good enough grades, joining the military seemed the best option. My avenue of going into the Army was a better option than a family situation that included physical abuse.

"I was the oldest of five boys, and four of us enlisted in the military, with three of us Vietnam veterans. Two Army, one Navy, and one Air Force. My relationship with my stepmother was like mixing oil and water, and my father was an alcoholic and physically and verbally abusive. My family was very far right conservative and very racist.

"I learned tolerance and grew up to be an adult early on in the Army. I had fellow soldier friends who were black, Latino, and female soldiers. I served with incredible human beings."

"When were you sent to Vietnam?"

"I was a Preventive Medical Specialist 91S MOS (Preventive Medicine Specialist) arriving in Vietnam on March 1, 1969. My job included mess hall inspections, trapping rodents to check for bubonic plague carrying fleas, distribute malaria medicine, and trap and identifying mosquitoes for malaria carrying species.

"My first job in An Khe, Vietnam was as a 91B medic, working in the emergency room, doing triage, IVs, cutdowns, giving out shots, cleaning up blood on the floors and also the stretchers, running shot clinics, treating wounded personnel and civilians, carrying wounded off Dustoff helicopters and any other related emergency room jobs.

"I grew as a human being, and really learned how great the other nurses, medics, specialists, and doctors were during that time. You really learn how good people are working under such stress.

"With one hundred days left (going short), I was moved to LZ English to replace a fellow PM specialist who was wounded during a mortar attack that hit the hootch he was in. I stayed in the same hootch for the remainder of my tour. Two 173rd Airborne soldiers in the hootch next door were killed during the same attack, and I still have photos of the memorial service. It was very sobering and caused survivor's guilt for a long time.

Mark then asked me if I knew who Sharon Lane was, and I answered, no.

"Lt. Sharon Lane was the only female nurse killed by enemy fire. She died on June 8, 1969, in Chu Lai, at the 74th Medical Battalion's 312th Evacuation Hospital in the civilian ward. I was in a bunker several hundred meters away when the hospital came under Viet Cong mortar and rocket fire.

"A Soviet-built 122 mm rocket hit the ward. She was killed instantly. We had one rocket fly right over us and exploded on the beach. I had just been transferred from An Khe a few days earlier. I saw the remnants of the hospital ward the next day; it was very sobering.

"My last day in Vietnam, I was sent to Cam Ranh Bay to wait for my 'Freedom Bird' flight home. I returned to McChord Field on March 1, 1970. I remember having a bad case of foot rot (trench foot). We flew to Sea-Tac airport in Washington, then to Southern California for thirty days leave.

"Landing at Los Angeles Airport, I was greeted and yelled at by members of the Hare Krishna. I made the mistake of wearing my uniform. My younger brother picked me up. I've never forgotten that my father and stepmother did not come to greet me.

"After my home visit, I was sent to Fort Benning with the same MOS. It was where I would meet my wife, Joan, who was a nurse. After I got out, I enrolled at a community college in '72, and I never let anyone know I was a Vietnam veteran. I had a history professor who was really helpful and understanding, and I started also reading self-help books.

"After community college, I worked for a professional photographer and loved it, so I enrolled at the Brooks Institute of Photography. Thirty-five years in the profession and twenty-five years owning my own studio. I have been married for fifty years and have two boys, Sean and Bryan."

Mark Derry is still living at the age of 71.

JIM GLENNON　　　　　　3rd Infantry
　　　　　　　　　　　　'The Old Guard'

I met at Jim at a local gym in Canby about six years ago. We would talk sports, mostly football, while riding the stationary bikes. He was heavily involved with the Canby Football Club that supported the Canby High School football team, and he even remembered me from my football coaching days.

About three years ago, Jim told me, "It's impressive what you have been doing for veterans over the years. I'm a Vietnam Era veteran, and I was stationed stateside." I asked him what he did during the war. He told me that he did funerals at Arlington. As soon as I heard that, I told him that I would love to include him in the book.

"I was born in September 28, 1946, in Philadelphia, Pennsylvania. My mom, Joyce, was just eighteen when she met my dad in Southern California. Jim was a Marine who served in the South Pacific. My brother, Patrick, was born during WWII, and I was my parents' second child. We moved to Philly, where dad was from. They divorced at four, and I never saw him again until I was in the Army.

"When I was stationed in Virginia, he called and said he and his new wife were going to be in Washington D.C., and he wanted to see me. We all went to a speakeasy (a retro style bar that replicates aspects of historical speakeasies).

"I remember his wife; my stepmother, was a really nice lady. She was an entertainer, and they traveled around country performing at nightclubs, big back in those days.

"I was still seventeen, but they were able to get me in the club. They were friends with Buddy Hackett and Jackie Gleason who were putting on a show that night. My stepmother went up on stage and sang a song for everyone.

"Later that night, I asked my dad, 'How come you never came to see me and Patrick?' He immediately responds, 'Well, you know how your mother is.' I said, 'I never want to see you again. Asshole!' That's what I called him.

"My brother was in the Navy serving onboard the USS Frank E. Evans when he was killed; seventy-four sailors were lost. Did you ever hear about the Evans? She had been shelling the North Vietnamese coastline after some R&R. They were part of Naval operations in total darkness in the South China Sea with The Royal Navy, Royal Australian Navy, and the Royal New Zealand Navy.

"An Australian aircraft carrier HMAS Melbourne cut the Evans in half in a collision in June of '69. The sleeping quarters were in the front of the ship, below deck. It sank in less than five minutes; my brother was sleeping there.

"They have been fighting to this day to get those 74 names on The Wall in Washington D.C. I will never understand why they are not on that wall," Jim said in a disgusted voice.

"That's terrible, I don't understand why either." Jim just shook his head.

"Every birthday, Veterans Day, Memorial Day, 4th of July, and the day he died, I fly my brother's American burial flag.

"When I got the news of my brother's death, I called our father and cussed him out, yelling at him, called him every name in the book. I was so angry. My half-brother, Patrick James, who was thirteen, told me later that he could hear me yelling over the phone. He told me it was the first time he saw our father cry.

"My mother remarried when I was seven, and we moved to her husband's farm in North Dakota. My childhood was a nightmare, constant verbal abuse, name calling, putdowns, and I was slapped a lot. He was brutal. He never knew what my name was, just always called me asshole or little fucker.

"He worked us like dogs on the farm. Up at 5:00 AM every morning to milk the cows, feed and water the pigs and chickens, cleaning stalls and other farm chores. He only paid us a dollar a week, and we would have to beg for it. He would just throw it on the floor and say, 'You don't deserve this.

"When my brother was a sophomore, he quit school and went to work for another farmer for a dollar a day. I don't know how he got away with that. I didn't. Our stepfather became a millionaire farmer but became an alcoholic and almost lost it all."

"What were your high school days like?"

"I went to a very small high school. We had a total of nineteen players on the football team and played teams who had up to sixty. I was only four foot eleven and a half as a freshman, but I was old-school tough and always listened to our coach. I would run through a brick wall for him. I was a very hard worker at practice, and I was very quick.

"My first helmet was a leather helmet, later got a one-bar helmet from my brother that didn't fit. I was a running back. My sophomore year, I grew over six inches.

"I graduated in '64 and walked on the football team at Minot State. I grew some more and was now 5'10" and 175 pounds, and I always had strong legs. I was 17 that fall, and some upperclassmen teammates asked me to come with them to a place called The Friendly Tavern. I was never asked for my ID. I had never drank or smoked before and here I am drinking a beer and smoking a Lucky Strike.

"Well, that winter term I started drinking too much, playing Pinochle, and I quit school. Weeks later, I ran into the Civil Service Board lady who asked why I was not in school. I told her I was taking a break. A month later I was drafted.

'It was November of '66. I scored very high on the math part of the Army test, and they offered to send me to Army Financial Management School, but it would mean another year, I said no, just two years for me. I was also a fast typist on those old typewriters.

"Basic training was a piece of cake. I maxed out the PT test, became a squad leader; everybody liked me, even my DI. After basics, a small percent of us were sent to Tigerland, Fort Polk, Louisiana which had swamps and tunnels for our basic training. It was there that we learned our MOS was we were all going to Vietnam.

"At Tigerland, we were treated with respect. While I was there, my mother mails me a letter and includes an article cutout from Parade magazine. It's about some rule that two brothers can't be in Vietnam at the same time. I threw it away.

"Later, I was on the front page of my hometown paper because I was 'Tiger of Week' out of the entire battalion. It was all because of my performance in a full gear twenty-six mile march. When a guy dropped out, we were required to bring his pack and rifle with us. I picked up one guy's pack and ordered another guy to carry the rifle. It was too slow just walking, so I started running. It felt good. While I was running, I passed the Battalion CO, who asked others about me. I guess he was impressed.

"We got our orders for 1st Cavalry. I was so excited to go to Vietnam," Jim laughs and adds, "Brainwashed. But I get called into the office and told that my orders are going to be changed because they learned my brother is over there. I got so emotional and started crying. I begged them to let me go. I told them I wanted to be with my guys.

"About a week later, I get my new orders to Fort Myer, Virginia right next to Arlington National Cemetery. I asked around, but nobody knew anything about it. Someone tells me they do ceremonies at the White House.

"Finally, I learn I'll being sent to the 3rd Infantry, 'The Old Guard." We were treated nice. There are four companies, A, B, C, and D. And each has a marching platoon, honor guard, a fife and drum corps, rifle team, and pallbearers.

"I was Company B, as a casket bearer, and we always thought we were the best company. We had to have perfect body, looks, arm length, etc., and many rules. We rotated days for the funerals at Arlington. On our off days we had to practice, practice, and practice again with sandbags in a casket. Sometimes some jerk would order more sands bags than required just to see us suffer.

"On a regular casket, you only needed six pallbearers, but because Vietnam KIA caskets were much heavier, it took eight guys. I was the drag man; I would pull out the casket or loosen the tie downs on the caissons (two-wheel, horse-drawn wagon). And then secure the flag.

"You never want to hear the word 'Refold.' That's a big no-no, a sin. Only experienced one refold that I was a part of. A retired Admiral had a specially made oak casket that was too heavy and had no handles for us. It was a disaster.

"I tried to pull out the casket, but with no handles to get a grip, plus it was so damn heavy, I couldn't get it to move. I requested help, another guy tries to help, but we can barely move it. We requested two of the rifle team to help us. We get it out, it's so heavy. I was constantly worrying about losing my grip and dropping the casket.

"It's even worse because it's a Catholic funeral and those are longer. We have to hold the casket while the priest prays and throws holy water on the casket. Two guys have to lift and turn the flag upward at an angle, so no water will hit the flag. Our arms were aching so bad. Then the flag does not get folded tight enough, and we hear, 'Refold.' Man, it was bad.

"One day got an order for an instant audience at the White House. We were ordered to sit in the crowd and observe President Johnson present a soldier the Medal of Honor. We all got to shake hands with the Medal of Honor recipient and then Johnson. Man, he had big hands!"

"How many funerals did you do?"

"Well, into the hundreds." Jim suddenly gets emotional, and his eyes get teary, and he says, "Well over half were Vietnam KIA's." He looks away and pauses.

"Can you tell me what that was like?"

Jim gets more emotional. "Those were just brutal, the hardest. God, I just hated facing the families. The children were the worse, but so were the mothers, the wives, even some fathers lost it. It hit me hard every time.

"But the most emotional funerals were Black funerals. I'd never experienced anything like it before. A grieving women tried to crawl into the casket once and other times a grieving woman would get in-between and under us while we were holding the flag above the casket. They would lie on top of the casket and just weep. It was tough.

"I had a lot of anger issues for years, and at forty-four, after my divorce, I went to see a shrink. We started off with my childhood and dad and stepdad. This shrink had me write it all down in a journal to bring back for our next session. When I started, I couldn't write, I started shaking, broke the pencil, ripped the paper. I'm crying, but I did it.

"I bring my homework to my next session, and he makes me read it to him. I had the same emotional reaction. But for the first time in forty-five years, it all felt like a weight lifted off my shoulders. Because of it, I think I'm okay with my military experiences, especially at Arlington. It's just very sad memories."

"How were you treated when you got out."

"There were no protesters in North Dakota. I flew into Grand Forks then hitchhiked in uniform, no problems. A trucker picks me up right away and drove me twenty-four miles out of his way to take me home.

"Later, I got a call that my stepdad had passed, at 61. It was the happiest day of my life. I celebrated. I can never forgive him. But I have four half-brothers and two half-sisters and found out about another half-sister just a few years ago. I'm doing okay!"

Jim Glennon is still living at the age of 76.

MICHAEL COON   Muscogee

I first met Michael Coon in November of 2008 when we honored Native American veterans at Milwaukie High School. Michael came from Oklahoma with his father Phillip, Army, WWII, Bataan Death March Survivor, Ex-POW, and his mother, Helen. All three of them came back to Oregon every year until Michael's parents passed.

Phillip and Michael were very proud of Michael's son, Michael Keith, who was serving in the Army and had two tours, one in Iraq and the other in Afghanistan.

Both Phillip and his son, Michael, were hoping to come to Oregon with Michael's son, Michael Keith, to be honored as a three-generation family of Army veterans, all of whom had served in war zones. Regrettably, it was not to be.

Phillip passed away in 2014, and his grandson, Michael Keith, tragically took his own life the following year. Several of Michael Keith's platoon buddies had taken their lives before Michael took his.

A month after his tragic loss, Michael still came to Oregon to tell high school students about his son. He said to me, "I will be there in November because all the veterans your students honor are my family, and I need to be around them."

Michael has kept alive the memories of both his father and his son. He has written a book entitled *A Soldier's Silent Prayer: The Survival Story of Phillip W. Coon.* There is so much more to Phillip's story. I highly recommend Michael's book. Phillip Coon's section is also in Remembrance Volume I.

Michael is also the steward for 'The War at Home Memorial' which was dedicated in Broken Arrow, Oklahoma on June 11th, 2022. The memorial pays tribute to the soldiers and brings awareness to veterans who have committed suicide as a result of their PTSD.

The memorial has a thousand pounds of steel ten-foot-tall silhouettes, each set in granite. There are twenty silhouettes and each bears the name and likeness of military veterans who died by suicide. One of those silhouettes represents Michael's son Michael Keith Coon.

Michael is also part of Mission 22, an organization that provides support to veterans and their families when they are in need.

"When and where were you born?"

"I was born on April 17, 1952, at Claremore Indian Hospital in Claremore, Oklahoma. In high school, I ran cross country and the two mile in track for Tulsa Central High School my sophomore year.

"I was offered a job at one of the leading architect firms, Hudgins Thompson & Ball. It was too good an opportunity to pass up, and my coach was mad at me.

"My first cross country meet I ran bare foot because I hadn't gotten my shoes. I almost beat the defending state champion. My coach gave me a pair of running shoes, and I beat him in a rematch," Mike laughed.

"I graduated in '70 and enrolled at Tulsa Junior College because my mother wanted me to pursue an education. I finished the first semester, then started the second semester, but dropped out. I decided to join the military because I knew I was going to get drafted, so I took the bus to Oklahoma City and joined and didn't tell my parents.

"When I got home, I told my father, and he was shocked. He only said, 'You have to tell your mother when she gets home.' I knew this would upset my mother as we had lost two cousins serving in Vietnam. One in '67 and the other in '69. My mother gets home, and I tell her, and she starts crying.

"My first order after basics I was sent to leadership school and graduated early. Fifteen soldiers were stationed stateside, some to Germany, and the majority were sent to Vietnam. We were told we are going to RVN. I asked, 'What's that?' Someone yells, 'You dummy, that's Vietnam.' My best friend calls his mom to tell her, and she hangs up on him.

"Me and a buddy are sent to Jump School at Fort Benning, Georgia. We thought we were getting out of going but are told we are still going to Vietnam. After graduating, I'm sent to Fort Bragg and told to go home for a 30-day leave. Take care of your personal business, papers, etc.

"On the way back, I call Joshua Randall, Army, Seminole, to tell him I'm driving over to pick him up. We flew home together and planned to drive back together. He said, 'I'm, not going with you because I'm not going to Vietnam. Well, the Army got him, and he was sent to Vietnam.

"I arrive at Fort Bragg, and I'm told I've been assigned to be on a General's staff. I was so upset. I wanted to be with all the guys I had trained with. They were all sent overseas.

"When I meet the General, I'm introduced by a SGM (Sergeant Major) and the General is told, 'His father served in the Army during WWII and was a Bataan Death March survivor.'

"Right away I called my dad. I was not happy. I asked him in an upset voice, 'Did you have anything to do with this?' He told me, 'No.'

"I'm then stationed at Fort Bragg, assigned to HHC XVIII Airborne Corps G2 C-119/C-130/C-141, Hueys and Chinooks. We did night jumps and water jumps. We were even sent to Greece to train with their paratroopers for a two-week field exercise. Being on the General's staff, we had access to extra chutes that had to be used, so our SGM would ask who wants to go jump from Hueys.

"One time I jumped, and only half of the chute opened, which means it was slowing me down, but I was still coming in hard. I didn't pull my reserve because it would cigarette roll around my main chute, so I climbed as high as I could up the chute ropes. I hit the ground hard but got up, no broken bones.

"A soldier in a jeep raced over to see if I was okay and gave me a ride back to the loading zone. The ambulance was looking for me and of course couldn't find me. By the time they found out I was okay, I was already up in a helicopter to jump again."

"Damn Mike, you are crazy." Mike just laughed.
"Well, to me it was just like a fast carnival ride, and you just got get back on it. In the over two and half years, I probably jumped over 20 times on top of the required jumps every three months. I loved it."

"So, even though you mostly served stateside, did you experience anything negative, protesters, etc. ?"

"We knew not to wear our uniforms off the base. Unbelievable isn't it. Hard to believe that today. We served many burial details for Vietnam KIAs also." Mike voice got emotional. "We were spit on during a grave site funeral once. Another time, the soldier was presenting the flag to the widow, and she spit on him.

"Damn, I'm so sorry. How did you react?" We just sucked it up, remained professional. You have to understand, during that time of the war, there was a lot of anger, and it was present and evident at many funerals. It was all so sad."

Michael had two sons, Jeremy Michael Coon and Michael Keith Coon. He has five daughters, Teri Lyn, Summer, Autumn, Raven, and Sky Herrod.

Michael Coon is still living at the age of 70. He has been honored as a Living Legend by the Muscogee (Creek) Nation.

———————— ⋆ ★ ⋆ ————————

MIKE MCMILLON

I have known Mike for many years because both of us supported and attended the Chosin Few, Oregon Chapter's many events. Mike's first wife was Lois Lane, daughter of Al Lane, Marines, Korean War, Chosin Few, whose section is in Volume II. I did not learn Mike was a Vietnam veteran until his daughters told me about five years ago. When I asked him, he responded, "Yes, but I didn't do anything." He is a very humble gentleman.

"I was born in a small town, Nashville, Arkansas, on October 22, 1947. My father, Norman, served in the Army Air Corps during WWII and was stationed in the Aleutian Islands. After the war he was a pipeline welder for his career and retired at Northwest Natural Gas as a welding inspector.

"My mother, Margaret, met at my dad at a USO dance in Oregon City. Her and her sister both met their future husbands at that dance. They got married, and because of the war, he was gone for four years."

"After the war, they traveled all over the country for pipeline welding work. Dad got a pipeline job in Arkansas, and I was born there. They ended up buying a home in West Linn, Oregon and that home was always our home base. Every summer we traveled with Dad wherever his work took him.

"From my eighth grade to end of my sophomore year in high school, Dad worked on the Titan Missile Program, and that took us to several states. When we returned to Oregon, they bought a house on the Clackamas River, and my current wife and I still live there.

"I graduated from Oregon City High School in '65, got a job and attended Multnomah Junior College on a student deferment. I was not a good student and was drafted in '68.

"I reported to boot camp on September 11, 1968, and we all knew we going to Vietnam. I tried not to give it much thought, it was not a big deal to me. I guess because I had no idea what it would be like.

"They gave us 'dream sheets.' Basically, a where-do-you-want-to-be-stationed-next form. As if we had a real choice. A few got lucky, but for the rest of us, we went where the Army wanted us to go.

"After boot camp, I was sent to AIT (Advanced Individual Training) at Fort Lewis and then NCO school at Fort Benning, Georgia. Graduated, my second MOS was for Operation Intelligence. We were the very first class.

After that, I was sent to Vietnam on September 10, 1969. Then sent to a forward Firebase. At first, they didn't know what to do with us. My Sergeant had me build bunkers and other labor type work. Sometimes, I filled in at the Operations Center, relaying messages for supplies.

"I never went out in the field or experienced combat, but I was blown up." Mike responded with a kind of forced laugh.

"What? What happened?"

"It was on Jan 5, 1970. Four if us were in our tents just relaxing, one guy was asleep, me and another were trying to fall asleep to take a nap. A young kid (a Viet Cong) asks if he could see my hand grenade, so I handed it to him. He pulls the pin and lets go of it. I quickly turned and rolled away from him on my cot. Then the explosion.

"The kid was killed, and rest of us are wounded. I'm stunned and seeing stars, but somehow I'm able to stand up and walk out of our tent. I see many soldiers running towards us. They all think it was a rocket attack. I'm medevaced with the most badly wounded soldier on the first helicopter.

"I watch as the medics work furiously to save him. He does not make it. Dies during flight. A second medevac retrieved the other two wounded soldiers. I'm in the hospital for two weeks, then sent to Japan for more surgery for a few more weeks."

"Were you awarded a Purple Heart?"

"No, and I've never even looked into it. I still have mixed emotions about receiving a Purple Heart anyway.

"After Japan, I was flown to Travis Air Force Base on a troop transport, and we avoided the protesters. I was sent to Fort Hood Texas until I got out on September 10, 1970. There were no protesters down there in that part of Texas. I came home, went to work, and just got on with my life."

They have two daughters, Michelle, Julie, and a son, Mike II.

Mike McMillon is still living at the age of 75.

ROBERT HALTINER   Purple Heart

I've known Robert since the late '90s. He attended several of our Milwaukie High School Living History Days, but I got to know him real well at the State Conventions of the Military Order of the Purple Heart. His two best friends were Dale Alby and Keith Kingsley. It took me months to get Robert to meet me for lunch and an interview.

"I kept putting this off, Ken, telling you I was always busy, but really was trying to get myself ready to talk about my experiences with you," Robert laughed after telling me that. "I'm very grateful," I told him.

"So, where and when were you born?"

"I was born in Tillamook, Oregon, down on the coast on April 13, 1946. Grew up in the small town of Hebo and my parents owned an 88-acre dairy farm. My dad, Jack, was a farmer. He was full-blooded Swiss who settled in the Hebo area because there were other Swiss immigrants living there. My mom, Frieda, was Swiss also, and she was a homemaker.

"Before and after school, seven days a week. I also wrestled for Nestucca High School for four years at 115 pounds (52 kg). I know that's hard to believe now," laughing. "We had a good wrestling program. The football and basketball coach was Barry Adams (Oregon Basketball Hall of Fame)."

I jumped in a said, "I know him. He was a starting spilt end at Oregon College of Education (Western Oregon University). His good friend and the QB of the team was Mouse Davis, my football coach at PSU. The Fullback was Erv Garrison, my high school football coach, small world."

"Well, Coach Adams taught history and let us know he did not like wrestlers. We had to earn our grades."

"Did you join the Army out of high school?"

"No, right after I graduated in '64, I went to work in a mill that summer and still had to do my chores at the farm. That fall, I enrolled at Lane Community College. It was a new community college and classes were held in a high school.

"While at Lane, I got a job helping out a disabled man. I'd drive him around for errands, and he paid me on the side. He was able to get me two deferments. But back at the draft board in Tillamook, I lost my temper because they refused to okay a third deferment. I was so angry, I stormed out of the office. Two weeks later I receive a letter saying I'm drafted. It was January '67," Robert laughs again.

"I was then sent to Vietnam in June of '67 with the 1st Infantry 2nd Battalion, 28th Infantry Regiment. We were called the 'Black Lions,' a brand-new company. But in September, I was transferred to 2nd of the 2nd Mechanized Division.

"I'm a driver of APCs (Armored Personal Carriers). Sometimes we would be sent out in the field by helicopter, and there were times when they couldn't land because of hostel fire.

"It was something else flying back to the base on a chopper. Arriving at the base, they never touched the ground, and you had to jump about five to six feet to the ground. You had about eight to ten seconds to get off the chopper or you went back out and nobody wanted to do that."

Robert started laughing as he told me this: "And going out, if you didn't get off in time and rode back to the base, you better have a good reason for not getting off.

"One time, we went out with the carriers and when we came back to our base, it was deserted. The squad that I was transferred out of had been ambushed by the VC, and everyone was killed."

Robert stopped talking and became emotional. Then started talking again. "You learn fast to not trust anyone. There were even kids throwing hand grenades into jeeps. After that, I didn't want to know anyone's names or where they were from.

"I'll never forget us walking through the jungle, and at the same time being sprayed by Agent Orange. We were told, don't worry about it. I saw leaves change colors when wet from the spray. So, I thought something is not right about this," Robert shakes his head in disgust.

"Can you share how you earned a Purple Heart?"

"On February 2, 1968, during the Tet Offensive, we were stationed next to the Cambodian border and attacked every night. We went out and went through a large village, found a VC, and killed him and attached our patch to his chest. We got lots of weapons. That night, we heavy artillery the village all night.

"The next day we go back out with four carriers and ground troops. I'm driving the lead carrier out front. As we get close to the village, all hell breaks loose. Rockets are fired at us, and we are being fired at from both sides. It's a four-hour fight. We run out of ammo for our 50-cal machine gun. I lost count of how many times I ran back and forth from our carrier to the second carrier carrying ammo.

"We were making no headway; tanks are called in and fire point blank into the jungle. We are ordered to pull out. I have my carrier almost turned around when three rockets are fired at us. One goes high, one is short, and the third hits our fuel tank. Big explosion.

"The gunner's wooden board seat breaks and he falls into carrier, wounded from shrapnel and on fire. I'm burnt bad on my back and hands. My jacket is on fire and another soldier pulls it off me and throws it away from me. I stand up, and run after my jacket, cause my wallet is in it. Then I fall to the ground and roll around and the fire is put out.

"I'm put on a tank and taken back to our base. From there, by helicopter, to the hospital for two days, then to a burn center in Japan." Robert pauses and looks away. "I'll never forget this. At the airport trying to fly out of Vietnam, the airport is being bombed with rockets. They put us wounded in the morgue for the night. Man, what a slaughterhouse. Bodies being put into caskets all night, so many bodies, and then into refrigerated trucks. I can't get that out of my head."

"After I heal, I'm stationed in Seoul, South Korea for eight months until I get out."

"Were you greeted by protesters?"

"No, I was very lucky, no protesters. It's just terrible what those protesters did to us. We're just defending our country and get treated like that." Robert had a very disgusted tone in his voice while shaking his head.

"But this was the best part of finally coming home: Before being sent to Vietnam, I met a beautiful lady, Karen, at a dance hall in Pacific City. We danced and talked for three hours and agreed to write each other.

"My last letter I wrote to her before I came home, I wrote, 'If you are not there when I come home, I'm going back to Korea.' Karen was there waiting for me, and we got married on May 30, 1969. Been married fifty-three years."

"How have you dealt with the memories?"

"I've had lots of nightmares, and sleep disorders. I still can't sleep well. First got help in '97. Before that they didn't believe us. Counseling has been very helpful. One-on-one counseling was the best though. But I stopped when doctors are in their twenties. They didn't know anything about Vietnam. Once I was asked to tell my story to a high school student who was writing about PTSD. She was Vietnamese American, and I just couldn't do it. Bad trigger.

"My Son Rob, in the Army National Guard, did a tour in Iraq, driving heavy equipment, anything that moves. We Skyped a lot and that was very helpful for me.

"Once my son, was shook up and said, 'One of our units got hit, I can't talk. We are a family, Dad.' I responded, 'I know son. I also have two daughters, Kimberly, and Becky. Big Oregon State fans! Love the Black and Orange. Same as my high school colors."

Robert Haltiner is still living at the age of 76. He is an Agent Orange related cancer survivor.

HERB HIRST

I met Herb well over twenty years ago when he started talking to Milwaukie High students and at Reynolds High School. He and a small group of other Vietnam veterans still go into high schools to speak to history classes.

Herb was awarded a Bronze Star, one of the military's highest awards, in addition to a Distinguished Flying Cross as well as sixteen other air medals while piloting over 500 combat missions for the Army.

"I was born on May 3, 1938, in Albany, New York and lived there until my dad, Harry, and my mom, Helen, bought a resort hotel (Kezar Lodge) in Maine in 1955. I had to transfer high school for my senior year.

"My dad ran away from home and came out west to Portland, Oregon. He just walked the streets, worked some lumber camps and restaurants. He said that men were still wearing six shooters and holsters on their hips. He worked as a cook in restaurants.

"Then, because of WWI, he joined the Army. He was a WWI era veteran who served in the Army, but the war ended before he was sent over. My dad got really sick in '48 and was hospitalized for six months and spent another six months recovering at home. Because of this, my folks went through all their money and savings, and mom had to work.

"I had to learn to cook at eight years old at home and take care of my younger twin brothers while my mother visited my dad and worked. My brothers didn't even look like each other and by the way, drove my mother nuts. Lots of energy and getting in trouble.

"First breakfast I cooked was bacon and eggs at eight years old. Growing up, we all had to work a shift at the restaurant my parents either owned or operated. I wanted no part of the restaurant business after that.

"School was not my thing. I didn't like homework, but I could listen to a lecture and ace the test. I didn't do any of my geometry homework assignments and was flunking the class. The final test, our teacher said, 'If anyone aces this test, I'll give them an A for their final grade.' The night before I studied anything and everything about geometry and aced the test. Boy, that teacher was so mad," Herb laughs.

"Right out of high school, I got a job fixing minor repairs, cleaning, and shining cars. The owner offered to send me to auto mechanics school, but I wasn't interested. I decided to join the Army because my brothers and cousins all joined the Navy. And I didn't want to swim in case our ship sank." Herb laughed out loud.

"I absolutely loved being in the Army and I went from a private to a colonel relatively fast. I would go back in a heartbeat if I was younger.

"I was one of the replacements to the Aerial Rocket artillery, A Battery, 2nd Battalion, 20th ARA, 1st Cav. We were the first replacements for the very first Air Cav, famous for the la Drang Valley battle. *We were Soldiers* movie and 'We Were Soldiers once and Young' written by Joe Galloway and Hal Moore. I met Joe Galloway at a reunion in San Diego a few years ago. I had talked on the radio with Lt. Col. Hal Moore during a mission.

"I did some stupid things as a LT before Vietnam. I went AWOL for a week in Seattle, based at Fort Lewis. A friend found me; I was drinking too much. My Lt. Col. could have had me thrown out, but gave me a second chance. I had to stay in my apartment for three months except reporting for duty.

"If I needed to buy groceries, I had to call and ask permission, call him when I got to the store, call when I was leaving and when I got back home. But I did it! I was the best soldier you could imagine. I didn't always do everything smart, but I really cared about people.

"I was sent to Vietnam in '66 and back to the U.S. in '67, but I was sent to Texas as a flight instructor. That was a scary job as the new kids often made lots of errors, and I didn't like it. I wanted to go back and tried.

"In Vietnam, we provided close aerial support for our infantry, sometimes right on top of them." Here is something funny for you, "I used to put a crayon mark on my windshield. It was my aiming stick. I was more accurate with that than I ever was with the sight," he said laughing.

"But there were a few times when we were ordered to fire at our own troops because they were overrun. The rocket would explode in a conical shape upwards and if you were lying down to the side, you might not get hit by the shrapnel.

"But the bad part about these rockets, they were not always accurate, some would go long and some short of the intended target. We flew sometimes six to seven missions a day with two-hour breaks to refuel and repairs.

"Other times we fly to a LZ before our troops were brought in, and fire rockets to clear it. The gunships would follow us. It was very intense; you never knew what was going to happen. It could be from nothing to all hell breaking loose. And we were not always successful in finding the enemy.

"We were shot at all the time. The rotor blades would get hit and create little holes. You could hear it when it happened as you could hear a whistle. Maintenance would have to rebalance the blades, sometimes they would just tape over the small holes. If they didn't, it would shake the chopper apart.

"The scariest was the nighttime mortar patrol. You couldn't see mortar fire unless you were right over it. We were an easy target, but many helicopters were shot down. We would do a two-hour shift, turn on armed forces radio, land, refuel, and go out again, plus the daytime shifts, too. You learn to sleep standing up. I probably averaged about three hours of sleep a day, except R&R," laughing.

"Hardest part was seeing tracers coming at you, and it seemed as if they were headed right towards my head. It happened so fast, looked big, but really small and scary."

"What last thing would you like to say about Vietnam?"

"It was such a gorgeous place. So beautiful, and the people were so friendly. Miles and miles of jungles. When I was in the hospital, I was able to walk to the downtown part and visit all the little shops. I tried to be friendly to everyone I saw. I was invited by shop owners to eat with them several times and I did. It was good, but I don't know what I ate," Laughing. "I have not been back and have no desire to go back.

"Were there any protesters when you returned home?"

"Oh yes! I landed at Portland's Airport, and a college kid walks up to me and spits on me. Now, remember just over twenty-four hours earlier, I'm still in Vietnam, so this triggers me. I was on top of him, beating the hell out of him, and I was truly going to seriously harm him.

"The airport police pull me off of him and got me out of there. They took me to a bar and told the bartender to give me anything I wanted to drink and as much as I wanted, and they would pay for it. But I didn't want to drink because I wanted to see my new '67 Thunderbird. And I did. Got out of active duty in '71. Joined the reserves and made my way to Colonel.

"Met my wife Cindy while in the service, and we have been married 44 years. She deserves a medal. She put up with a lot with me. In about 2002, she told me, 'You are going to get some help, or I'm out of here.'

"Around that time, I was becoming more and more angry, nightmares, and taking it out on my wife. I went to the VA for testing and was diagnosed with PTSD. I just can't get out of my mind the men we lost and why not me? The counseling was very helpful for me. They taught me breathing exercises, and techniques to recognize triggers."

"Have you had any Agent Orange related health issues?"

"Part of my PTSD is from Agent Orange. I don't want to talk about it."

Herb Hirst is still living at the age of 84.

JAMES 'DOC' WILSON   Medic
                           Two Purple Hearts

Doc is a really smart and interesting guy. He was the sommelier at Jake's Famous Crawfish in downtown Portland for thirty-two years. He attended all of Milwaukie and Reynolds High School's LHDs since 1996 and spoke to the students every year. He and a couple of his close friends, also Vietnam veterans, bailed us out many times over the years at Reynolds.

One year, the Principal, Jeff Gilbert, wanted to put all of the students in the main gym for the Assembly of Honor with veterans sitting on chairs on the gym floor. The gymnasium was to be overflowing sophomores, juniors, and seniors and we still had the freshmen to seat.

Just as I was asking what do we do with the over five hundred freshmen, Doc and his buddies volunteered to speak to them all in the auxiliary gym that he was using for his pictures from Vietnam. The feedback from some teachers were that they did a great job and had the freshmen in the palms of their hands. "They were awesome and funny," a freshman told me afterward.

"I was born in Portland on September 8, 1944. My dad, James Riggs, served in the Coast Guard during WWII and never went overseas. He played the trumpet in the Coast Guard's band at dances for the Navy's Pier 91, in Seattle, Washington.

"We lived in Tekoa, Washington, close to Palouse and the Idaho border. My mother, Doris, divorced when I was three years old. She married Talbot Wilson who adopted me and had my sister Judy. She was a stay-at-home mom. Talbot was a dentist in the Reserves and left-handed at that.

Living in Seattle, my mother divorced again when I was nine years old. I lived with my grandparents during grades six thru eight in Portland and was sent back to Seattle and lived with my mom again.

"I graduated from Queen Anne High School and enrolled at University of Washington. My freshman year at UW, I majored in pre-dentistry but flunked out because I changed my major to playing pool, bowling, and attending just my gym class," laughing.

"Moved back to Portland to attend Multnomah Junior College, or as we called it, MIT (Multnomah In Town). After Multnomah, I transferred to Portland State and took a full load, going to night school five nights a week while also working forty hours a week at Meier & Frank.

"I was tired, so I dropped from a full load of fifteen hours down to nine hours. That move cost me my college deferment.

"I was drafted in '68 and reported to Fort Lewis for basic training. I took two days of testing and qualified for NCO, OCS, and Green Beret. They asked if I was interested, and I said, "No, No, and No.

"Because I was majoring in social psychology, they wanted to send me to Fort Sam Houston for a sociology program, but after I failed a color-blind test, I was disqualified from the school. So, they put me down as a clerk typist because I could type forty-five words a minute.

"Somehow out of two hundred forty trainees in Basic, sixteen of us went to Medics Training Camp at Fort Sam Houston in July of '68. It was ten weeks of vigorous training. The graduating class before us are all assigned to hospitals in Korea, Panama, and Germany and the same with the class after us. In my class of ninety-nine, eighty-eight were sent to Nam.

"On September 7, I flew to Vietnam and celebrated my birthday when we crossed the international dateline and had only four hours left in the day to celebrate.

"After landing at Bien Hoa Airfield near Saigon, I was assigned to the 9th Infantry Division. I spent five days at training at Reliable Academy (9th Infantry's nickname was 'The Old Reliables') where we learned how to cross log bridges, use night vision scopes, and deal with being in water. All this because we were going to the Delta where the rivers rose and fell with the tides of the sea. We had good boots, but wool socks. Not good when wet.

"Dong Tam was the 9th's base. We operated in the field out of the town of Can Giuoc next to a river. We used Tango boats (Armored Transport Carriers) with .30 caliber machine guns on them. We would go up the river hoping no VC were around with rockets. I was scared shitless.

"At Can Gioue, there were aluminum billets built on stilts. During the rainy season, we had to wear flip-flops to get to the shower. We medics would spend six months in the field going out for three days with an infantry line unit trying to intercept VC supply lines.

"We were always on the lookout for Punji pits, which inside had sharp pointed bamboo with cow dung on them. If a guy steps on one, he could get a bad infection. We eventually got boots with steel bottoms to handle the sharp bamboo.

"We learned to trust no one. A VC would be a family man during the day, but at night he was the enemy. You also never knew when a sniper was around. I learned fast not to walk to close to the Point, or the Rear, or near an officer, or a radioman. They were always targets. And I always carried an M16 to look like a regular soldier because medics were a main target.

"My first Purple Heart was when a VC machine gun had us pinned down under a hootch. VC shoots a rocket that misses the hootch but explodes next to it in a rice paddy. I'm hit with shrapnel in my knuckle, pulled out, bandaged, no big deal.

"You have good days and bad days; good days sit around and drink beer and play cribbage. One of the bad days was at 'Ambush Alley.' this went from a dirt road to paved Highway 4 (main road from Saigon to the Delta). Snipers would pick off truck drivers one at a time. They would go over sixty miles an hour to avoid getting hit.

'There was this one guy, Forrest Pierce, only eighteen years old from Idaho. He walked point and had amazing sight. He would always see a booby trap, a hand grenade attached to a tree. They usually had a ten second delayed timer, so the soldiers in behind would get blown away, and the shrapnel will hit lower extremities.

"My worst day ever: Ralph Martin was walking point, and we were in a small hooch area. Five men in my platoon stepped over a small hump covered by dry palm tree leaves. The sixth man, Specialist Keith Organ, tripped a booby trap, probably made with B-40 (rocket) rounds. I was four men back of him. The shrapnel shredded his whole left side. The blast broke both ankles of the man behind him and caught two more men in front of him.

"The radioman and the corporal ahead of him caught shrapnel in the back and rear end. The radioman, Dorel Horsmann, had smoke grenades tied to the back of his PRC-25 Radio. They detonated and I heard screams ahead of me and everything was surrounded in yellow and purple smoke. As I pushed up to render first aid, I was followed by my platoon sergeant Randall Zimmerman holding his left bicep. He had caught a piece of metal in his arm, and he still has it today.

"The kid who tripped the wire was in real bad shape, but still conscious. I put pressure dressings, as many as I could, on his wounds and got an IV in his good arm. I'm talking to him the whole time, keeping him from looking down at his leg, and trying to keep him calm.

"Luckily, I had taught other members of the platoon an intensive class on everything in my Aid Bag, and its use. They took care of the other injured men while I concentrated on keeping him alive.

"Zimmerman took my morphine syrettes and gave shots to the other three wounded. Martin was so upset because he missed the booby trap he knew was for him. He made sure he grabbed litters from the medevac helicopter that had landed in an open area and brought them to the casualty area.

"It was then that he discovered another trip wire on the only trail to the Chopper's LZ. We had no time to blow it in place, so we carried the three litters out while we had spotters from the platoon on both sides of the trip wire to make sure we got the men out safely.

"I carried Orgon's IV bottle as I gingerly stepped over the wire. Orgon lost a leg, an arm, and an eye, but survived. I learned that Keith Orgon from Wisconsin became a father just two weeks before getting hit.

"All our wounded lived, but I was fried and exhausted after the chopper took the causalities to the Evac hospital. Later, Ralph Martin went back to sniper school in his home state of Hawaii. This left us with the most astute and cleareyed point man we ever had; Herman Atalig from Guam, and we just called him Guam.

"We went on a three-day Bushmaster OP in an area contested by the VC. As we headed down a trail, we found a huge cache of rice with VC signs on it. We blew it up and rice rained on us for about a minute. Then the 3rd Platoon followed by the 2nd Platoon goes on a fork to the right.

"We started to follow them, but Guam stops us in our tracks. He spots a daisy chain across the trail. It was three grenades strapping the trail covered by dead palm leaves. Over forty-eight men from two platoons stepped over it without tripping it. We moved back and set a charge on one of them and a synesthetic detonation set off the other two.

"We moved up the fork and took the left-hand trail. We go about thirty yards when Guam raises his hand. He had spotted another trip wire. One end of a monofilament fishline was attached to one tree and across to a tension spring tied to the base of another tree that led to a B-40 rocket five feet above the ground on the back of the tree. If it had exploded as an air burst, it would have been a busy day for me. It was just one example of how Guam saved a lot of lives.

"After spending six months in the field, I'm rotated to a Battalion Aid Station in Dong Tam at our Division Base Camp. There, I handled sick call, gave shots, and handled ambulance duty.

"Our aid station had a concrete floor with a front entrance to an open compound area with a large sand bagged bunker in the middle. Next door about 20feet away was a small officer's club. It was 10 PM and I was near the front door showing off my 35mm Canon SLR Camera with the lens cover off.

"Seven others were sitting inside when all heard a *whump*. The Officer's club took a direct hit from a mortar round. Luckily, the Philippine bartender had just stepped out, so nobody was in it. The blast shook dust down from our rafters in the aid station and many of my fellow medics headed to the door and to the safety of the bunker.

"I proceeded to place both covers on my camera so the dust wouldn't get on it. I was the closet to the door but the last one out. As I ran into the dark toward the bunker, I heard another *whump*, and something hit my foot and knocked me off stride. But I kept going and got safely to the bunker. They sounded the all-clear and I walked back to the aid station. As I came into the door, I saw our medical platoon sergeant talking to the Battalion Commander, a full bird colonel!

"He was asking Master Sergeant Lemare if there were any causalities from the attack. MSG Lemare answered, 'No sir, we didn't.' Then he looked at me and said, 'Wilson what happened to you?' I looked down and saw blood pooling on the floor underneath my right foot.

"It was then I started to feel pain. Evidently, a piece of shrapnel had cut through the top of my boot and almost severed a tendon in my big toe. A quick trip to the hospital for a sew-job and back to duty.

"In July of '69, Nixon pulls the 9th Infantry out of Vietnam. We landed on July 13th at McChord Air Force Base in Tacoma; the day Nixon and Westmoreland were at a parade in Seattle. We were not greeted by protesters, but I would never wear my uniform again until joining the Oregon National Guard in '78.

"I was a platoon sergeant assigned to a medical company and served for twenty-three years, retiring in 2002. I also went to work for Jake's Famous Crawfish (a seafood restaurant in downtown Portland, Oregon, founded in 1892) as a server and wine steward for thirty-two years.

"I had worked for ten years when the owner, Bill McCormick, called my mother and asked if she had a picture of me in Vietnam. She did and sent him one with an article from the North Portland News about me coming back home. The picture and article still hangs in Jake's today!"

"How did you deal with the memories, any PTSD?"

"When I was sent overseas, it really helped that at twenty-three years old, I was more mature, dealing with officers, and I had more patience. I take everything one day at a time. The VA has helped me a lot. I'm very lucky."

James "Doc" Wilson is still living at the age of 78.

RANDALL JOSHUA   Seminole

I first met Randall years ago when he was pressured to come to Oregon by Rex Hailey (Army, Iraq, Commander of the Seminole Nation Veterans Honor Guard of Oklahoma) and several other Seminole veterans of the Honor Guard. They had been coming up to Oregon for several years joining us in speaking to high school students.

They are a great group of guys and every year have given me and my wife the most beautiful handmade Seminole gifts. We are so grateful for their support.

Everyone felt Randall coming to Oregon to attend our scheduled visits to schools would be healing for him. When he finally did come, he was quiet the entire time and to me he appeared as if he was not having a good time. He only spoke a few words.

It wasn't until over a week later that Rex called me and said, "Randall went into every class with us and tried to talk about his experience in Vietnam but could not finish as he broke down and cried. When we came home, Randell thanked me for bringing him as he felt he needed to try to talk and was somewhat relieved."

Randall agreed to be interviewed by me when I talked with him during our trip to Oklahoma. We planned to do the interview over the phone, but I was never able to do it because he passed away. His friend Rex Hailey was kind enough to tell me about some information on Randall.

"Randall was born on February 8, 1952, in Talihina, Oklahoma. His father, Edmond Sr. was an Air Force veteran. He was sent to Carter Seminary Boarding School in Ardmore, Oklahoma. He was a hell of a football and basketball player his high school years.

"Before finishing school, he joined the Army on March 12, 1971, and served in the 101st Airborne Division. While in Vietnam on Christmas Day, he accidently ran into his two brothers. They told him, 'What the hell were you thinking? You should have stayed home.' It was the last time he spent with them.

"They were killed in an ambush, and Randall also lost a lot of buddies. He carried that guilt all these years. When he came home, he was greeted by protestors and Randall fell into a deep depression and became an alcoholic. He struggled with PTSD for years and years until he told his wife that he needed help.

"He admitted himself into the VA Hospital, but it didn't help. After the years of struggling, he found the Lord, which helped him find peace within himself and it helped greatly with his guilt. He truly became a man of God. In 2017, he went back to school, graduated, and earned his diploma."

In November of 2021, I traveled to Tulsa and Broken Arrow, Oklahoma, for the first time to have veterans speak at Sequoyah High and Sapulpa Junior and High Schools. One of the evenings, we gathered about fifty veterans including some spouses in a small banquet room for dinner.

Most everyone knew each other from previous trips to Oregon. After eating, Chris Spence presented a gift to Chosin Few veteran Bill Chisholm. The gift was a Tootsie Roll Canister filled with Tootsie Rolls. Bill Chisholm. Well, Bill laughed and then for the first time ever he tried to tell the story of how Tootsie Rolls saved troops at the Battle of the Chosin Reservoir. He couldn't finish as he broke down and cried.

Well, this led to other veterans opening up and telling all how our Living History Days have been so healing for them. Each veteran ended speaking with tears in their eyes. It was such a powerful evening.

Towards the end, Randall stood up and gave his personal testimonial. He started to talk about when he and his buddies were ambushed in Vietnam. He starts crying and says, "I'm sorry, I've never spoken of this before to so many people. But being around you all feels so safe and healing. Thank you."

Rex Hailey wanted everyone to know that, "Randall Joshua was extremely proud to be a Seminole Nation Veteran Honor Guard representing his tribe."

Joshua Randall passed away in February of 2022 from illness associated with exposure to Agent Orange.

JERRY GOMES

Jerry and his lovely wife Kaye have attended many of our events over the years. They used to have a summer barbecue at their home for the 101st Airborne veterans who lived in the Pacific Northwest.

In 2013, the 101st Airborne's National Reunion was held in Portland, Oregon, and I was asked to speak, and my beautiful Malinda was asked to sing. Malinda sang a few songs and ended with, 'You'll Never Walk Alone.' She starts singing, 'You'll Never Walk Alone', and suddenly everyone in the banquet room stands up and starts singing. We see many of the veterans crying. We looked at each other both thinking, 'What have we done?' We learned afterwards that it was their song.

A special moment for all was when our three-year-old granddaughter, Tianna, climbed up to the podium and told all, "It's my turn to sing." She then sang 'Twinkle Little Star' and received a standing ovation. Tianna went to many veteran events with us and always sang the WWI song 'Over There' with Malinda.

Malinda and I drove up to Jerry and Kaye's home out in the country close to Mt. Hood to interview him in June of 2022.

"I was born on July 12, 1947, in Topo, on the northeastern corner of Calheta on the island of Sao Jorge in the Azores Islands near Portugal. My grandfather, Germano Jose, stowed away in a whaling ship to America. He traveled west and met my grandmother in California. It was there that dad, Germano Leonardo, was born. But they later moved back to Portugal during the early depression years.

"My name was Germano also, but they called me Germino, which means 'Little Jerry.' I'm the first ever American soldier in my family's history. My older brother served in the Portugal Army; his serial number was 445. That should give you an idea of small their military was.

"My parents lived in Topo, where they had Marizania, Antonio, Madalena, Joao, Germano III, Luis, and Teresa, and a set of twins that died very young. When I was eleven, we came to America for the first time. My father loved America and wanted his family to live in California. Later he, my mother, and sister Teresa returned to Portugal to take care of my elderly grandparents.

"I remained in California and worked on the farm in Newman, California, milking cows and going to school. In '67 when I was nineteen, I got a job milking cows at a dairy in Petaluma, California. I got the job because I was not a fluent English speaker.

"My co-worker was a Korean War veteran, and he told me, 'You'd better just get it over with. You will go someday anyway if the draft gets you. You might as well sign up. You can always have this job when you come back.'

"So, I went to the recruiter in Santa Rosa and enlisted 'RA All The Way' (appointed into military as opposed to drafted). After that the most memorable part of my life began. At first, I wanted to join as a heavy equipment operator, but the recruiting sergeant in Santa Rosa told me that there were no openings because all slots were full. I was hoping for a better future than milking cows.

"That sergeant was an E-7 Master Parachutist with a 1st Cavalry combat patch and spit shined boots. He pointed to a poster on the wall of a trooper in full canopy and said, 'What about that?' I asked what it was. He said, 'You get to shoot a lot, and you won't have to walk. You just jump in and when you get those Silver Wings on your chest, the girls won't be able to resist you.'

"My answer was, 'Well, that's for me.' By the way, I wore out my first pair of boots and was working on the second pair while in Vietnam. He lied about the walking part!

"Basic training was in Fort Polk Louisiana in March of '67. The weather was almost like Vietnam, hot and muggy. Basic was tough. We didn't walk anywhere; we ran everywhere. I was in good physical condition, but I wasn't good enough to be first. But oh, how I tried!

"We were stationed in the one-story cement block buildings that housed WWII German prisoners. The latrine and showers were in a separate building. This barracks had one stairway coming down, and with the lower floor opening into the same stairway. There was only one door to get out. We all kept practicing to get out to formation quicker, in order to beat everyone outside. But someone got hurt, and the practice had to stop.

"I had two bunkmates that I liked; Frank Griffo and Dan Gaworecki. We ended up in Jump School together and in the 3rd Brigade 506th Infantry in Vietnam. We were kept lean and mean. I learned to eat lettuce and oranges, including the peels. Anything that hit the tray was devoured. The only way we got to eat was to do the entire length of overhand bars to get to the chow hall.

"For the PT test to go to Jump School, we ran everywhere and started losing guys that couldn't keep up. We were also trained in hand-to-hand training and pogo stick fighting; then push-ups and sit ups.

"I loved the shooting, and my favorite weapon was the trusty M14. I carried the M14 as my choice weapon in Nam. Getting up at 5 AM and then late training at 10 and 11 PM was normal. We were always tired and sleepy. Anytime your ass touched the ground your eyes slammed shut.

"I had a friend of Mexican descent, Hernandez, who wanted to be airborne so bad. He did everything to qualify except he could not do the overhand bars. We nicknamed him 'VC' because his features were similar. I felt really bad when he couldn't go to Jump School with us. He ended up in the 11th Cavalry.

"Jump School was at Fort Benning in Georgia. It was the best chow I ever had. Jump School was three weeks with the first Ground Week, second Tower Week, and third Jump Week.

"Jump School is training for the basic paratrooper (military parachutist) where if upon passing the training soldiers earn their 'wings'; a silver dress badge pin with an open parachute flanked on either side by wings that curve upward.

"We were up at 3:30 AM for PT and a seven-mile run around the perimeter. If you can't complete the run, you're out, or if you're lucky, you get recycled. Lots of the guys, they got sent out to the leg units (low-entry ground soldier), which is a huge disappointment.

"We had training for when we would jump off a 34-foot tower, basically a platform mounted on telephone poles. Our first time at the tower, the stairs were all loaded with jumpers, and the sergeant at the top rocked the tower back and forth. It moved a lot!

"When my turn came, I climbed to the top of the tower, waited for the Sergeant to shout my name and my number, 242, before I would jump. I forgot both and got booted in the ass off the tower! After many more trips, they were satisfied, and I was qualified to jump out of a C-119.

"Years later, was in the same exact spot to pin my wings on my daughter at her Jump graduation in May of 2010. She was an Army ROTC Nurse student. I was glad to see the new towers were now made out of steel instead of wood. She is now an Army Captain at Landstuhl Regional Medical Center in Germany.

"After the 34 Tower jump, we then progressed to the 250-foot tower. I was excited until I reached the top and had to release the safety line. Boy, that's when the pucker factor got big.

"Third week, Jump Week, was really exciting and scary. My first and second jump I had my eyes closed. After that it got easier. What a feeling- one-one-thousand, two-one-thousand, three-one-thousand, four-one-thousand, check canopy, and your chute is full. So exciting. You really start feeling invincible. After the fifth jump you can do anything!

"After getting our wings pinned, we rode buses to Fort Campbell Kentucky. At the repo depot (replacement depot), eight names were read out, including my own, and we were assigned to the 3rd Brigade 506th Infantry. The cadre laughed, and we had no idea why. They knew what we didn't: that the 3-506th was already packed up for Vietnam. We left thirty days later. While at Fort Campbell we finished packing, but most of the battalion equipment had already left.

"I was assigned to the S&T Platoon (Supply and Transport) to drive a truck. I didn't like it. My buddy, Dan Gaworecki, went to the Currahee Shock Force, and I badly wanted to go with him. Later though in Vietnam I was able to transfer to Currahee Shock Force by trading with a soldier, Guilermo Bigatti, who was from Argentina.

"We flew to Oakland, California and boarded troop ship USS General William Weigel and spent twenty-seven days sailing to Vietnam. We stopped to re-fuel at Midway Island and then stopped at Subic Bay with a mechanical problem.

"Life on the ship was just lots of PT and practice shooting BB guns up close. No aiming, just point and fire. With lots of practice it works, as the majority of our contacts with VC were up close. Finally, we landed at Cam Ranh Bay. After some speeches, we rode trucks to Phan Rang Air Base, home of the 1st-502nd, 1st and 2nd-327th and the 502nd Infantry.

"The Currahee Shock Force was a small company of two platoons consisting of the AT (Anti-Tank) platoon and the Recon platoon. Our platoon Sergeant Philip R. Chassion was loved by all. Our Commander First Lieutenant David M. Peason was one of the most decent officers I ever met. His call sign was 'Paladin' because he wore a gun just like the cowboy Paladin in the TV show *Have Gun - Will Travel*.

"I was assigned to Sam Jacob's team, who was from Texas. Other teammates were Gene Carne, Tim Howard, Doc Wendelshaefer, and Leonardi. They were great guys and took me under their wing, since I was a cherry.

"Our training as LRRPs (Long Range Reconnaissance Patrol) was to gather intelligence without being seen or heard. We worked in six-man teams with camouflage jungle fatigues, painted faces and Boonie hats (no helmets). We were inserted at dusk by Huey helicopters and patrolled for five days. At the end of five days, we got picked up and back to base to get ready for the next mission.

"All of the battalion's infantry companies were in heavy contact with NVA and VC Forces approximately fourteen klicks north of LZ Betty, Phan Thiet. One platoon from C Company 3-506th was pinned in a rice paddy by elements of the 186th Main Force Viet Cong Battalion and a Sapper Company (elite combat engineers) of the 240th NVA Battalion.

"They had casualties and medevac helicopters were unable to reach them due to the intensity of enemy fire. There were no units available to reinforce them. C Company platoon had three KIA and eleven wounded out of a small platoon.

"I was leading a six-man reconnaissance patrol of E Company, call sign Romeo 4, in the jungles northeast of Phan Thiet when we were called to end the recon mission and meet helicopters to take our team to reinforce Charlie Company.

"Our three LRRP teams landed at the Forward Base LZ Sherry, and the next morning, we climbed on the tanks. LZ Sherry was an artillery and armor base consisting of M48 Patton tanks belonging to the 1-69th Armor.

"We rode to the contact area through rice paddies, about twelve to fourteen klicks from Phan Thiet. The tanks didn't drive on Highway 1. When the tanks moved out, our radio handset was caught in the tank tracks and ripped off the back of PFC Wyatt who was a new radioman on SFC Olan Payne's team. This was Wyatt's first day on the job. We always carry a spare handset. This still bothers Wyatt to this day.

"Riding on the back of these loud, slow-moving tanks was unusual for a recon platoon, and we felt very uneasy about being so exposed. We got off the tanks and patrolled suspicious locations like hootches ahead of the tanks before the tanks could move on. It took a few hours to get to the pinned down platoon of Charlie Company. The ride seemed like forever and was so noisy.... we all felt naked riding on those tanks.

"Upon arrival to the forward edge of the contact area we dismounted and crept up to Highway 1 and took cover in a rice paddy at the edge of the road. The road was about three feet higher than the surrounding rice paddies and provided good cover. We came from the west perpendicular to Highway 1. Charlie Company was pinned east of the highway and the enemy was right in between in a banana grove, dug into spider holes small enough for one Vietnamese to crouch in and also in bunkers which were camouflaged.

"As we crouched in the rice paddy, RPD machine guns raked the top of the road and bullets snapped over our heads. The enemy fired numerous B-40 rocket propelled grenades at us and at our tanks. American artillery and airstrikes were called and coated enemy positions with napalm and HE explosives (High-order Explosives). A few enemies were killed in the barrage, but many were not.

"We kept our heads down below the top of the road while our tanks hammered away at the enemy. While the tanks fired relentlessly into the banana grove hot shell casings fell on us. The concussion from the shells blew us down or backwards. To our right were approximately a hundred ARVN South Vietnamese with three or four U.S. advisors.

"They were unable to maneuver due to the volume of enemy fire even with the tanks engaged. The enemy was throwing hand grenades at the tanks and the enemy was within fifty feet of us. The tanks advanced towards the banana grove, which prompted First Lieutenant Roos to jump up to the road yelling at us, 'Come on!' Bullets flew all around him and hit near his legs and feet. I was frozen paralyzed with fear as were the others. We had not planned to get on line with no cover and attack a VA and NVA Battalion. The Lieutenant jumped back down next to us in the ditch.

"This all seemed to happen a hundred miles an hour and slow motion all at the same time. We were keeping low, and we all looked at each other realizing that we were going to have to go over the road into the banana grove. SFC Payne looked down towards the ARVNS and American advisors (who wore steel helmets) and raised his camouflage Boonie hat and said, 'Would anyone like to trade a steel pot for a beautiful camouflage hat?! No!? OK!'

"And with that, the men followed SFC Payne over the road into the banana grove assaulting the enemy. We were not going to let one guy go alone. We followed Lieutenant Roos and SFC Payne into the banana grove. It was a miracle that no one got hit by the enemies' grenades, rockets, machine guns or AK47 fire.

"The tanks fired their machine guns and main cannons directly into the NVA positions as we assaulted. The NVA popped up out of their spider holes to toss grenades and fire B40 rockets at the tanks and at us. Other NVA laid down streams of fire from RPD machine guns and AK47 rifles towards us.

"The ground was pockmarked from the earlier artillery barrage. We bounded as the tanks fired; banana plants chopped in pieces littered the ground. When the 90 mm tank cannon fired it knocked me down. The sound of the cannon and gunfire made my ears ring.

"We were all running and lying in the prone position when I heard screaming and turned my head. The ARVN soldiers that were behind us were pulling the enemies from their spider holes, giving them rifle butt strokes and killing them. The spider holes were so well concealed that we ran right past and over them. Some of the spider holes were right next to where we took cover in the course of our advance.

"The ARVN soldiers had been watching earlier that morning and spotted where some of the enemies were hidden in spider holes and bunkers. We didn't know that there were any spider holes. If it wasn't for the ARVN soldiers, we would have all been killed.

"Then I felt something warm on my hands, saw blood on the sites of my M14 and felt blood dripping from my chin. I thought I had been hit. Luckily it was just a nick, a small cut from shrapnel or from hitting my chin on the sites of my M14. I didn't call for a medic.

"It didn't seem that important at the time. I'm proud of that scar although I didn't get a Purple Heart.

"We finally reached the end of the banana grove and the edge of the rice paddies where the platoon of C Company was trapped. I don't remember anything after we reached C Company other than being on guard big time. The American dead and wounded were evacuated by Hueys, and it began to get dark. A perimeter was set for the night and there was no more shooting. The rest of the night was quiet.

"The next day, we policed up the enemy bodies and enemy weapons. One machinegun, one sub-machinegun, one B40 RPG with numerous rounds, three AK47s and one sniper rifle with large scope were found. It gave me shivers to think that someone may have looked at me through the scope of that sniper rifle.

"While we were policing, I found a spider hole with a dead Vietcong. As I pulled him from his spider hole, his brains rolled out of his head like Jell-O. They were what we call a 'stay behind.' They would stay behind to fight us in order to give their friends enough time to get away. They were sacrificing themselves so the rest of the NVA could escape.

"The enemy dead had ammo and pre-cooked rice only and photos of their family, but no money or watches. There was one that had a photo of a little girl and his wife. I still have the pictures. It didn't bother me then, but it does now. We left the bodies lying on the ground when we left.

"I don't remember if choppers or trucks came and got us when we were finished with the mission. When we got back to Phan Thiet, life went on as usual. It was just another day.

"It was only until three years ago that I met some guys from this battle who we went to help. In 2005, at an Army Reunion in Branson, Missouri, I met two men from C Company that we helped that day: Steve Trambaugh, of Loogootee, Indiana and Kenny Jones from Springfield, Missouri. and their platoon sergeant and several others that I don't recall their names.

"They were glad that we came to their aid and so were we. Their Platoon Leader, First Lieutenant James R. Magouyrk, was awarded the Distinguished Service Cross for his actions that day. I hope to meet him someday.

"Magouyrk stayed in the Army and retired a full bird colonel. PFC Billy Frank Harper, SGT Salvador De Los Santos Rios, and SP4 Robert W. Hook, were killed that day. SP4 Hook was posthumously awarded the Silver Star for his heroic actions that day.

"I'm so glad to be able to sit with my buddies who all made it out of this mess alive today. We all call each other every February 12. For my actions on that day, I was awarded the Bronze Star with V Device from the US Army and Gallantry Cross with Bronze Star from the Government of the Republic of Vietnam. I was not the only one to be awarded the Bronze Star but ALL of us should have been awarded one.

"I loved the camaraderie. My service ended; I ended up doing two more tours with the same unit. I didn't want to leave the guys. I came back to 'The World' in June of '69 to Fort Bragg, North Carolina, and was in the 82nd Airborne 2nd-508th LRRP Team. February 28, 1970, was my last day in the Army."

"Did you run into any protesters?"

"I was very lucky; I never ran into anyone, but I knew of some 82nd Airborne buddies who put on long hair wigs to look like a hippy. Hell, it was impossible trying to meet women back then. As soon as they learned I was a Vietnam veteran, they wanted nothing to do with me. I was even called a baby killer.

"Being form Portugal, no TV, no news, I knew nothing about America and even while working on the Dairy farm, I still knew nothing about the antiwar protests and riots. I didn't even know what certain American holidays were such as Memorial Day.

"I had a friend in Vietnam, a black guy who finished his tour and went back home. Within a couple of months, he was back with us. 'Why are you back?' I asked. He said, 'They don't want us.' I just couldn't understand it.

Jerry got very emotional, "I served with Americans of several different races. Great guys, all of them, and every single one of their blood bleeds red.

"Back home I traveled to Oregon to visit two dairy farm friends who were working at Timberline Lodge on Mt Hood. I fell in love with Oregon and never left."

Jerry Gomes is still living in Oregon at the age of 75.

MILTON JACKSON — United States Military Honor Band

I met Milton through my wife Malinda, and she told me he is a great musician and that he was also in the Army band.

"Tell me, where are you from and when were you born?"

"I was born on March 11, 1956, in Atlanta, Georgia."

"How old were you when you learned to play an instrument?"

"I started right after I was born," Milton laughs very loud. "Actually, I started playing the drums in kindergarten in a talent show. I ended up learning how to play the trumpet and the trombone, but my thing was drums and percussion.

"I played drums in the band in grade school, junior high, and in high school. I was the drum section leader for the George Washington Carver High School Marching Band. When I was a freshman, our band was just thirty-nine strong, and we marched in a parade that included the five hundred strong Florida A&M band.

"Our band director, Augustus Cook Jr., decided to start having summer band camps, inviting grade school, junior high, and high school kids. It was incredible. By my senior year, we were over three hundred strong.

"Augustus and a couple of us formed a small band and every summer we played for many outdoors events and festivals. We were good. It was then that I decided music was my passion, and I wanted to devote all my energy into it.

"Florida A&M, the number one Black college band in the world, was going to offer me a full scholarship to attend. My band director, Augustus, set up a meeting at Carver High in the band room. The band director of Florida A&M came in person to meet me.

"Well, it was Senior Week, and that week was filled with different activities. The day he came to offer me was a Switch Clothes Day. Girls dress up as boys and boys dress up as girls. I wanted no part of that. Lots of seniors skipped and so did I. I completely forgot about my 1:00 PM meeting in the band room. Both band directors were extremely disappointed in me. Augustus was very upset with me. The Florida A&M band director wanted no part of me now. Couldn't be counted on is what he said. I've regretted my mistake ever since.

"Two weeks later, an Army Band came to our school with the FORSCOM Band from Fort McPherson. Augustus made me stay for their concert. I didn't want to play march music because I could do that in my sleep. But I was blown away. They blew my mind playing from different genres of music.

"I walked up to the stage during a break to check out their set up. A Colonel with the band talked to me about joining the Army to be in the band and told me, 'You don't have to play soldier.' Augustus then tells me, 'You better take this offer as you screwed up. The word is out on your standing up Florida A&M.

"So, I joined the Army in '74, and after basics I had to take AIT (Advanced Individual Training), and then Administration and Logistics (Supplies). After all that, I'm sent to the United States School of Music, where I auditioned and made the United States Military Honor Band. It was made up with the best musicians from every branch. These were the best musicians in the world," Milton laughs.

"I performed with them for ten years. Played for many impressive events including in the White House for President Carter and President Reagan, in the Capital building, and much more.

"Sometimes, some of us would get together and just jam. We only worked on our days with gigs. The rest of the time was relaxing, rehearsing, or learning new music to play."

"So, I need to ask you this question. From '74 to '75, you are considered a Vietnam Era veteran. Even though you were stateside, did you ever have any negative experiences? Protestors?"

"Yes, I made the mistake of wearing my uniform while flying home for some R&R from D.C. As I'm walking to my departure gate, an older white man walks up to me and says, 'You don't deserve to wear that uniform.' I just saluted him and walked away.

"After getting off the plane in Atlanta, a white lady looks at me with an angry look and spits on the floor in front on me. I just shook my head and continued to walk. I felt it was very demeaning for her. I only told a couple of people this before because it's just too upsetting. I mean, I was serving our country.

"In 1984, I wanted to reenlist and stay in the band, but the Army and Marines changed some policies. You had to play soldier for a while before going back to the band. I did not want to do that. I know that both the Army and the Marines lost a lot of highly trained men. It had to hurt them.

"A buddy of mine, Ron Gaines, decided to stay in and reenlist. He was riding on the back of an Army truck when the truck ran over a big pothole. Shockingly, he fell out of the truck. His right leg was jammed into his chest breaking ribs, but his leg was so badly damaged it had to be amputated.

"He was only given thirty percent disability and ended up becoming so angry and depressed, he ended up losing his wife, his child, his home, everything.

"I lost track of him for decades and tried to find him on Facebook, but no luck. One day, I'm riding my bike in Washington D.C., and I ride right by this homeless man in a wheelchair. He has long scraggily hair, a long beard, and he is filthy, but I recognize his eyes. I yell, 'Hey Gaines, It's Milton Jackson.' And he remembers me.

"We talk for a long time. He tells me, 'I was going to drive my wheelchair into the Potomac today. I just can't deal with it all anymore.' Right away, I called a friend working for a colonel who connected us with his friend in the VA. Six months later, Gaines is in a home, has a new wheelchair, has a van, he can drive with his left foot, and got one hundred percent disability benefits.

"When I got out with some of the others who got out also, we formed a band and played in a lot of gigs around D.C. One time after a performance, a man walks up to us and asks, 'Who's the leader? I need a backup band to open up for a big act.' I respond, 'We are not a backup band and who is the big act?' He said, 'Roberta Flack.' We took the offer and toured with her for three years.

"I'm happily married to Bennie White Jackson, living in Atlanta. We had three children together, plus I had one from my first marriage, and she had two from her first marriage. We raised them all in a blended family."

Milton Jackson is still living and playing music at the age of 66.

NAVY

I am a United States Sailor.

I will support and defend the Constitution of
the United States of America and I will obey
the orders of those appointed over me.

I represent the fighting spirit of the Navy and
those who have gone before me to defend
freedom and democracy around the world.

I proudly serve my country's Navy combat team
with Honor, Courage, and Commitment.

I am committed to excellence
and the fair treatment of all.

~The Sailor's Creed

JOHN 'MIKE' McGRATH   Naval Academy
                                 Fighter pilot
                                 Ex-POW Hanoi Hilton

I brought in Mike from Colorado in 2012 for our high school Living History Days and a special event to honor Ex-POWs at Evergreen Aviation & Space Museum. He not only graduated from the Naval Academy but was a great wrestler for its nationally tenth ranked wrestling team.

As a Navy pilot, Mike was shot down on his 179th combat mission by enemy gunfire over North Vietnam, on June 30, 1967. He was taken as a Prisoner of War and held captive for 2,075 days and was released during Operation Homecoming on March 4, 1973.

After being shot down he received a broken and dislocated arm, and fractured vertebrae and knee. Then while a POW the brutal torture sessions he was given resulted in injuries to his other shoulder, as well as his elbow being dislocated. He also spent many months in solitary confinement.

As a Prisoner of War for nearly six years, he participated in communication and organization efforts to resist the enemy. I highly recommend for everyone to read about his experiences in his book, *Prisoner of War: Six Years in Hanoi*.

I also recommend watching the American Experience Film, *Return With Honor*. In it, you can see drawings that Mike drew himself. He taught himself how to draw and he drew his first picture on a prison wall with his own blood. You can also see many of them online.

The first time I spoke to Mike over the phone was when he was the NAM-POW's Historian. When I asked him what he did there, he sadly informed me that much of his and his fellow Ex-POW's work was to expose phony Vietnam POWs.

After our conversation, I was able to convince Mike to come to speak at LHDs. While speaking to the students, he was very brief about his experiences being beaten or tortured. He didn't go into detail. He reminded me of so many of the tough wrestlers I have known. They don't complain or brag about being tough.

Mike said, "I have many physical ailments from the brutal torture and beatings, and I have never been able to raise my arms above my eye level." He then showed the students that he could not raise his arms very high. But immediately said in a loud, commanding voice, "But I never complain about it though as I'm grateful to be alive."

When one student asked him how he was able to endure for so many years he said, "In all my years as a POW, I was constantly sustained by faith in my friends and in my country. I never lost hope because I thought about everything about American life, from peanut butter sandwiches to peaceful Sunday mornings in church. And I had faith that someday I would see them again."

In January of '22, I called Mike again to ask him a few questions in as I wanted to hear from him directly concerning a question I wanted to ask him. Although I already knew what his answer would be before I asked.

"Can I assume that your wrestling background helped you get through those years as a POW?"

"Oh yes. It was tremendous help. You see, wrestlers have been beat up, hurt, thrown, pinned, and humiliated in front of crowds after being beaten. There is no quit. I can't imagine going through what I went through and if I had never competed in a sport before. While in captivity, I remembered the joys of victory and the agony of defeat as a wrestler at the Naval Academy. Because I had participated in sports, I had the determination, strength, and stamina to resist and survive."

"Can you tell me about your wrestling background from the beginning?"

"My first year was as a high school freshman in 1953. I was a 112 pounder, and I was pinned on a regular basis.

"But I didn't give up. I was a district champ as a junior and placed third in the regionals. I did not place at the state meet because of an injury. My senior year I was undefeated and favored to place but was upset in the regional. I learned about, 'The agony of defeat.' I was devastated.

"My senior year, I applied for the Naval academy but was denied, so I took an offer of a scholarship at the University of Colorado where I wrestled as a freshman. I applied for the Academy again and this time I received a Congressional appointment and was accepted."

"Were you accepted as a wrestler?"

"No, I had good grades. The Navy wrestling coaches knew nothing about me. I was a walk-on, and every wrestler on the team was recruited, and everyone of Navy's wrestlers were state champions in high school. It's damn tough to make it as a walk-on. The coaches didn't even like me because they didn't recruit me.

"In order to make the freshman team, I had to defeat, on a weekly basis, a two-time state champion from Pennsylvania who had been recruited by the head coach, Ray Swartz. Eventually he quit the team because he couldn't beat me anymore." Mike laughs.

"At the Naval Academy I lettered all three years, placed fourth in the Eastern Intercollegiate Wrestling Association as a junior and third as a senior. I was captain of our team my senior year. We were ranked tenth in the nation, the highest ranking ever for a Navy Wrestling team. I qualified and wrestled at the Nationals both years."

Recently Mike emailed me a short bio of himself written years ago and gave me permission to use it. I include parts of it as it is further proof of the kind of man Mike McGrath was and still is.

> ... at age 15, Mike had his first brush with "courage." Mike saw a construction worker fall into the Colorado River, flounder and be swept

downstream by the current. Mike dove from a bridge abutment into the cold waters of the river and swam to the man who could not swim a stroke. Mike was able to pull the man to safety about a quarter mile downstream as he saved the man from certain death…

… Mike went on to complete a Navy career that saw him in uniform for a total of 24 ½ years. He served in many areas of responsibility including command of a combat ready attack squadron during the Iranian hostage crisis. Shortly before he retired as a Navy Captain, Mike had one more opportunity to display unusual courage above and beyond the norm. While aboard a naval vessel at anchor, he witnessed a patrol boat come along side and crush the gangway because of rough seas. Two women were thrown off the gangway into the patrol boat while two women were thrown into the water between the hulls of the two vessels. Everyone but Mike stood spellbound and actionless. Mike quickly descended hand-over-hand down the collapsed gangway to the patrol boat where he grabbed a life preserver, jumped into the water between the crashing hulls and pulled the two women to safety. For his action in preventing possible death or injury to the two women, he was awarded the Navy-Marine Corps Medal for heroism…

Finally, I asked Mike about his return home, which was a major event.

"I was able to join my wife, Marlene, and my two sons in San Diego on March 7, 1973. I was thankful to be home with them and to find them okay. Right away, we took the kids out of school, bought a motor home, and travelled around the States for seven months."

Mike's family means the world to him. He can also be proud that his son and grandson both graduated, 1987 and 2015, from the Naval Academy in Annapolis.

Mike lives in Monument, Colorado with his wife Marlene. They have two adult sons, and six grandchildren.

Mike McGrath is still living at the age of 82.

DOUG BOMARITO   Naval Academy Class of '68

"I served in active duty in the United States Navy from June 1968 through August 1972. During that time, I had three tours of duty. The first on a Navy Destroyer that made a WESTPAC Cruise (Western Pacific) in the Vietnam Area. My second tour was in the Mekong Delta of South Vietnam attached to a River Patrol Boat Division. And the third and last tour of duty I had was as an officer in charge of Officer Recruiting at the Navy Recruiting Station in Portland, Oregon."

Doug attended several Milwaukie High LHDs in the late 90's through the 2000's and served on our RAH Board of Directors from 2002 to 2008. I first learned he was a graduate of the Naval Academy when he asked me to speak at an Oregon Southwest Chapter Naval Academy Alumni Association lunch.

"Please tell me about yourself."

"Well, I attended Detroit public schools and graduated from Southeastern High School in Detroit, Michigan in 1963 and was a three-sport athlete in football, basketball, and baseball, and was also the 1963 Senior Class President. My senior year, I received a Congressional appointment to attend the Naval Academy in Annapolis, Maryland. Every midshipman has to participate in some level of athletics, either varsity or intramurals."

"What did you do?"

"I played baseball on the varsity team. I started at first base and batted over .300 in my senior year. An early teammate was Roger Staubach, Heisman Trophy winner, quarterback for the Dallas Cowboys for eleven seasons, including five Super Bowl appearances, and NFL Hall of Fame. Roger was the Captain of the baseball team when I was a sophomore. He was one of the best athletes I have ever known, personally, and a fine human being."

"What was it like watching the Army - Navy games?"

"It is an amazing experience, just terrific. I'll never forget Roger Staubach leading Navy to a 21-15 victory over Army in 1963. We were ranked number two in the nation that season."

"What was your major?"

"Engineering, but it was a struggle. Math was tough on me, and my coach helped me to graduate. He was an excellent coach. I graduated in June of '68 and that summer was assigned to a destroyer CIC (Combat Information Center) off the coast of Vietnam in late 1968 and early 1969."

"I thought you served on a Navy Gun Boat over there?"

"Not exactly. In '69 I volunteered to go to Vietnam. I was attached to PBR Division 532 (Patrol Boat River) that conducted mostly night ambushes. My job was as a patrol officer in that division.

"In the Spring of 1970, we were ordered to conduct new tactics. It entailed more dangerous daytime exposure. The goal was to draw the enemy out. On my seventy-fifth patrol, we were transitioning to an ambush site when both the lead boat I was on, and the cover boat were hit by B40 rockets and small weapons fire.

"Many of us were wounded, and two other sailors and myself were wounded seriously. I woke up in an Army hospital, and after two weeks was transferred to a hospital in Saigon, then a Navy hospital in Japan for a month, and lastly a Navy hospital in Bremerton, Washington. Later I received a Bronze Star, along with a Purple Heart.

"After healing from my wounds, I was given new orders to the Recruiting Office in Portland. We did the recruiting for the Oregon, southwest Washington, and Idaho area. My job was to recruit officer candidates for the Naval Academy and for NROTC midshipmen (Naval Reserve Officers Training Corps). I had visited Portland once before on my first ship, and I loved the people and the area. And I have been here ever since."

"What was it like recruiting during those days of the anti-Vietnam protests?"

"It was very challenging. At the University of Oregon, I was allowed to set up my table with displays and brochures in the far corner of the basement of the Student Union. Oregon State, Boise State, and Southern Oregon were the best because the faculty and staff at both institutions were the most helpful and pleasant. There was a lot of support from the administration of both schools. The Navy decided it was not necessary to recruit on campus at PSU as the protests were getting ugly there.

"I was discharged from the Navy and attended Lewis and Clark Northwest College of Law. I passed the Oregon State Bar in 1976. I practice family law, wills, probate, real estate, and personal injury. I still work at my law practice three to five days a week."

"How did you deal with the memories, nightmares, PTSD, etc.?"

"Working with so many civilians while recruiting in Oregon helped me a lot with transitioning back into civilian life. I enjoyed working with all those people. A VA therapist shared with me how to cope with my PTSD issues. Basically, I try to remember the positive experiences in my life and minimize any negative effects. The theory is fight or flight, and try to make a choice and then follow through on that choice.

"I have kept in touch with my shipmates and crew from the PRB, and especially the cover boat captain who immediately came to our rescue during the fire fight. The reunions of the PRB crews have helped greatly. The greatest healing of all was helping to build Oregon's Vietnam Memorial in Washington Park in the 1980s. But my late wife, Jean, who was a nurse, was always at my side. She died in in 2018. I miss her very much. I am still relatively happy. I am very blessed."

Doug Bomarito is still living at the age of 77.

JOSE HERNANDEZ — Navy

Jose is a good friend of both Malinda and me. We have known Jose for over twenty years, and he has attended LHDs all over Oregon since 1998. His personal life story has been and still is an inspiration for many students.

For years at the events, he would set up a display of all the Hispanic American Medal of Honor recipients that included pictures of the recipients and their citations of their 'Above and Beyond the Call of Duty' actions.

I have heard him speak to students from different high schools several times. He would always start off with, "I was Born in Olmito, Texas and had to work in the fields starting in the third grade. In elementary school we were not allowed to speak Spanish on school property. The teachers would make us eat a bite of Ivory soap when we were caught speaking Spanish. I remember the 'Whites only water fountains' at the grade school.

"I dropped out of the seventh grade during the first month of school and then worked full-time in the fields until I joined the Navy at seventeen in 1956. I was assigned to the 144th, at the US Naval Training Center in Illinois. My first Sea Duty Assignment was the USS Lake Champlain CVA-39, on which I served from '56 to '59 at which time I received my discharge and returned home to Olmito, Texas.

"I re-enlisted in December '59, reported to Long Beach Naval Station where I was assigned to the USS McGinty DE-365, which was a Naval Reserve Training Ship stationed in Swan Island, Portland Oregon.

"The McGinty was commissioned in October of '61 and deployed to Vietnam. We were one of the first seven ships assigned to help train the South Vietnamese in Saigon and on the Mekong River. We returned to Portland in July of '62. I continued to train Reserves on the McGinty until mid-1965.

"The McGinty is famous because of its connection to Portland, Oregon. It was honored by the state of Oregon in 2019 because it provided assistance to emergency teams and went on lifesaving missions in Oregon during a flood in late December of 1964.

"In 1965, I completed ten years of sea duty and upon completion of my two years of shore duty, I volunteered to return to Vietnam and was selected as a Blue-Ribbon Crew to reactivate the USS New Jersey in Philadelphia, Pennsylvania, which was then going to deploy to Vietnam.

"However, on the seventeenth of July, while still under travel orders, I was a passenger in a vehicular accident that caused me to be hospitalized and unable to report to my assignment.

"While I was a passenger in Navy van with other sailors, a Semi-Truck crossed over lanes and hit our van head on. I was thrown from the van and badly hurt. The Navy discharged me because my right arm was permanently disabled. I had served twelve years, and I was very disappointed as I wanted to stay in Navy for a career."

Jose was quite the joker too. During his talks to students, he would grab hold his right arm up and with his left hand would twist and turn his right arm all around and then laugh. At first the students would gasp but then started laughing.

He may have been a joker, but he was also smart. "While in Navy, sailors would buy *Playboy* magazines every month, but I would buy *Reader's Digest* to learn new words from the Word Power section. It helped me greatly when I attended college and earned my degree at Portland State University graduating with a 3.7 GPA (Grade Point Average). I was also heavily involved with the Oregon Democratic Party for many years and formed the Latino Democratic Caucus."

I asked him how he was treated when he came back from Vietnam. He said, "When I first came back there were no protesters yet. But while I was stationed stateside, the protests started. One evening I finally got some time off, so I got dressed up in my Navy dress uniform to attend an event off base. It was my first time off base in weeks, so I was really excited. As I was walking in town off the base, I was hit with a couple of eggs by some protesters.

"I was so upset because now I had to go back to the base and only had one set of Navy dress uniform and now could not leave the base."

Jose was a very good public speaker and did a great job inspiring high school students to stay in school and do their best.

Jose Hernandez is still living at the age of 83.

ANN COPELAND

I invited Ann to our Living History Days a couple of times, but she told me she just couldn't do it. In 2011, Ann sent me a notebook of poems she had written years ago that was very helpful for dealing with her PTSD. I contacted her and interviewed her. I'm so grateful for her opening up and sharing her story. She is a strong survivor!

"Tell me about your parents and your childhood."

"My Dad, Frank, was a Radioman in the Army Air Corps on a Transport plane. He joined on December 8, 1941, the day after the Japanese attack on Pearl Harbor. After boot camp, they were sent home and told to settle their estates in case they didn't make it home. He served in North Africa, Italy, and England. After being rotated back to the states was then sent to Burma till the end of the war.

"My mother, Ceal, was intelligent, beautiful, and very evil. She worked during the war in Madison, Wisconsin, and met my dad at a club. My dad was at navigator school there at the time. He became a radioman because after several times sitting in the navigator's seat, he would pass out during takeoff. His blood pressure was always low and because radiomen would lay down during takeoff, they tested him for that job, and he was fine. They were married in the spring of '44, and during their honeymoon, he was ordered to India.

"I was one of nine children born in Laramie, Wyoming. I was so desperate to get away from my mother, I asked my aunt, my mother's older sister and the Mother Superior at the convent in Chicago, if I could go there to become a nun (Franciscan Sisters). She convinced my mother, and I enrolled at fourteen. The church was my refuge.

"I didn't want to be a nun. I did it because I thought I would be safe. I was deeply afraid of men because at thirteen, a friend of my father's almost strangled me to death, and my father did nothing. Plus, I could get away from my mother.

"It was a horrible experience and I lasted only two years and quit just six months from taking my vows. I came home and finished my junior and senior year at Laramie High School, graduating in '65.

"My dad moved the family to Lander, Wyoming, a small town with no jobs or young adults. I had no money to go to college. My mom told me if I didn't get a job, she would pack my suitcase and kick me out.

"I finally got a job for a small businessman who was a German Nazi and proud of it. About that time, I received a letter from a classmate at the convent. She had joined the Navy and she loved it and said I should join too. But she warned me that the sailors only had one thing on their mind.

"My younger brother was eligible for the draft in '67 and was very nervous about being drafted and being sent to Vietnam. He was not a fighter, and I was. I fought my brothers all the time. I truly believed that if I signed up and requested to be sent to Vietnam, my brother would be exempt from being drafted," she laughed.

"I knew also that I would not have to worry about meals or housing, got paid, and would have money when I got out to go to college. Another reason, I was very patriotic and back then only one percent of the military were women. And I believed it would be the best way to conquer my fear of men.

"I decided to join the Air Force as I was interested in being an air traffic controller someday. I told my boss I needed a day off to drive to Denver to take tests to join the military. He said, "If you join the military, I'll fire you. I went and he fired me.

"I got the highest entrance exam score in Wyoming since 1950. I was a straight A student all through school and high school. But I received a rejection letter from them saying I was not pretty enough," she laughed.

"I asked a recruiter why I was rejected, and he contacted the Air Force recruiters who told him, 'She was not the cream of the crop material.' He told them, 'But her scores are high.' And they said again, 'She is not the cream of the crop,' and the Air Force wants only the cream of the crop.

"My father had to approve of me joining, and women had to be twenty-one, be in the top ten percent of their class, also be a high school graduate, and have impeccable behavior. My father told me the Navy had more planes than the Air Force anyway. And there was also a horrible stigma from men gossiping that a woman in a uniform was not good. They are just interested in sex.

"So, I drove back down to the recruiter's office to join the Navy. While I was signing up, the Navy recruiter went down the Air Force office to get my files. She came back so excited and says, 'The Air Force always gives us great recruits.' When I got back home, the Air Force recruiter called saying they changed their mind, but I said, 'Hell No!' Two weeks later, I was sworn in and sent for boot camp at Bethesda, Maryland for the next ten weeks.

"My instructor was in the very first class of WAVES (Women Accepted for Volunteer Emergency Service). They were just used for clerks and nurses. They told us the very first thing they were told when reporting was, 'You think you're men now? Well you will be treated like men. No excuses about being on a period. And feminine supplies will not be available. If you are a problem, we will kick you out.'

"It was rough, and it's still rough today. They did not want us there and still don't. The Navy was the last of the military branches to accept women and made it tough hoping women would just quit."

Anne then starts telling me about being stationed in San Diego, and about her horrible experience there in complete detail.

"It took me thirty years to say the word 'rape.' One evening we were all at the NCO Club and a Chief Service NCO was talking to me. At the time, I felt something was off about him, but I just shrugged it off.

"He offered to walk me back to my barracks. Right in front of our barracks was a three-story high building where huge refrigeration machines were built for big ships and aircraft carriers. He was telling me all about it, and it was interesting.

"He then asked me if I would like to go in, and he would give me a tour. I said yes because I felt physically safe. I was taller than him, and he was skinny. And I could fight.

"As we entered the building, he shut the huge medal doors and locked them from the inside with his key. I knew I was in trouble. The lights were out, and it was dark. I saw that there was a break room nearby, the windows were very high and darkened, there were '50s style furniture. There was a sofa, a couple chairs, a couple filing cabinets. I thought I could hide from him, so I hid behind the sofa"

As Ann was telling me this, I could only sit, mesmerized by her memory and attention to such detail. I wanted to interrupt her and tell her she didn't need to tell me everything, but I remembered listening to Holocaust survivors tell their story, and I understood that I had to let her talk. This was very difficult for me though.

Ann continued, "So 'RAT Face,' what I nicknamed him, yells 'where are you?' He finds me, throws me on the sofa. I fight back, but he overpowers me. He yells at me to stop talking so loudly. I was praying to God. Please God, I'll be perfect, just let me die until the pain goes away."

Anne laughs and says, 'Prayer never worked. My whole childhood, I would pray to the Virgin Mary, begging her to show me a sign. I would pray to her, 'Please let me die and come live with you. You are my real mother.' My prayers were not answered before, and they weren't again now."

Anne stopped talking. There was a pause of maybe ten seconds, so I said to her, "I am so sorry."

Again, there was a long pause, and Ann began to speak again, "I was in a hurry and had just walked out of that building and immediately ran into this tall man. I said I'm sorry, and I looked up and saw these beautiful blue eyes. I said to myself, 'I've met my guy,'" she laughed after that.

"After that, I was sent to Hawaii on a top secret Crypto Clearance assignment (Navy cryptographic systems and classified information). I was one of only four women in the Navy since 1950 to have clearance.

"We saw each other a couple of times when he was ordered to Vietnam. He asked if I would write him in Vietnam. I said no because I'd witnessed too many women with broken hearts. He then asked me if he could write me. So, I said, 'If you write me, I'll answer every letter you write me.' I believed he would never write me, but I was wrong. He wrote me whenever he had a chance. I still have a big box of his letters today."

Ann's husband Chuck did a total of five tours in Vietnam, the first before '65', involved with training South Vietnamese soldiers. And the other four tours from '65' to '69. He was with the 3rd Marines who were the first in Da Nang. It was there that he earned a Purple Heart.

"He was sent to Camp Pendleton in California for Recruiting School and that's when we started dating, while I was still in San Diego. We were married on May 29, 1970, and we had two children, one boy and one girl.

"In 1987, he was diagnosed with cancer that had spread all over his body and every organ. He passed three months after being diagnosed. I believe his cancer was from Vietnam, Agent Orange Cancer. He's buried at Fort Logan National Cemetery in Colorado. For many years, once a week. I would drive the hundred miles one way to visit his grave and then get back in my car and drive home.

"When he died, I did not want to live anymore. I believe if I did not have children to live for, I would have not made it."

After a short pause, Ann said, "I could never remarry ever again. He was one of a kind. I still dream about him and talk to him all the time. His funeral was huge and many, many of his friends asked to be a pall bearer. Thank God the Marines took everything over and handled it all.

"Absolutely none of my family attended the funeral. It was okay though because my mother had treated him so badly and disrespectfully since we first got married. She died in '93, and I felt as if the weight of the world came off my shoulders. The chains came off, and I felt freedom. My father had passed in '90, and his passing never bothered me because he always supported his wife and not me."

"Is there anything you would like to end on about serving in the Navy?"

"Yes," she laughs. "You know the book *A Tale of Two Cities* and the quote, 'It was the best of times and the worst of times?' Well, you heard about my worst of time, and the best was that I learned a lot, made some good friends, and met my husband."

Ann Copeland is still living at the age of 75.

TIM MYERS   Naval Academy

I have known Tim since he and his wife moved to Oregon. He has spoken to students at Living History Days, and to this day continues to speak to high school students in the Portland area about Vietnam. I knew he was Naval Academy Alumni and a Vietnam veteran. Over the years, I've met many Military Academy Alumni and all of them are very impressive and very successful men. While interviewing Tim for this section, I learned even more about him and just how impressive he was and still is. Tim has lived an amazing life.

I learned firsthand about Tim's standing at the Naval Academy back in February of 2011. My wife and I were asked by a Mega-Black Church in the Washington D.C area to coordinate an event with Tuskegee Airman Alex Jefferson. The day after the event, we had some free time to sightsee, and Alex asked if we could drive over to Annapolis and visit the Naval Academy.

It never crossed my mind that we would not be allowed to walk on the campus as we were quickly denied access by the guard at the front gate. After a few moments, I called Tim who was back in Oregon hoping for a longshot miracle. I explained our situation and he said, "Give me about ten minutes. I'll see what I can do."

To his word, about ten minutes later, we see two black officers approaching us from the gate. They greet us by saying what an honor it is to meet Lieutenant Colonel Jefferson, and then proceed to give us a first-class tour, including buildings not assessable to the public.

One of the highlights happened while we visited The Naval Academy Chapel and Crypt of John Paul Jones. It was closed for the day as the Academy's Gospel Choir was rehearsing, but our Naval Officer tour guides took us in there anyway. It was a special moment for all of the choir members as they were surprised to meet Alex Jefferson.

Thank you again, Tim!

In 2022, I met Tim for coffee and asked him many questions and about halfway through, he offered to email me a transcript. He gave me permission to use it as I wished.

> I was born on the 9th of August 1941 in Wilkes-Barre, Pennsylvania. My dad, Richard, was working as a salesman for an auto store. Four months later right after Pearl Harbor was attacked, Dad joined the Navy. Because he had a college degree, they gave him a commission in the Navy as a Lieutenant, junior grade, and sent him down to Miami for about six weeks of school and then they brought him back to New York and sent him on a Murmansk Run.
>
> A Murmansk Run normally was a hundred and forty ships or so, with maybe ten combat ships to protect all the other ships that were hauling oil and parts to Great Britain or to Russia. This was very dangerous, because you had to cross right in the middle of the Atlantic where packs of U-boats were sinking ships. After coming back, the Navy sent him to the Pacific, as a Gunnery Officer on a destroyer. He was in many of the major battles for gunfire support in the Pacific.
>
> In 1943, he had made Lieutenant, and was getting ready to make Lieutenant Commander, when the navy orders him back to Boston and assigned him a hotel ship. The hotel ship, USS New Yorker, had over one thousand rooms on it and it had no engines. So, he and a tugboat crew from Boston, towed it down through the canal, and over through the Pacific to a place called Ulithi (360 mi (580 km) southwest of Guam).
>
> The Navy was going to get a fleet ready to invade Japan, about 1,500 ships. It was anchored there, and the mechanics, doctors, lawyers, and strange ratings all lived on the New Yorker and my dad was a hotel curator, basically.

Probably the best birthday present I have ever had in my life, was on August 9th, 1945. The second atomic bomb was dropped on Nagasaki. The Japanese surrendered and Ulithi became a thing of the past. Had my dad been in the invasion force, who knows what would have happened? After the war, he got out of the Navy, and went in the reserves, and when the Korean War breaks out, he's recalled and sent to Gainesville, Florida to take over the Naval Reserve Training Center.

It was 1951 and I was ten. We lived over a mile from the campus of the University of Florida. I walked up there and next thing you know I am the mascot, and the water boy for the University of Florida football team. My first year of playing baseball I struck out practically all the time. So, every night my dad took me to the park and would pitch to me. Then we would come home, eat supper, and then he would hit the ball to me. If I could catch a hundred in a row, I got to stay up an extra hour.

In high school, I was a very good student and very good athlete. I played football, baseball, basketball, and I made All-County in all three sports my junior and senior year. I was the only freshman that made the varsity. So, at the time I was a pretty big kid. I pitched a bunch of games. I never lost. And I was averaging sixteen of eighteen outs, and sixteen strikeouts a game. The kids were petrified of me because I was pretty big. I threw the ball pretty hard.

I take the SAT and get 740 in math out of 800, but in English, I get a 420. I tell my dad there were too many words I didn't understand. My dad looked at me and he says, "We're gonna take care of that." So, each night we would finish supper my dad would take the New York Times and I would have to read out loud, word for word, the front page every day for six months.

If there was a word I didn't understand, I had to write down the definition (of the word), write two sentences and then I had to come back and tell him what the word meant and read my two sentences before I went to bed. We did this for six months, seven days a week. Needless to say, my vocabulary got a little better.

My parents pushed me into the places that they knew I should go, so that I could leave this little burg in Pennsylvania and go somewhere and make something of myself.

The Naval Academy is very interested in me, and I'm very interested in the Naval Academy. Navy's football coach visits us and says, "We don't like you're SAT score. So, we are going to send you to Admiral Farragut Academy Prep School for a year. Your English will become better, and you'll get through the naval academy much, much easier."
I played all three sports. The prep school was a typical Ivy League prep school, and we played all these other prep schools.

I was a thirteenth grader playing ball with high school kids. I was just coming from western Pennsylvania which was the hub of high school football at that time. So, we get down there and it was almost like a joke. After two tackling sessions, the coach pulls me to the side and says, "You can't tackle with these kids. You're going to hurt them. I said, "OK. I'll tackle them easy." They said, "No, you're not going to tackle them."

I was the middle linebacker and I averaged about twenty-five tackles a game. Because of this, I made first team All-League Private Schools, and I made first team All-State New Jersey. So now, we get to basketball, and we had nobody that could shoot except me. So, I averaged 39 points a game. Again, first team All-League. First team, All-State New Jersey. Then we get to my good sport which is baseball. I pitched twelve games maybe; I can't remember the exact number. Half of them were no hitters and won all those and then of course, first team All-League and first team All-State.

I got accepted to Naval Academy and I thought to myself, "Ha. There's nothing to it." I'll just go down and play three sports at the Naval Academy. I just didn't understand that there was more to it than what I'd just been through. But my plebe year (first year), I started on the plebe football, basketball, and baseball teams. The plebe freshman couldn't play varsity at that time.

I went to my first football practice and there were 300-plus plebes out of a class of about 1,200 who wanted to be football players. There are nineteen centers, seven of them had been first team All-State in high school from different states. That's the type of talent that you were competing against. I was just amazed. I said, "Holy Cow!" My freshman football coach was Steve Belichick, and met his son little Billy who was about eight years old. Today, little Billy Belichick is the current Head Football Coach of the New England Patriots.

I had no problems with academics except for engineering drawing. It's not that I didn't understand engineering drawing, but I was slow! I'm the starting center and middle linebacker on the plebe football team and I get a note to see the coach. He says, "I want you to go to 'Stupid Study'(what they called it). All this week, you won't come to practice. That means that you will not dress for next week's game." I really worked hard and after three days, I got to come to practice. I actually got to dress but I hardly got to play and that was a wake-up call for me. I got better in engineering drawing.

During the summer the baseball coach does not want me in the weight room lifting but the football coach does. My sophomore year was my last year of playing football. I was centering for a punt, and I went down to cover the punt and a guy clipped me and broke my ankle. So, I finally said, "Ah, this is too hard." So, I switched and just went all baseball.

My senior year, I was sitting in a weapons class and taking a test. The teacher walks into the room and says, "Everybody, turn in your test. I know you're not done but turn in your test. Go back to your room and tune your radio to a news station (no televisions at that time). President Kennedy has just been assassinated in Dallas."

John F. Kennedy, being a Navy guy in World War II, used to come down to the Naval Academy sometimes for a weekend. It was really kind of amazing that the President the United States was walking around the Academy.

Shortly thereafter, I was one of 120 seniors selected to march in his funeral. The Army was right behind the casket, and we were right behind Army. There were people mourning on every street, maybe two or three deep and you could see little kids cry. You'd see men and women crying. They really loved John Kennedy. So, we marched for almost seven hours and then finally ended up at Arlington. Then, we just disbanded, went back to our buses, and went home. It was a long day.

My biggest disappointment was during my junior year for my annual physical. They said, "You know, you have a refraction problem in your left eye and that means that you can't be a pilot." I graduated in Class of '64 and when it came time to pick your selection, I selected a ship out of San Diego.

About a month later, I'm told, "They got this new program in Pensacola called Naval Aviation Officer. You can't fly an airplane as the pilot, but you can be the bombardier or a tactical coordinator or a navigator." I go down to the main office and tell them I'm interested and a couple days later I'm selected. They sent thirty people just like me, to the base in Florida to start this new program.

I finished up Pensacola Flight Training just about the same time as the Gulf of Tonkin incident in Vietnam. Then they sent me the Corpus Christi. I immediately get assigned to a squadron and the squadron is already in Vietnam. That's where I joined the squadron. I end up going over to Vietnam in May of '65. It was a Seaplane Squadron at Cameron Bay, which is right in the middle of South Vietnam. Cameron Bay was just this gorgeous, large bay with the whitest sand you've ever seen.

Well, these seaplanes were interesting. They were huge and designed for reconnaissance and anti-submarine warfare. We had a crew of thirteen of us in the airplane. They would put an anchor down and put a buoy there and we would tie up to the buoy, sleep on the airplane, cook on the airplane, do everything on the airplane. The next day we'd fly a mission.

They brought in a seaplane tender (boat or ship that supports the operation of seaplanes). A seaplane tender went out and would take care of the five buoys that were put in. There would be five of our airplanes sitting there. They'd bring our meals out to us, and once a week we would get to go on the seaplane tender and take a shower, and eat a meal on the ship, and see a movie. All the rest of the time we were on the sea flight. We had beds on the side that were just a cot that folded up against the wall, against the bulkhead. I did a total of three six-month deployments. In between each deployment I would be sent stateside for six months.

We had only one tragedy during my deployments. We were very big and very slow and because we flew real close to the shoreline, we were shot at. Occasionally they would hit us, and it would put a hole in the hull. Now, don't forget we landed in the water. After we got about ten of these holes, we flew our plane to Sangley Point in the Philippines and the holes were plugged. A bunch of our mechanics had never flown.

So, they all get to have a flight and also see the rockets on the wings fired. At about 5,000 feet, a rocket blows up on the wing and blows the wing off. Down they go. Everybody's killed. So, this was as real as you can imagine for a squadron that had never lost an airplane. This was a huge tragedy.

Our mission was reconnaissance, and this is where Agent Orange came in. The VC were coming down from the south on the Ho Chi Minh trail. It was inland about seventy miles off the ocean. It was a small trail that was widened so trucks can come down. We got a problem. There is so much overcast in the jungle that we can't see them down below.

So, Agent Orange starts getting sprayed and in two days all the leaves would be gone. It would just eat the leaves away and we could now see down there. Of course, they had no idea what Agent Orange was going to do to people. I was out of Vietnam in '68.

When I left the first time, Vania (my first wife) was pregnant. I came back to a baby. The second time I left, she was pregnant again and the baby was born right after I got back. So, I had a lot of time away from my wife and a lot of families didn't fare very well because of that.

We went on our honeymoon to Sea Island, Georgia. We were there for a week, and she was dark to begin with because she's Brazilian and she must have laid in the sun six to eight hours every day and by the time we were done she was real dark. So, now we leave, and we head down to Pensacola. We get into Mississippi, and this is 1964. We go into this restaurant and we're sitting there, and sitting there, and sitting there. So, I said to the person, "Could we get some service please?"

He said, "We don't serve Negroes in here."

I said, "She's not a Negro. She's Brazilian." He said, "She looks black to us, and she can't be served in here."

Boy, that took me by surprise because I had never had anything like that in my life and so, we went to another place.

I went from Vietnam to the U.S. Navy's test pilot school. I was the third NFO (Navel Flight Officer). I was selected for test pilot school; I was number three to be selected to go to the test pilot school. Which was a real honor because I was coming from a reconnaissance squadron. So, when I got there, they really didn't know what to do with me, but it was good because I'm in test pilot school—Well, what do you do with a guy that isn't a pilot?

In 1970 we get ordered to fly a multi-engine, propeller-driven, turboprop heavy plane to take a world record away from the Russians. We flew out of Japan and waited for almost four weeks until we have a tailwind for most of the way. We'd been flying for about eight hours, climb up to almost 47,000 feet. That's a new record. All we have to do is land and we've got the distance record. So, now we got two of the three. Next day, we went out on a closed course and broke the speed record. So, all three records now belong to the United States, and we've taken it away from the Soviets.

While I'm there, I'm helping develop an anti-submarine warfare airplane (S3) to land on a carrier. Well, here I am, eleven years in the Navy and I've never landed on a carrier because my airplanes didn't land on carriers. I eventually had command of the first squadron of S3 Viking on the USS Constellation.

While I was there, I screened for the executive officer of the USS Ranger. Tony Less was the Commanding Officer of Ranger and he was not a Naval academy graduate. He was the First Commanding Officer of the Blue Angels when they became a squadron and from there he went to the Commanding Officer of the Ranger.

I ask Tony, "Wait a second, am I going to be the Executive Officer?" He says, "Yeah. In time. But I'm losing my Operations Officer which is right under the Executive Officer and makes all the decisions for the carrier, and I really wanted you for that, but you'll eventually be the Executive Officer." So, I became the Operations Officer, and we went on a deployment up in the northern Indian Ocean, up by the Persian Gulf.

Then I became the Commander of the USS Ogden, and they gave me four Seal teams and four Marine Recon teams, about nine hundred men. About that time, the Exxon Valdez runs ground up in Valdez, Alaska and we're sent up to Valdez. Most of the oil had drifted into Prince William Island, Prince William Sound and down to Smith Island, a game preserve. We dropped all the Marines and Seals off when we left Long Beach and we picked up eight hundred civilians, who would make around $35 an hour to clean up oil. Every morning at four o'clock they'd get up and eat breakfast. They get in boats; we'd take them down and drop them off on the beach and they would clean oil.

We would heat the water. We had these little boats that heated the water. It would make the oil come to the surface and it would go ashore, and they could clean it up. It was a big job, and they were working seven days a week and they were working from six to six. We stayed for three months and cleaned up as much as we could clean up.

After the USS Ogden, I became the Commander of the USS Peleliu when the Iraqis invaded Kuwait. The Peleliu and about 130 ships are all sent to the Persian Gulf. I got there just at the end of that war. I was one of the last big ships to come in there, they left me with five ships under my command to stay in the Persian Gulf. The Iraqis had put a whole bunch of mines in there. With a bunch of EODs, Explosive Ordnance Disposal guys we get rid of the mines.

We went down to Abu Dhabi, and we pull in and there's the Sheik. He's also the mayor. He comes aboard and says that he wants to take me to dinner. So, next day we go to this is a really nice restaurant. We go downstairs and the restaurant gets nicer as you go deeper. We go around the corner and who's sitting there? The dinner guest is Muhammad Ali.

I can remember him coming over, he extends his hand and says, "You box?" I said, "No, Champ. I don't box!" We talked a lot about the world, and he says, "The world needs to be friendlier. We need to find ways to make sure everybody gets taken care of." He talked a little bit about hunger in Africa. Ali was a really nice man.

We hosted the Bob Hope 50th Anniversary of Entertaining the Troops but there were some of the high muckety-mucks in Hollywood there too. Bob Hope came on the Peleliu with his wife in an armored vehicle waving to everybody. Then we took him our gym and renamed it the Bob Hope Gym. He cut the ribbon. He had a really, really nice time on the ship and it was a wonderful celebration for everybody on the ship.

I had twenty-eight years in the Navy. I leave the Peleliu and found out for the first time that politics even played into the military. The Navy brings me to Washington DC to be executive assistant under the Secretary of Defense with the possibility of making Admiral. Well, I had one tour in Washington, and I didn't like it.

So they gave me the NROCT at Northwestern University and I ended up being in command of the NROTC Programs at eight Chicago universities known as the Chicago Consortium.

I retire from The Navy and get a call from the Principal of a Zion Benton High School in Northern Chicago by the Great Lakes. He said, "I would like to put a Navy Junior ROTC in my high school." The school had about 2,500 kids.

The kids in the beginning didn't understand us. Here we are with ninety years' worth of Navy service retired! And we're in khaki uniforms and none of us have ever taught school. So, it is the first day and we were told by the teachers to just go stand outside your room when the bell rings and make sure that the traffic goes by. The bell rings and we all go out. Here's the Master Chief SEAL and he's standing there.

Things seem to be going OK and then around the corner comes a girl with a guy on her shoulders. So, he calls him over and says, "You, get off her shoulders. Stand right there. You, young lady, you get to class.

Now!" So, now the traffic is beginning to stop, and he looks at this kid and he says, "Give me fifty push-ups." The kid says, "I don't have to give you fifty pushups. I'm not in your program!"

The Master Chief reaches down and grabs him by his shirt, pulls him right up right in front of his face and he said, "Son, you have five seconds to start doing push-ups or you're going to wish you had never seen me." The kid thinks about it for two seconds. Down he goes. He does his fifty push-ups. Master Chief grabs him by his belt. Picks him up by one arm. Looks him in the eye and says, "Son, those were damn fine push-ups. Now, you go tell the principal you want to join Junior ROTC. Got it?" He drops the kid and away he goes. Next day, here's the kid in the front row, "Here I am, Master Chief. I joined." He turned out to be a good guy and good kid.

While there I coached football, wrestling, and baseball. At the end of about four years we had over three hundred kids in our JROTC. It's getting really big. We ended up sending eight to United States Naval Academy, a couple to West Point, and a couple to the Air Force Academy. All graduate and all of them have served their country and they're all doing well.

I had nine really, really good years there but in 2003, we move to Lake Oswego, Oregon because my second wife, Mary loves Oregon. There's a group trying to bring the decommissioned, carrier Ranger to Portland. They learn that I'd been the executive officer of the USS Ranger and wanted me to become the executive director of their group.

For the next seven years, I go all over the state talk to everybody from the governor on down but eventually they said, "No." I kept telling them the number one reason I would like to bring it here is what if there's a disaster, suppose we have an earthquake and Portland is leveled—and there are people laying all over the street.

Number one, if you had the carrier here, you would have a helicopter platform that you can pick up the really severely wounded in a helicopter and bring them, put them in the hospital. We have two hospitals. We have 6,000 beds on the carrier. We can store up to a seven million gallons of potable water. We can put a billion, maybe more, meals ready to eat—we can store them on the carrier.

The other thing beside that, you could turn this into some kind of a classrooms. You could train kids there. It could be a museum—a museum that ties Portland to World War II and the shipyards and that is a story unto itself. The amount of ships that were made in the Portland

and Vancouver Shipyard during World War II. So the Navy sends it to Texas, and it's scrapped. We really lost something that could have been quite nice to Portland.

While living in Oregon, I joined the Naval Academy Chapter and became President of that organization. But my love has been playing softball. I've played one-hundred-fifty to two hundred games, every year since I've been here. The camaraderie is great. In the 75 age and above category, we been World Champions three years in a row.

Tim and his wife, Mary live in Lake Oswego, Oregon.

Tim Myers is still living at the age of 81.

VIC WOOD   Yakama

I've known Vic since 1997 when he and many other Yakama Warriors would travel down from Toppenish, Washington to participate in Milwaukie High School's annual Living History Days. Even to this day, the Yakama Warriors support us.

"I was born September 4, 1949, in Modesto, California but was raised in Toppenish, Washington. My father, Victor, was going to join the Marines when the Korean War broke out but broke his leg right before he went to sign up. He used to call me 'Little Vic' and I hated it. He drove logging trucks and was a cattle rancher. We had forty acres. He also started a Rodeo business called 'Let er Buck' for forty years."

"I also did rodeo. I was a pick-up man and competed in team roping. My mom, Colene, worked a lot of different jobs, mostly warehouse work and was the rodeo team advisor.

"I attended White Swan High School, played trombone in the band, played football, basketball, and ran track." Vic started laughing and said, "I wasn't that good at the trombone, but it was fun getting on the bus with everyone and traveling places.

"I graduated in '68 and went to work in the forest, and that fall I enrolled at Yakima Community College where after five months I changed my major to partying.

"I had dropped all my classes but one, Bodybuilding. So, I receive a nice letter saying, 'Due to your GPA, you are now eligible for the draft.' This was right after the Tet Offensive, and they were drafting anyone who could walk," laughing again. "I talked a buddy into joining the Navy in the spring of '69.

"Two years before my interview with Vic, my wife and I traveled to the Yakama Warriors' offices in Toppenish for a veterans event. Vic showed me a newspaper article on his wall in his office. It was about a crash that happened on the USS Midway during the Vietnam war. All he told me was, "I was on the Midway when that happened.

"We were off the coast of Vietnam in the Gulf of Tonkin, it was October 24, 1972. My job was Aviation Ordinance with the 161st F4-B Fighter Squadron, part of the air wing. My job was maintenance of weapons systems on the flight deck, arming planes before taking off, checking the safety on fire pins, all ordinance, fuses, and bombs.

"Did you know that the flight deck is called the most dangerous four and one half acres in the world? We were always told, 'Keep your head on a swivel.'

"It's in the middle of the night, and an A-6A Intruder comes in for a landing. After a plane lands, we check weapons ordinance for safety. My buddy, Clayton Blankenship, yells at me, 'It has no bombs on it! Go ahead a go back to sleep! I'll handle it!' I go down the elevator to the catwalk and the crash horn goes off.

"The jet had hooked on the No. 2 arrestor wire and the jet's right main wheel axle snapped off. The jet slid and crashed into planes parked on the bow of the flight deck

"Clayton is killed. The pilot, Lt. Bruce 'Klaw' Kallsen survived, but the Bombardier/Navigator Lieutenant Mike Bixel punched out in the water, but it was dark, and we didn't know. By the time we found out, it was too late, he was gone.

"A sailor passes me on my way back up and yells, 'Don't go up there.' I was one of the first to the wreckage, and pulled Clayton out from the wreckage and got him below. I went back up and the fire was just put out, I helped drag out the other bodies.

"The Galley was turned into a triage," Vic pauses and shakes his head. "I helped carry one of the badly wounded with burns. He kept telling me over and over, 'Don't let them tell my mom.' I promised I would, but I had no control over it. I don't know why, but he refused to talk to anybody but me.

"A total of five men were killed in the crash: Lieutenant Bixel, Aviation Ordnance Man Clayton Mitch Blankenship, Airman Daniel Parks Cherry, Airman Robert W. Haakenson, Jr., and Airman Apprentice Robert Allen Yankoski.

"I didn't find out till later that Clayton was married with two kids. I always wanted to write his parents, but I just couldn't do it. I've looked up his name on The Wall every time I'm back in D.C. The other four are there right next to him."

"How have you dealt with all this?"

"I never felt I had PDST, but I had the same dreams over and over again. A Navy plane would crash on our ranch, and I could not get the jet's canopy open. Another dream is I'm all alone on the flight deck.

"I must have been good at stuffing it all these years until this last year when I completely broke down while trying to talk about it with another Veteran, Shawn Marceau, Marines and Yakama Nation Veterans Affairs Program Manager. Shawn told me, 'You are getting help.'

"Oh, I want to add, one of our pilots, Lieutenant Victor Kovaleski, shot down the last MIG of the war in 1973. It was also the 197th MIG shot down during Vietnam. Two days later he was shot down also, and he punched out over water, and we were able to save him."

"How were you treated when you came home?"

"Serving on a carrier, I didn't have to go into any airports. I was lucky. But right after basics, we had some leave time to go home. Me and a buddy, we thought we were so cool, decided to go to downtown Seattle and walk around in our uniforms.

"A group of teenagers, about fourteen or fifteen years old, see us, runs up to us, and spit at us and laughs and runs away as fast as they could."

Vic Wood has been the Head Warrior of Yakama Warriors for the past eighteen years and is still living at the age of 74.

WAYNE SCOTT

I first met Wayne in 1995 when I bought a home in one of his home developments named Willow Creek Estates. After moving into Willow Creek, I was immediately told by my Canby coaching friends, that I was living in Wayne's World. When I said it to Wayne one day, he just laughed and thought it was funny. Wayne and his lovely wife Marlene attended the majority of them. Both were always very kind and friendly.

Wayne is a very successful business man and has impacted the town of Canby with many positive improvements, many different businesses, home neighborhoods, apartments, etc. He is a very impressive big man who has a commanding presence when he walks into a room. Wayne is well respected and admired in Canby.

It wasn't until later that I learned that Wayne was a Vietnam veteran. Upon hearing this, I invited him once to attend our LHD at Milwaukie High School in '98, but he politely refused. I was told later by a friend who knew Wayne, "Don't ever ask him about it. He does not talk about it."

I respected this until in the winter of 2021. One night when my wife and I went to Backstop Bar and Grill in Canby for dinner sitting at a table were Wayne and his wife Marlene. Then, after walking to his table to say hello, I told him, "I've been interviewing Vietnam veterans for Volume III, and several live in Canby. I would sure be honored to include you."

Wayne looked at his wife and said, "Well, I think it's time to tell my story." When we met in May of 2022, Wayne said to me, "This is the first time I've ever talked about Vietnam. So, this is historic and I'm very grateful to you."

I started with, "Are you originally from Canby?"

"No, I was ago born in Wallace, Idaho on January 7, 1947, and my parents moved our family to Canby in 1949. My father, Albert had a concrete business where Canby Landscape is now and a cement company in Woodburn. He was a hard worker. My mother Virginia was a stay-at-home mom, a homemaker.

"I graduated from high school in 1965 and enrolled at Portland State with an education deferment. But that all changed in '66 when the deferments were revoked. My dad had a friend on the draft board who told him I was going to be drafted. I tried to join the Air Force, but the turnaround time was too long, so I walked across the street to the Navy recruiting office and joined the Navy in April of '66.

"I became a corpsman specializing as a Dental Tech and am told I will be stationed in a hospital in the states. But that didn't happen because I was sent to Vietnam. On the plane there were only two dental techs, me and another guy.

"During the flight, an officer approaches me and asks me, 'You have a choice of being stationed at Camp Tien Sha or Danang US Naval Hospital.' I picked the hospital thinking it would be the safest.

"Camp Tien Sha was never shelled; however we were shelled every night. Spent every night in a fox hole. Every other day, I was in the operating rooms helping during surgeries."

I stopped writing and looked at Wayne and asked, "Dental surgeries?"

He looked at me squarely and said, "No, wounded. It was horrendous, very gory." Wayne stopped and looked away. "It was bad." After a pause, he added, "Days off I worked the Helipad bringing in the wounded from the choppers." Wayne paused and stopped talking.

"It was bad, really bad. I just counted the days to get out. Now as I look back, it was a worthwhile experience and I'm proud of being there, although history has proven the war was terribly mismanaged. I was in Vietnam from December of '68 and was sent home in December of '69. Then I was discharged after serving three years, eight months, and twenty three days."

"Did you encounter any protestors?"

"That is the major reason why so many of us never talk. It's so upsetting that we all got lumped together. It was really distasteful, but I guess it was the popular thing to do, was to protest returning veterans. I was required to wear my uniform on my flight to Portland's Airport and was greeted by protestors screaming obscenities and spitting at us." Wayne just shook his head.

"So you came back. What did you do next?"

"I should back up and tell you that I married my high school sweetheart Marlene Kraxberger after high school. We actually had been friends since the first grade. The Kraxberger family has roots in the Canby area for many generations. There's even a road named after them just south of Canby.

"Came back and went back to school. First Clackamas Community College, then transferred to Portland State. Attended classes during the day and worked my way through college at night. First as a night janitor at Ackerman for six months, then at gas stations in Portland. I was accepted to Dental School but decided against it because I had done some research on real estate, and I believed if I worked hard enough and did it right, I could make it. I guess I was lucky," Wayne laughs.

Wayne will be 75 years old in January of 2023.

AIR FORCE

> I am an American Airman.
> I am a Warrior.
> I have answered my Nation's call.
> I am an American Airman.
> My mission is to Fly, Fight, and Win.
> I am faithful to a Proud Heritage,
> A Tradition of Honor,
> And a Legacy of Valor.
> I am an American Airman.
> Guardian of Freedom and Justice,
> My Nation's Sword and Shield,
> Its Sentry and Avenger.
> I defend my Country with my Life.
> I am an American Airman.
> Wingman, Leader, Warrior.
> I will never leave an Airman behind,
> I will never falter,
> And I will not fail.
>
> ~The Airman's Creed

LT. GENERAL RUSSELL C. DAVIS — Tuskegee Airman

We first met this impressive veteran with a commanding presence and his lovely wife Shirley Davis in April of 2010 at the Army-Navy Club in Washington D.C. for lunch with Tuskegee Airmen Bill Holloman and Alex Jefferson. This was a historic place and very beautiful, similar to a museum, and I was in awe. There were strict rules, and I had to borrow a sport coat and tie to enter.

I had set up speaking engagements for Bill Holloman and Alex Jefferson at Unity Baptist Church, NAACP (National Association for the Advancement of Colored People) Washington D.C. Chapter, Howard University, NABVETS (National Association of Black Veterans) Washington D.C. Chapter, Dunbar High School, Ballou High School, Faith Community Baptist Church, and Walter Reed Hospital.

At Walter Reed, Bill and Alex were able to meet and talk to wounded soldiers from the Iraq and Afghanistan Wars.

General Davis and his wife would travel from D.C. to Oregon to speak to high school students. He was such an impressive public speaker that I always had him speak to the larger groups. He always used a small pocket size copy of the constitution and would incorporate it during his talks.

General Davis was the kind of man who, when he walked into a room, you knew he was important. Hell, I still cannot even say his first name and always refer to him as only General Davis. And I only address him as, Sir.

We are, I feel, very good friends. However, the General never stops laughing when he reminds me, as well as all the Native American veterans every year without fail, of the time I introduced him to the student body of Gervais High School. I approached the podium, grabbed the microphone, and said, "Our Keynote speaker is Lieutenant General Russell Davis. Students, do you know how many stars a three-star general has?"

Immediately, every veteran started laughing and then the student body followed. All I could do was laugh at myself, and try not to turn as red as a beet.

When I spoke to the General over the phone during the winter of 2020, I didn't have to ask many questions as he just started talking. I was fascinated.

"My dad, Marcus, was a top student at Tuskegee University and then worked as a business manager at the university. My mom, Winfred, graduated from there also. During WWII, she packed parachutes.

"I don't remember this much as I was four and five years old, but mom told me about George Washington Carver. She said that Mr. Carver, wearing a white lab coat, would come out to the playground from his work and give us candy.

"My grandfather was good friends with Mr. Carver. My grandfather worked with him as a farmer also. Thanksgivings were at my grandparents, and this was old school with lots of family and friends there, and Mr. Carver would come too.

"From 1941 on, we would walk over a block from my grandparents' home to Moton Field to watch the Black pilot cadets train. It later became Tuskegee Air Field, which as you know, was the home of the famous Tuskegee Airman."

The Tuskegee Airmen were the first Black military aviators in the U.S. Army Air Corps (AAC). They flew more than 15,000 individual sorties in Europe and North Africa during World War II. They also earned more than a hundred fifty Distinguished Flying Crosses, and helped bring about the eventual integration of the U.S. armed forces. Their stories are in both Volume I and Volume II.

"At fourteen, I joined the Civil Air Patrol because I wanted to fly, and all the instructors were ROTC Air Force officers. At Tuskegee Institute High School, I was heavily involved in sports and also played in the band, sang in the choir, and as a Senior had the lead in the big high school play. I soon became a lieutenant in the Civil Air Patrol. I knew I could lead.

"After that, I joined the Air Force in '58 as an aviation cadet and received my commission in 1960. I was assigned to Lincoln Air Force Base in Nebraska as a bomber pilot and attended and graduated from the University of Nebraska."

"Did you experience any racism while serving in the Air Force?."

"The majority were good people for the most part, and I got along with the majority of them. There were some who had interesting ideas on how they felt about what Black Americans' role in the Air Force should be.

"There were some who would never look or speak to me. But I did not let that affect my focus. I knew teamwork; working together and not apart led to success. I chose to rise above it. The Civil Rights movement was very big then and my entire family was involved. My Aunt taught Black college graduates how to register to vote.

"After serving in the Air Force till 1965, I went into the National Guard as there were more opportunities, and I wanted to take advantage of those and ended up with the 132nd Fighter Wing, Iowa Air National Guard in Des Moines.

"My family was always supportive and pushed us into getting a higher education with an advanced degree. Actually, it was expected of us all and that expectation continues even today with my grandchildren. I asked my own children and grandchildren what kind of lifestyle they want as an adult. And do have the tenacity and focus. And how will they handle failure.

"My family's thinking in this regard comes from our great-great grandfather, Lewis Adams, who was born into slavery. His mother was a house lady (house slave). Lewis's older half-sister and his brother taught him to read and write. After the Civil War, Lewis pushed getting an education with family, friends, and especially former slaves. He could speak several languages.

"He even started a school for former slaves. That came about when a former Confederate Colonel, W.F. Foster, who was a candidate for re-election to the Alabama Senate, was seeking Negro voters in the 1880 election and asked my great-great grandfather for help. So, he made a deal to deliver voters.

"The deal was that in return, the Alabama legislature would pass a bill to establish a Normal School for colored teachers at Tuskegee. He also insisted on having a Negro principal and Booker T. Washington was hired. Lewis was a respected leader of the black population in Macon County, Alabama. Forty-three of his descendants would graduate from Tuskegee.

"I have something fascinating I learned from my grandfather that he learned from his grandfather. Ken, do you why Pastors or worship team leaders would sing the first line from a hymn and then the congregation would sing the line?

"The reason is that it was against the law for the enslaved to read or own a book. So the Pastor would memorize the hymns. Churches all over the America still sing the hymn that way today, but most people have no idea why it was done like this. In fact my great-great grandfather died while leading the worship singing at Sunday School in April of 1905."

"Did you ever have any bad experience with protesters?"

"I never personally experienced harassment by protestors but knew it was happening. We did not wear our uniforms off the base. I was asked by someone once why I didn't volunteer to fly in Vietnam. I had two brothers who served in Vietnam, one in '66 and '67 and another in '68 and '69.

"My mother and father were both WWII veterans, so felt I was serving our country and had a job to do here in the states in Air Defense. One year I flew two hundred days while attending law school full time. As a family, we felt we did our part in serving our country.

"I'm proud of my service in the Air Force and the Air National Guard. I loved to fly. But I never personalized comments from others, I was too focused on my personal goals."

General Davis was always really great with the students when he spoke at any event. Every time he would advise them by telling them, "Do and try many different things. Get and stay focused. Set personal goals. I set goals for five years, and ten years. Understand that this takes time, you can't do anything over night.

"I knew I wanted to fly as a young teenager, so kept moving forward, truly believing that I would achieve my goal. I also understood that my goal was not possible in a short time, so I set a ten-year goal to become one. I also set leadership goals, because I knew I could lead."

His citation for his Air Force Distinguished Service Medal says it all:

> The President of the United States of America, authorized by Act of Congress July 9, 1918, takes pleasure in presenting the Air Force Distinguished Service Medal to Major General Russell C. Davis, United States Air Force, for exceptionally meritorious and distinguished service in a position of great responsibility to the Government of the United States. General Davis distinguished himself as Vice Chief, National Guard Bureau, the Pentagon, Washington, District of Columbia, from 18 December 1995 to 31 July 1998. During this period, the extraordinary professional skill, remarkable leadership and ceaseless efforts of General Davis resulted in major contributions to the effectiveness and success of the National Guard at every level-- internationally, nationally and locally. As the Vice Chief, he was the primary representative of the Chief of the National Guard Bureau on virtually every issue in every forum, in the Chief's absence. General Davis was instrumental in streamlining and realigning the National

Guard Bureau to respond to the downsizing of the national security establishment. General Davis provided the inspiration and guidance in the development of new initiatives in the areas of Extremist Activities, Sexual Harassment Issues, and the Quadrennial Defense Review. Every airman has felt his impact at every unit and state. General Davis stands above others because of his visionary leadership abilities, his pragmatic approach to solving problems, and his unswerving devotion to the organization and its people. The singularly distinctive accomplishments of General Davis reflect the highest credit upon himself and the United States Air Force.

In addition to all that, General Davis was the first African American to be named a general officer in the Air National Guard. And also in 1988, he was the first African American to serve as National Guard Bureau Chief.

He is a truly a great example of a leader because he shows us that when one envisions the way, then goes towards, and continually works towards it, they will achieve it. He is just another great example of the wonderful people we were and still are able to have speak to students at Living History Days.

Lieutenant General Russell Davis is still living at the age of 84.

JIM WILLIS

The first time I met Jim was at a veteran related event over fifteen years ago, and my first impression of him was how he carried himself. When he entered a room, it was obvious he was a natural leader. He attended many of our events over the years, and as he was an outstanding public speaker.

Many times we had Jim be the keynote speaker. During one of his talks to McMinnville High School students, he told them, "Did you know that German teenagers in the '30s and early '40s had to hide to listen to their favorite music. They loved American Jazz and dancing to swing music played by popular big bands of the era. There was a big problem though, the Nazi party had outlawed that genre of music. Germans caught listening to this music were arrested.

"Students, when you think about the freedoms we enjoy in America like listening and enjoying your favorite style of music, we are very fortunate. I'm remembering back in the '90s; I heard this loud booming beat coming from my daughter's bedroom. I went back to tell her to turn that crap down, and I asked her what the hell is that kind of music.

"She yelled back at me, 'Dad, it's RAP and I like it.' Now, I didn't understand it or like it, just like my parents didn't like Rock and Roll, but thankfully we live in a country where we have the freedom to listen to whatever style of music one likes."

Jim could have been a great teacher.

"I was born in Portland and lived in Oregon's second largest city, Vanport, for the first five years of my life. Vanport was created for all the Americans who came to Portland's shipyards for work during WWII. After the war, it was home for many people who were struggling financially and included most of Portland's Black population."

"Do you have any memories of the famous Vanport Flood?"

"Oh yes. I can vividly remember our house floating away down the Columbia River. We moved to Albany, and I attended elementary, junior, and high school in Albany."

"What were your high school years like?"

"I played trombone in the marching band and stand-up baritone in the orchestra, wrestled for all four years in high school, and ran the low hurdles in track. I graduated in '61 and was going to join either the Army or Marines because of my father."

"I know you are an Air Force veteran, so what happened?"

"Well, I asked my father for his advice. He was a WWII veteran who served in the Army in the 104th Timberwolf Infantry Division in Europe. They took part in many battles including the Battle of the Bulge.

"I was born when he was overseas. I asked which branch I should join, the Army or the Marines. He immediately responded with a loud, 'No Army and no Marines.'

"Later, I told him a buddy was going to join the Air Force and wanted me to join with him. My father gave his approval by saying, 'Good Choice'. My friend Ken Bancroft and I enlisted under what was called the Buddy Program.

"We graduated on the second of June and started boot camp on the fourth. My buddy and I were together the entire eight weeks and then I never saw him again for forty-five years."

"When were you sent to Vietnam?"

"In '66, but I wasn't supposed to go there. I re-enlisted in '65 because I was offered a quarantined three-year tour as an MP at the new NATO Headquarters in Paris, France. I was so excited. It would have been a great time because I could see all of Europe during my times off.

"However, late in '65, I get called to see the First Sergeant. As I entered his office he says, 'I got orders for you and you're not going to like them. You're going to South Vietnam.' Less than half a second after I yelled, 'What? What about NATO?' He said, 'Do you see this small print at the bottom of you re-enlisting contract? It says the Air Force can send you wherever they want to.'

"Straight away I ask, 'Where am I going?' And all he proceeded to tell me was that I was going to APO-96321 (Air Force Post Office 96321).

"I flew out of Travis Air Force base in a C-141 Starlifter. It had no seats and only webbing, so I sat backwards the entire time. The plane was loaded with men from every branch. We landed in Hawaii to refuel, and the pilot announces that we have a three day lay-over due to maintenance issues. We all thought that that didn't make any sense, but we found out the crew wanted to take three days off to enjoy Hawaii, so they made up the maintenance problem.

"Most would think I was lucky but not me, cause I'm stuck at the airfield with no money. So I take out my blue tube, has my pay records in it- you protect those with your life- and ask someone for a draw. They give me $60 and now I had beer money."

I was going to ask Jim what he did in Hawaii for three days, but he kept talking.

"We flew to Guam to refill and then to Clark Air Base in the Philippines. I'm standing at the booking counter, and I see a grease board on the wall with the destination of APO-96321 written on it and where to go. I go and it takes me to a C-123 Provider. I notice that it was an Arizona Air National Guard plane, and it was being loaded with big Tarnex boxes. I talk to the pilot, who is a young Captain, and ask if I can hitch a ride. He says, 'Sure, you're now the loadmaster and you can sit with me in the cockpit.'

"Wow, what a flight, that plane flew like a rock, bounced all over the place. We landed at Phan Rang Air Base and man it was hot and humid. On the tarmac was a big, barreled chest man wearing a baseball cap standing next to a garbage can filled with Carling Black Label cans of beer floating next to a big block of ice. The man offered me a beer. I found out later he was a full colonel.

"I reported to my CO at the Air Force Military Police base and the First Sergeant gives me a twelve-man tent to set up. He says, 'If you want a place to sleep before dark, you better get it up.' I'd only set up a pup tent in boy scouts but got some others to help me. Eventually, I stayed in there, with other guys, on cots for several months and then got Hollywood beds with frames and mattresses and mosquito nets.

"I was a small weapons specialist in the gun room the entire time. Plus, a firearms instructor and gun range instructor. There were many times we delivered gun jeeps, machine guns, grenade launchers, gas, oil, heavy machinery, and even crates of beer thirty miles northwest to Cameron Bay.

"We also did air base security providing combat convoy escorts between air bases. Now that wasn't fun. We were fired upon many times because the convoy can only travel as fast as the slowest vehicle."

"When were you sent home?"

"In March of '67. I was given a 'dream sheet' and told to pick three bases where I could be stationed. We all knew it was just a joke as those 'Son of a Guns' would just order us somewhere not on your sheet. Soon after that I received my orders, and I couldn't believe it. I'm ordered to Kingsley Air Base in Klamath Falls, Oregon. Well, I didn't tell anyone as I didn't want to risk the order being changed."

"Were you greeted with protestors?"

"No. You see, Klamath Falls is a red, white, and blue kind of town. It was a great place to live during the protest years. There were two other men who served in Vietnam there and the three of us became good friends. We were our own little support group."

"When did you get out of the Air Force?"

"In August of '67. My staff sergeant asked me to consider re-enlisting again because I could make Tech and then Master Sergeant. But during the interview, I'm told if I re-enlist I'm going back to Vietnam. My wife and I discussed it and because my son was one, we decided against re-enlisting."

"I know you were the State Director for the Department of Veteran Affairs. What did you do before that?"

"I went into civilian law enforcement. My first job I was a Deputy Sheriff in Roseburg, Oregon for fifteen years. After that, I became an Under-Sheriff when a good buddy of mine became the Sheriff of Washington County and asked me to work for him. I was too low a rank, but he didn't care because he said he want me for the job.

"For the first two years I worked, and I took many leadership and management courses from the state. Finally, I was promoted while working for the Police Academy.

"Then the State decides to merge several departments under a new bureau in the State Police Department and gives me the Command job. I'm loaned to the State Police for one year. But my boss tells me I won't come back. I didn't, and I became bureau commander for the Oregon State Police in Salem for ten years, until taking over as director of the Oregon Department of Veterans Affairs in 2003.

"Up till that time, I had been volunteering with veterans work and serving on an advisory committee for Governor Kitzhaber. When his former director retired, he asked me to take over.

"Again, I talked it over with my wife, Dee, and she says, 'You need to take it. I don't want you home alone with any power tools,'" Jim laughs. "She was working and had never forgotten about the one not-so-little mistake I made in her kitchen using a power tool," Jim laughs again.

"The next day, I'm sworn in as the State Director for the ODVA and served for the next ten years, finally retiring in 2013. I am also still very active with American Legion Post 10 and VFW 584 (Veterans of Foreign Wars) in Albany and the Vietnam Veterans of American 585 of Lebanon.

"I also helped spearhead the development the second Oregon Veterans' Home located in Lebanon. And helped build two memorials dedicated to those who fought and gave their lives in service to their country."

"I also remember seeing you at a pow wow at the Confederated Tribes of the Grand Ronde and you were dressed in Native clothes. Do you have Native Blood in you?"

"Unfortunately, no. But I've always had a strong affinity for Native American veterans. They have the highest percentage of service than any group in the United States.

"I started a state-wide program hiring Native veterans for Native Service getting help receiving their benefits from the VA. The majority of Native veterans could not get help from white service officers. But when we had Native service officers, we were able to get many their benefits. I've been honored three times by three different tribes with a blanket wrapped over my shoulders and even given a Native name.

"At my naming ceremony, the Chief told all, 'As the winds blow and the waters flow, from this day forward you will be known as Broken Wind." Jim and I both laughed.

Jim passed away in June of 2021 at the age of 78 from Agent Orange related cancer.

RON KOENIG   Milwaukie High Class of '63

I met Ron at Milwaukie High School as his son, Jason, was a very good three-sport athlete from the Class of '92. Jason took Strength Training from me three years in a row and was a starting strong safety on our varsity football team. Ron and his son Jason were both class act gentlemen. Ron was very supportive of me and the football program with donating and organizing fund raisers. I've always been very grateful to him.

After the very first Living History Days, Ron started donating to our cause. The first time I called him to thank him, he told me he was a Vietnam veteran. It wasn't until I was finally able to talk with him that I was really able to thank him for his service.

"I was born in Portland, and in the fourth grade, my family moved to Milwaukie. I was a two-sport athlete, first team All-Metro League as an offensive halfback and defensive back for legendary Coach 'Mouse' Davis.

"I was selected to play in the Shrine game but got sick and lost over twenty pounds. Right after the game, my dad took me fishing and noticed my neck was swollen. I had mono. That fall, I enrolled at the University of Oregon and played football on the freshman team.

"I only played one year because I felt I needed to improve my grades. I majored in biology and joined the ROTC (Reserve Officers Training Corps) my junior year. I had to put my uniform in my bag when I rode my bike to the campus ROTC building. It was not safe at that time as Anti-Vietnam War protesters were protesting on the campus. I was there when they fire-bombed our building."

"I remember watching that on the news. So why did you join the Air Force?"

"I wanted to fly. I applied to flight school and was accepted, sent to Reese Air Base in Lubeck, Texas, and commissioned as a Second Lieutenant. We were then assigned by grades, and I was assigned to fly KC-135 Straddle-Tankers, a four-engine jet. We performed mid-air refueling.

"After that training, I was sent to Sacramento for upgrade tanker training to perform two at a time. We were also a part of the Nuclear Defense Program providing fuel for the B-52s in case of an attack. We were on alert every seven days."

"When did you go to Vietnam?"

"In June of '68. I was sent three separate places in Thailand for about four months at a time. We would refuel planes doing air strikes over Vietnam. At 24,000 feet, we would fuel four to five F-4 Phantoms and after their strikes, we would top off their fuel tanks so they could make it back to their base. We also supported rescue missions with close air support. Back in the States, we were put on Alert for the B-52s again."

"When you came home, were you greeted with protestors?"

"No, I was very fortunate, very lucky. I came home to a Military air base. Using the GI bill, I enrolled in dental school and was a dentist in Milwaukie for my career."

"When did you marry your wife?"

"She and I were good friends since junior high school and started dating my senior year in high school. We got married my senior year at U of O and we've been married for over fifty years."

Ron is still living at the age of 77.

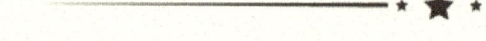

BOB BOYER

Bob and the Oregon Chapter of the National Association of Black Veterans (NABVETS) have been supporting our events for over ten years now.

Bob was twenty-two years old when, in 1961, the Air Force ordered him to a local airbase vehicle maintenance division. When I asked Bob why he joined, he said, "Because a judge gave me the choice of joining the military or jail. And joining the military saved my life. Running the streets of North Philly (Philadelphia) was a rough life.

"As a kid I was bullied, so I started taking boxing lessons at the same gym and time as Boxing great Joe Frazier and quickly became good, even boxing professionally earning the nickname 'Jaw Breaker'. I was also a standout football, basketball, and track star in high school.

"While in the military, I was a communication specialist and was told I would be sent to Vietnam in '62. But I loved cars and fell in love with the '62 Pontiac Staff Car and transferred to Auto maintenance. After my service, I started boxing again at Knott Street Community Center in Portland. I never experienced any harassment. Maybe because everyone knew not to mess with me." Bob chuckled after saying this.

"Working with NABVETs, we helped lots of Vietnam Veterans get millions of dollars in benefits over the years. Ken, did you know NABVETS was founded in the '70s just to help Vietnam veterans. I've helped many get help with their PTSD."

Bob worked in railyards and was also a longshoreman. While working, he went to night school to get his associates degree from Cascade Christian College, which he and others lobbied to rename Portland Community College. He also became the first African American to graduate from Marylhurst University with a degree in business management.

He has been heavily involved in many community causes over the years and is well respected. He even served as an Oregon State Senator in the '90s. One of his passions has been mentoring and motivating inmates at the Oregon State Penitentiary and McLaren Youth Correctional Facility.

Bob is one of the many veterans who continue to serve their country even after they come home.

Bob Boyer is still living at the age of 81.

NORM MAVES JR.

I first met Norm when he covered high school football games when I was the head football coach at Milwaukie High School. I've always admired and respected his sportswriter skills. It was only a few years ago that I learned he was a Vietnam Era Air Force veteran.

When my wife, Malinda, and I met Norm for his interview, he was wearing a red T-shirt emblazoned with the letters R.E.D. His jacket was zipped only half-way up, and I could not see the phrase below the letters.

I asked, "What does R.E.D. stand for?"

Norm responded, "It's 'Remember Everyone Deployed,' and you wear it on 'Red Fridays.' It's for all the troops who are on duty right now. I feel it's very important."

I've always known he was a respected sportswriter for decades, but interviewing Norm, I learned that he is extremely supportive of all who currently serve. And he has a special place in his heart for veterans, especially Vietnam veterans.

As we sat down, Norm, who knows I played for Darrel 'Mouse' Davis and that I love hearing any story I can about him, says to me, "I've got a great Darrel "Mouse" Davis story for you. By the way, I've always called him by his real name, Darrel, just out of respect, I could never call him 'Mouse.'"

I, of course, over enthusiastically replied, "Really!? Let me hear it."

"When he was the football coach at Milwaukie High School back in his last season at the school in 1964, we (Beaverton High School) played Milwaukie at home. Well, he had his several big stud offensive linemen take three-yard splits and they ran the ball at will. We couldn't deal with it."

We laughed. "Coach is known for passing the football more than running the football," I said. "Two years later, at Sunset, he installed the run and shoot. The rest is history.

"So, let's start at the beginning," I said next. "When were you born and where?"

"April 18, 1948, Nashville, Tennessee."

"Tell me a little about your parents."

"My dad, Norm Sr., was the oldest son of a big Canadian family, and served in Royal Canadian Air Force. He joined right after Germany invaded Poland in September of 1939. He wanted to fly but was color blind. He had worked in a bank, so during WWII he served as a paymaster in Europe.

"My mom Margaret's first husband, John Edgar 'Jack' Cornelison, was shot down over the Netherlands on September 29, 1944. My mom became a widow with a fourteen-month-old daughter, Diane."

"So, she's your half-sister then?" I asked.

"NO, she's my sister," he said in a raised voice. "We don't do half of anything in our family. Mom went to work during the war and raised her daughter alone. She met my father, Norm senior, and in '46, they got married. He adopted my sister, and I was born in '48. My youngest sister, Meg, was born in '54.

"There's a huge coincidence attached to the story. On September 29, 1972, a buddy of mine, Air Force F-111 pilot Robert Arthur 'Lefty' Brett, was shot down over Laos. I knew him when I was stationed at Adair Air Force Station north of Corvallis, and he was a student at Oregon State.

"His body was not found until late 2001. He left a widow and a little girl named Camille. The widow, Patrice, and I got married in 1977 and became a family. We buried Lefty at Arlington National Cemetery in the summer of 2002.

"So, I'm the second Norm Maves to marry a widow with a little girl of a pilot shot down and killed in action each on the exact same day September 29, twenty-eight years apart. We added a son, Michael, in 1987."

"Wow, that's unbelievable! That's incredible," I responded.

Norm continued about his high school years. "I first attended Sunset High School my freshman and sophomore years, then transferred to Beaverton High School. My senior year I played defensive end for Coach Duke Moore. And we got Milwaukie back in the opening game. I was a writer for both school newspapers, too. I graduated in 1966."

"What did you do after high school?"

Norm starts laughing. "I spent a disastrous year at the University of Oregon," he said, "and became draft eligible in the summer of 1967. I was not ready for college; I was about as mature as a glass of water. I flunked out.

"I was terrified of being drafted. In 1967, just before the Tet Offensive, over a thousand a day were drafted. I managed to secure an enlistment into the Air Force and shipped out to Lackland Air Force Base for basic training on November 21, 1967.

"These were some crazy times. Everyone was starting to take sides. You were either with us or against us. Kids my age were forced to make decisions they weren't mature enough to make. Society collapsed that way.

"I was sent to the Air Weather Service (AWS) Chanute Airbase in Central Illinois to go to Weather Observation tech school. My first duty assignment was Adair Air Force Station, seven miles north of Corvallis. I was attached to 26th Air Division, Western North American Aerospace Defense Command (NORAD), Air Defense Command.

"It was a Semi-Automatic Ground Environment (SAGE) assignment. SAGE was an early system that linked data from all the radar sites in the air division and put it into a computer that took up an entire floor of a four-story building. You could do the same thing today with a cell phone.

"When Adair closed in September of '69, I was shipped to Siskiyou County Air Base. It was a tiny backup base for a fighter squadron, eleven miles northeast of Yreka, California, just outside of the even tinier town of Montague. I was a one-man weather observer station working with civilians on the runway of the Montague Flight Service Station.

"Siskiyou closed in March of 1971, and I finished the last eight months of my stitch at McChord Air Force Base. From there back in SAGE again with the 25th Air Division of Western NORAD.

"I was discharged in December of '71, and I never had a permanent assignment farther than three hundred miles from home. Not much of a career, but my discharge was honorable."

"How do you feel about serving in the Air Force?"

"I'm grateful to the Air Force. It gave me a framework for life. It was kind of harsh, but I learned discipline. I was on my own for the first time in my life, and I had to learn how to handle it. Some say the military makes you grow up fast. I'm still working on that part, but life in the Air Force showed me how.

"I'm so grateful for the GI bill. I used it to buy my first house, and it paid for my formal education. But the best thing I learned in the service was the concept of duty. We all have duties that are larger than ourselves. You live by those duties. The service taught me that. And survival in the service was sometimes humorous, too.

"My basic training drill sergeant at Lackland, Technical Sergeant Robert Perkins, he sounded just like Mouse Davis, straightened me out once on the subject of questioning how things are done."

Norm then proceeded to imitate this man's intense sounding voice. 'Don't argue with the Air Force. You won't win. Just keep your eyes on your duty and save yourself a lot of trouble.' He was right."

Norm's last day of duty at McChord was eventful.

"So, my last day of duty before getting out of the Air Force, we were just doing our daily routine when a big commotion stirred over by the forecasters. An airline passenger plane at Sea-Tac International Airport was highjacked. McChord sent some chase planes up to follow it, but they lost it in the clouds. It was the D.B. Cooper hijacking. A few days later, I was a civilian."

"Wow, that's crazy," I said. "Even though you were stateside, did you ever run into protesters?"

Norm laughed. "No protesters in Yreka, California. But few of us wore our uniforms off duty. You never knew who approved of the military and who didn't. I did wear my uniform a couple of times to get lower airfare rates. I also wore it for pictures at home; one time, in Milwaukee, Wisconsin, I wore it, very proudly I add, to take my grandmother to church.

"I was out at twenty-three on December 1, 1971, and I went back to college. Did two terms at Portland State and finished up at the University of Oregon.

"After that, I have worked in newspaper journalism for almost all of my career. My newspaper career started before the military though, because I got my first job with the sports department of the Oregon Journal as a high school senior in December of 1965.

"I was answering phones, sharpening pencils, and typing up assorted things. In the times when I wasn't directly employed by a newspaper after that, I did a lot of free-lance work for anybody who would pay me. Or sometimes not pay me. It was too much fun to be too picky about it.

"I was the sports editor of the Springfield News in 1975 to 76, then got my permanent job with the Oregonian in September of 1976. I covered just about everything. In 1989 I transferred to the Living Section for four years, then over to the regular newsroom for the next eleven.

"I covered everything there, too, but it was also where I did most of my coverage of the Oregon military and veterans issues. Those fifteen years outside of the sports department, the people I met and the stories they shared, gave me a perspective on life that really opened my eyes to realities.

"In 2004, I transferred back to the sports department, where I covered high schools, Portland State athletics, and Oregon State baseball. I took all three trips to the College World Series in Omaha with the Beavers, which included two national championships. I retired on December 27, 2007."

"I was pleasantly surprised to see you at the Vietnam Memorial Dinner and meeting in February. Why did you become involved with them?"

"For years I've visited Oregon's Vietnam Memorial at Washington Park to remember and honor my buddies from my high school days, and my whole generation, who were killed in Vietnam.

"Terry Lee Thompson was a great defensive tackle at Beaverton High. He was a graduate of the class before me in '65. He was in the Army, and they were ambushed. Terry was running to get on a chopper and the soldier behind him got hit. As I understand it, Terry turned around to help him and he was shot and killed.

"My class of '66 also lost two men: John Sidney Rasmussen and Gary Grant Lamb. Rest in glory, boys.

One story that has always bothered me is somebody I knew at Sunset High School: Craig Albers, Class of '66. He was the best athlete at Sunset but had a difficult life. I'm being evasive here on purpose.

"Craig dropped out of Sunset in January of his senior year and joined the Marines. At nineteen, he was clearing a mine field when a mine exploded, and he lost three limbs. He survived and made it fifteen more years doing the best he could but gave up the will to live.

"He and passed on April 15, 1982. But he is not considered a Vietnam KIA because he lived an additional fifteen years and died in Portland. I've always felt, and written often, that his dying process started in that mine field and that he's just as worthy of any honor for a KIA as anyone else.

"I help read the names of the number of Oregonians KIA in Vietnam, every Memorial Day at the Vietnam Veterans Living Memorial in Washington Park. One year, I went off script and included Craig Albers. I didn't ask permission. I just did it because Craig deserved it as much as anyone else.

"But I've always had some survivor's guilt about my service. So many smarter and better men than me died over there. I am just so lucky."

Norm gets tears in his eyes and gets emotional about the subject of the war. He also is still in the habit of saluting the flag whenever he has the chance.

"You know, Ken," he said, "I salute the flag every time I hear the national anthem. The Department of Defense encourages veterans to salute, so I always do. I always I see my friends' faces, and the faces of the boys of my generation. I owe them a lot. We all do."

Norm Maves Jr. is still living at the age of 74.

PUBLIC SCHOOL TEACHERS-COACHES-ADMINISTRATORS

JIM GADBERRY   Army

Jim Gadberry is quite the man. He is a retired high school teacher, head wrestling coach, and high school principal. He coached wrestling for fifty years and is in the National Wrestling Coaches Hall of Fame. Jim has earned the love and respect of his classroom students, wrestlers, and staff wherever he has been and whatever he has done.

Jim never spoke about his time in Vietnam. In fact, I did not even know he was a veteran until we started doing the Living History Days. I can never thank him enough for his undying support since the very beginning, and most of all, thank him for his friendship.

"I was born in Longview, Washington in 1948, and my father, Odis, moved our family to Brookings, Oregon in 1950. He relocated to Brookings because his uncle and another family friend had just built a sawmill in the town. My father also built a small, one-man sawmill, and it was rumored he paid for it with money he won gambling during the war," Jim laughed.

"Odis was a Tail Gunner in a B-24 assigned to the 15th Air Force during WWII. On his third mission, his plane was badly damaged from German flak, and the pilot ordered all to bail out right after entering Italian airspace.

"After bailing out, my dad's parachute was hit, making the last sixty feet a free fall. Somehow, he was able to aim what was left of his parachute for a large pile of tilled up soil in a vineyard. Even then, upon impact, his back and hip were crushed.

"He was rescued by the vineyard owner, whose beautiful daughter helped nurse him back to health, with lots of wine. I never knew if my father and the farmer's daughter had a romantic relationship," Jim laughed again.

"What were your high school years like?"

"Believe it or not, I was a hell of basketball player but fell in love with wrestling in the seventh grade. I played football, baseball, and wrestled and was the Student Body President my senior year. Was also voted the 'Outstanding Senior Boy' and was the Class of '66 Valedictorian.

"After that, I attended Southern Oregon College (SOC) from the fall of '66 and graduated in June of '70. I was also the Student Body Second Vice-President at SOC. But in December of '69, my life would change drastically.

"About seventy-five male students would meet in the library to study several nights a week. On a cold and wet December night, I was sitting in my car in the library parking lot, listening to the National Draft Lottery on the car radio.

"Young men, ages eighteen to twenty-five, with a draft number under 180, were going to get selected by their local draft board for two years of military service. For anyone with a number over 180, their chance to avoid the draft was much better. However, if you were in school, you were allowed to finish. My number was number 88.

"My birthday was called, and then number 88, my number, and it brought me to tears. All I could think of was, 'God, I'm drafted and going to Vietnam.' When I walked into the library, half the guys were cheering, and the other half were angry. Those with numbers under 180 wanted to punch the guys celebrating.

"I was so upset, I wanted to drop out of college, but my father chewed me out and said, 'You finish up school.'

"I had a college deferment from my local draft board in Coos Bay. If you dropped out of school or graduated, you were immediately eligible for the draft. They then proceed to tell me that within two months after graduation I would be drafted.

"Five months later, in May of '70, my high school classmate and wrestling team member, Wes Davis, a helicopter pilot, was shot down and died over Cambodia.

"During my four years attending SOC, I had three close friends, and our draft experiences represent the common scenarios that most American males experienced with the draft. My senior year, two of these friends shared an apartment with me and the third friend was always at our place, living for free!

"One of my roommates failed his military physical because of poor health and weight issues. He was never going to get drafted. My other roommate had an 'Ace in the Hole.' His Aunt was the head of his local draft board. She told him he would be drafted, but she would make sure he was stationed stateside. Sure enough, after he's drafted, he lands a clerk job at the Presidio in San Francisco.

"My third friend passed his draft physical and is in great physical shape. Upon graduation in June 1970, he returns home, awaiting his local draft board to tell him to report to the military induction center in Portland, Oregon.

"On August 11, I report to the center and who do I see but my buddy, with the biggest grin on his face, and an official form in his hand declaring him 4-F, physically unfit for military duty. I asked him how he pulled that off and he said he got a doctor to verify he had a bad knee.

"He knew that the Army would be very skeptical of the knee injury, so he took speed before his physical. He told me that when the doctor put his stethoscope to his chest, his eyes rolled back and looked shocked. He asked him if he was okay. My buddy said, "he could see my heart beating through my skin as I talked to him!'

He escaped from the military and Vietnam, and later moved to the Reno/Tahoe area to build homes and achieve financial success.

"I, unfortunately, did not have connections, or any medical conditions, so passed my physical and was told to report. Us draftees had a three-hour wait to be officially inducted into the Army, so we left the center and found a tavern just down the street and drank as much beer as we could.

"Later, back at the center, we lined up, and a sergeant orders us to take a step forward. Well, half step backwards, some don't move, and some step forward. The sergeant then yells out, 'I don't care what direction you step, forward, backwards, or sideways, you are all inducted into the United States Army!'

"After a three-hour bus ride, we reached Fort Lewis, Washington for our basic training. The first three days, we are in the Reception Center. We were issued wool blankets and the rumor was, if you were allergic to wool, you could get out. I wake up the first morning with a rash from my neck down to my knees.

"There's no sick calls on Sunday and nobody is manning sick bay, so I'm sent in an ambulance to the hospital. At the hospital, a Sergeant gets furious with me and says, 'There is nothing wrong with you.' Later, a Captain yells at me, 'You are a chicken-shit! There is nothing wrong with you! You're going back!' And guess what? My rash went away within two days.

"During the first three days at Fort Lewis, prior to beginning basic training, each new soldier was interviewed to determine what specific job or Military Occupational Specialty (MOS) they should be trained for after basic training.

"The soldier interviewing me says, 'I see you speak a foreign language?' I took two years of Spanish in high school. 'Well, that's an affirmative check. You play a musical instrument?' I took piano lessons in grade school. 'That's a second affirmative check. And you are a college graduate? Third.

"I was then told they needed interpreters in Vietnam. Also told the Vietnamese language has five different tonal sounds and because I had an ear for music, I was qualified. The last question was when I wanted to go to Vietnam.

"I was given a choice: After eight more weeks of advanced infantry training (AIT) or wait a year. I say, "I'll wait the extra year.

"By the summer of '70, the Army was beginning to expand its withdrawal of troops from Vietnam. Normally, because of the expense to train linguists at the Defense Language Institute (DLI) in either Monterey, California or El Paso, Texas, soldiers had to commit to a four-year enlistment in the Army. However, the Army was now desperate for linguist/interpreters in Vietnam. Thus, for about a month the Army was offering two-year draftees an opportunity to go to DLI to learn Vietnamese.

"Additionally, the Army completed a thorough background check on each linguist as each would be given a top security clearance because they would be assigned to the Army Security Agency (ASA) upon arrival in Vietnam. Furthermore, if both of your parents were not born in America, the security clearance was denied.

"One of my best friends at DLI, El Paso, fell into this situation, as his mother was Canadian. The Army, after he graduated DLI in June of 1971, changed his MOS, and he never went to Vietnam... lucky for him!

"The DLI school, El Paso, was thirty weeks, five days a week, eight hours a day. Nixon was promising he would end the war. We were hoping it would be over soon. Our instructors were Vietnamese nationals, some who had left Vietnam when France was overrun by the Communists in '54 They taught us their country's history. It's three hundred years of war. And how most of the country was still very tribal.

"It didn't take us long to realize it didn't matter what our grades were or if you even passed the final test, we were going to Vietnam. Many of us stopped studying at night. I know I did not pass the test, but the Army said I did.

"The private sector company that taught the classes and administered the test were paid for the success rate of the test. The system was rigged to benefit the private contractor. The teachers always received a one-hundred percent success rate for each class of Vietnamese they taught.

"I finished and then was sent on leave to visit my parents for thirty days before being sent to Vietnam. My dad drove me down to Presidio Base in San Francisco where I would be shipped to Nam. I've only seen my dad cry twice in my life. The first time is when he dropped me off to go to Vietnam and the second time is when my mother died.

"From the Presidio, we are bussed to Travis Air Base in California and loaded on a plane, but the plane has engine problems, so all one-hundred and fifty of us were unloaded and bussed to a hotel for the night. At the hotel, there were ten to a room, and beds everywhere. We closed the bar down and refused to leave. There were brawls all over and the MPs were called. The next day, everyone is hung over with guys throwing up everywhere. The stewardesses were really pissed."

From here Jim became very serious and told me that what he wanted to say next he felt very strongly about and should be included.

"There was a huge difference about serving in Vietnam in the early years compared to serving in Vietnam in the later years. When we were sent to Vietnam in '71, the majority of us were draftees and did not want to be there. The morale over in Vietnam was bad.

"The war had become extremely unpopular in the states, and we knew President Nixon had promised to end the war. The attitude was most of us didn't want to die for a war that we believed was going to end soon. Most people don't understand the differences between the Vietnam veterans who served in Vietnam from 1963 to 1969 and those from 1970 to January 27, 1973.

"The first group, in the beginning, understood the need to be there because everyone believed it was not only patriotic but the right thing to do to stop Communism.

"Most people today would not understand at all what it was like serving in Vietnam in the early '70s. But it was real. I saw it. And being a coach, I can understand that bad morale is not good. It can impact winning and losing in sports. Bad morale certainly impacted my tour of duty in Vietnam.

"In early August of '71, eight to ten linguists from my DLI class, including me, arrived at the base in Phu Bai, southeast of the city of Hue in I Corps. We were assigned to the 8th Radio Research Field Station (RRFS), a part of the Army Security Agency (ASA), one of the least known Army units in Vietnam. Our group of linguist/interpreters, known as 'lingies', joined a large group of four-year commitment linguists who were bitter with resentment and hatred because we only had two years.

"The first two weeks, we were in transition, waiting to be assigned a workstation in the operations building. The operations building never closed. It was open and manned twenty-four hours a day, seven days a week. During those two weeks, we had to lay razor wire and serve guard duty every night at the ammunition dump.

"Finally, we were assigned to a group to begin interpreting tapes, collected by spy planes using Airborne Radio Direction Finding (ARDF). Most of the chatter on the tapes were from villages, rice paddies and farmers, nothing of military value. However, anything collected from the Ho Chi Minh Trail was a high priority because of usage by the Viet Cong (VC) and the North Vietnamese Army (NVA).

"If it was a high priority, we had twenty-four hours to send the translations up the chain of command. Our chain of command included the Army, the Central Intelligence Agency (CIA), and the National Security Agency (NSA) personnel, who worked with us in operations. Within two months, all of us new linguists were struggling, and our incompetence was showing.

"About the end of August in '71, I received a letter from my girlfriend back home with terrible news. Her younger brother, John Brannon, was killed in his third week in Vietnam. This was devastating news for me. Now a total of three soldiers from Brookings, Oregon were killed in Vietnam. Also, included at the end of letter she wrote, 'I'm begging you to stay alive, I can't lose you too.' That motivated me a lot.

"By October of '71, the need for a replacement 'Ditty Bopper' up near the Demilitarized Zone (DMZ) at a small outpost called Alpha 4 started circulating in our unit. The outpost was situated on a hill overlooking a NVA training base, which mortared the outpost almost daily. A Ditty Bopper is a Morse Code Interceptor who listened to a series of Vietnamese numbers and recorded them. The encrypted messages were then passed on to the RRFS at Phu Bai.

"I know I don't want to be the one picked. I actually talked to a Ditty when they returned to Phu Bai near the end of their tour in Vietnam. He was shaking and crying until he couldn't even speak because of combat stress.

"So, I start to become worried because the guy in charge of our unit of does not like me. Mostly because I was a two-year linguist draftee. He is a Harvard grad, speaks five languages and was told by the Army when he requested to go to language school (DLI) that he must sign up for two additional years.

"For committing to four years, the Army said he could select which language he wanted to study. He accepted the Army's offer, went to DLI after training, thinking he was going to study German. Instead, the Army switched him to Vietnamese and now has two more years in the Army after Vietnam.

"Well, he tells me I'm replacing the Ditty Bopper at Alpha 4 and will be sent up north in forty-eight hours. I tell him, I'm sorry you were lied to by the Army, but I'm not trained for this work, I'm only a linguist/interpreter, not a Ditty Bopper.' He yells, 'I don't give a shit! You are going! And now! Get the fuck out of here!'

"The next day I go to the officer in charge of our unit, a Captain, to ask him about my new orders. He was not aware of my new assignment and tells me he will look into it. Well, the next day he informs me, 'You're not going, and I'm reassigning you to work with the ARVNS.'

"The ARVNS, soldiers of the South Vietnamese Army, provided our field station with a variety of intelligence on a daily basis. Several linguists manned a remote space near the perimeter of our post to receive and process information given to us by the Vietnamese soldiers. Once processed, we sent it on to the main operations site to be interpreted by the linguist/interpreters.

"Our space was primitive and lacked few amenities. My limited language skills were now appropriately being utilized by the US Army. I spoke everyday with those soldiers. I really enjoyed working with the ARVNS as they were our only source of intelligence the last two months before I returned to the States.

"My last three months in-country saw in I Corps a build-up of VC and NVA. Phu Bai was the last major base in the region. The 101st Airborne Division had left the area, leaving just a platoon of infantry soldiers to assist our field station.

"During that time, we rotated daily for guard duty, Ammo Dump, sometimes during the day, sometimes at night. We saw this twice. Kids would jump of a bank onto a truck as it drove down the hill going slow. They would jump off when it stopped, steel ammo and disappear through the bush.

"Also because of the build-up of VC and NVA, the response by our base was a set of orders requiring most of us to begin digging out the dirt and vegetation in the long trenches surrounding the base which was built by the French. It was hot, dusty, and dirty work with lots of poisonous snakes to deal with. The purpose for this order was in preparation for us to defend our field station because we no longer had a large presence of infantry to provide combat support for us.

"During my entire time in Phu Bai, our M16 rifles and ammunition were stored in an armament building. You checked them out and then again in whenever you had guard duty. As the enemy build-up continued, our commanding officers decided to conduct a 'timed drill' on how quickly soldiers assigned to the armament building could disperse our weapons and ammunition.

"Once we got our weapons and ammunition, we would assemble in the trenches in preparation for a firefight. Well, the guys in charge of the weapons were the biggest bunch of stoners, always high.

"So, the drill was a cluster, and our officers ordered us to go to the trenches without our weapons. So, around seven hundred soldiers climbed into those trenches as day turned to night.

"My trench was in front of the 'Lifer's'. They were career enlisted soldiers and they had air-conditioned trailers. A bunch of us grab rocks the sizes of baseballs and get everyone down the long trench to do the same.

"On the count of three, we all throw the rocks onto their roofs. They all came running out of their trailers, pistols drawn, and panicking. We all laugh, they cuss us out and go back inside. We never had to do that drill ever again.

"Our weapons would be locked up every night and checked out to you when going on guard duty. The Standing order was to fire at anyone trying to sneak in to steal anything, but if you fired your weapon and there was not a body on the wire, it was an automatic bust down to E-1, Buck private.

"I do have one funny story. Well, it's funny now, but could have got ourselves in big trouble. Six of my buddies and I fly to Bangkok, Thailand for our seven days of R&R. The Army, because of heavy drug use by GIs, had created a drug testing procedure before anyone could go on R&R. However, it used up one full day of your seven days.

"So, when all of us got to Saigon, we had learned from other GIs on how to avoid losing that day. Also, none of us used drugs! We managed to avoid the drug test (by not taking the drug test!) and saved one day.

"Then, as we were waiting to board our commercial flight at the Tan Son Nhat Airport, several MPs approach our group and ask to see our drug clearance cards. Just as we start playing stupid, they receive an emergency call to report immediately to another part of the airport. As the MP's depart, our group is told to board our plane.

"Then, as we taxi down the runway for liftoff, the MP's, in a jeep, drive alongside the plane, trying their hardest to get it to stop. It did not happen, and the plane lifted off. We had a lot of much needed fun in Bangkok, but what happened in Thailand stays in Thailand," Jim laughed.

Jim must have seen my face because he added, "It's ok to include that. My wife, Darlene, already knows."

Jim came back home in March 1972, returning to SOC majoring in Education. In the fall of 1974, he was hired as a history teacher and a wrestling coach at Milwaukie High School. Here he started a path that would lead him to his over forty-year coaching career at six different Oregon high schools.

Many people do not know that because of his Vietnamese language skills, Jim helped many of new students who had come over from Vietnam. He would personally meet with the parents to help them. They all were very grateful.

Something else many people do not know is that Jim has climbed the highest peaks in all fifty states. Something very few people can lay claim to doing. He has climbed Mount McKinley in Alaska, and even Mauna Kea in Hawaii, and of course Mt. Hood many times.

He even took my stepson Benjamin Blair, who helped me write these books, up Mt. Hood, in Oregon. Something Benjamin says he will never forget.

Jim Gadberry is still living at the age of 74.

LEN KAUFFMAN   Army

In 2011, I attended the Oregon Chapter, National Wrestling Hall of Fame to support Jim Gadberry who was being inducted that evening. I was in awe of the many greatest wrestlers in Oregon history from Olympians to Collegiate All-Americans.

After the ceremonies, most went into the lounge to visit. I noticed there was a large group of former great college wrestlers from around Oregon sitting at the same table. So I walked up, introduced myself and asked, "As a football guy, I'm curious as to who is the toughest SOB in this room?"

Everyone, at practically the same time, said, "Len Kauffman." Everybody laughed and someone said, "And it's not even close." A former wrestler stated, "Len Kauffman is considered the toughest wrestler in OSU history."

Len is arguably the best wrestler ever to compete at Oregon State. He pinned every dual meet opponent during the 1964 and 1965 seasons and broke the school record twice for falls in one season. He earned three conference titles and earned All-American status three times as well. He was a four-time AAU All-American, including National Freestyle titles in 1964 and 1969.

Len still holds records set during his college days. His .949 college winning percentage stands third in Oregon State University history. He also has the title 'pinningest college wrestler in history,' with eighty-four percent of his matches ending in a 'Kauffman fall'. His NCAA record still stands today.

Len agreed to meet and be interviewed. "I was born in Lebanon, Oregon on December 12, 1942. My father, Leslie, who went by LJ, grew up on a farm in Montana and dropped out of school because my grandfather needed him to work on the family farm. My grandfather did not believe in school.

"My father came to Oregon in the mid-thirties during the depression looking for work. He bought a hundred-acre farm and also got a job at a lumber mill making plywood decking for Navy Ships. Because his job involved supporting the war effort, he was not drafted for the military. My mother, Sylvia, was from Lebanon.

"My two brothers, Darrell and Don, and I, were all state placers in high school wrestling and all three lettered at OSU wrestling. Our sister Carolyn was toughest of all of us though. She boxed me many times.

"My father always pushed and supported our education from high school through college. But he had to pull us out of school to help out on the farm. We had chores every morning and evening, milking cows, feeding the pigs and chickens. I was so unprepared for high school, so I was way behind academically.

"I went out for wrestling because I fell in love with the sport watching my older brother wrestle for Lebanon High School, so I went out as a freshman. I qualified for the state tournament all four years and was a state champion my senior year.

"University of Washington offered me a full ride to wrestle, and Coach Dale Thomas of Oregon State offered me fifty bucks a term. I went to OSU because my older brother was wrestling there, and I thought Coach Thomas knew everything about wrestling.

"The NCAA National Championships were at Gill Coliseum at OSU in '61. My teammate and good friend Don Conway won his weight class and was a national champion. I followed Don as the head wrestling coach at PSU. Oh, and did I tell you I loved wrestling?" he said laughing.

"Why did you join the Army?"

"Well, incoming freshmen were required to be in the ROTC program both their freshman and sophomore years. It was because of the Land Grant Institution Program that was ended after my sophomore year. But I stayed in all four years.

"I signed up during a lunch break. I went down to join the Air Force, but the line to sign up was very long, so was the Navy and Marines. The Army line was very short, so I joined the Army, and had plenty of time to eat lunch before my next class. I decided to stay in all four years and upon graduating in '65 was commissioned as an officer.

"Because I was still wrestling, after graduation I asked and was given permission by the Army to postpone my duty for a year to wrestle freestyle for the United States Team in the World Games. Because of the postponement, I started working on my Master's, and was an assistant wrestling coach for Dale Thomas.

"In the ROTC, I also applied to a pilot license program offered to seniors. I passed the exam and learned to fly while in the ROTC and got my pilot's license.

"Because of that, the Army sent me to Flight School in '66 learning to fly Huey helicopters. I graduated second in my class, and they sent me and the top pilot to USC (University of Southern California) for their Officer's Aviation Safety Management Flight program. This course in the past was only available to experienced pilots, and we were sent as an experimental test to see if we could handle it. It was by far the most valuable course I ever took in the military.

"I was sent to Vietnam in January of '68, just three weeks before the Tet Offensive. I was attached to the 174th Assault Helicopter Company attached to the 11th brigade America Division."

"Anything you want to share about your experiences in Vietnam?"

Len paused and looked away. Considered by many as one of the toughest men many have known, Len got tears in eyes and said, "Ken, I've never talked about this to anyone, ever! I just don't think I can do it. I lost too many very good friends over there.

"It was tough, dangerous, and very stressful. We delivered soldiers and brought out the wounded. You've heard of My Lai the massacre. We brought troops in all day and brought the wounded out."

Len then became silent for a very long time, but then started speaking again, but had changed the subject.

"After one year, I had over a thousand hours flying and was disappointed that I couldn't fly more, but they were always giving me assignments on the ground, Intel, and such. I just wanted to help save more of our men.

"I got out in '70 but signed up for the Oregon National Guard, Air Division out at the base by Portland's Airport because I loved flying. I flew helicopters and then the Mohawk plane (a triple tail attack plane used in photo observation and electronic reconnaissance). At the same time, I enrolled back at OSU to finish my Master's and coach for Dale Thomas again."

"Were you greeted with anti-war protestors returning home?"

"Oh, yes." Coach instantly became upset and in a more intense tone of voice said, "Too many experiences, and I will share only one. I was almost late to my next class, and I was walking fast. And across the street was a young ROTC cadet wearing his uniform trying to walk away from about five or six hippies who were harassing him, calling him names, and shoving him.

"I instantly became very angry. I wanted to cross the street and help him out. But something told me to just go to class. I'm still upset with myself for not helping him. I regret my decision to this day. I still see it vividly today."

Coach was very upset telling me this. I'm glad he listened to that small voice as I believe he might have seriously hurt some of those hippies.

Len was the head wrestling coach at Portland State University from '75 to '84. He also was a pilot for American airlines for sixteen years, and retired from the Army as a Colonel in 1992.

Why join the Military? "I truly believe in an all-volunteer military as you only get who really wants to be there. I really admire those who choose to serve. I wouldn't want to pressure or sell someone. It should be their choice."

While speaking at a Veterans Car show a couple years ago, there was a flyover right after Malinda sang the national anthem. The MC announces over the loudspeaker, "Thank you Colonel Len Kauffman for the impressive flyover." I learned coach had done many flyovers over the years.

Len Kauffman is still living at the age of 79.

TOM W. DOUD   Marines

Tom Doud was a great guy and an extremely intense man. In 1982, I was hired to be the Defensive Coordinator at Milwaukie High School. I knew I needed to learn fast, and I remembered Tom Holley had told me Tom Doud was the best Defensive Coordinator he had ever known, the most knowledgeable, and also one of the most intensely competitive guys he had ever known.

I set up an appointment with Coach Doud and spent an entire Saturday afternoon at his home. Tom put on an impressive clinic. Watching his intensity while teaching me about his defensive philosophy is something I'll never forget.

In a very loud voice, Tom started off by telling me, "Everyone must be on the same page and every defensive starter and player must be talked to individually. I tell them, you are just one of eleven defensive players on the field. You must commit to the other ten players that you will do your job first and then pursue to the ball."

Tom stopped looked at me and said, "Do you understand?" I nodded my head yes. Tom then hit my upper arm with an open hand and the blow almost knocked me off my chair. He asked me again, "Do you understand?" This time I said in a loud voice, "Yes, I understand." He then yells, "No, you don't understand," and begins to explain it to me again, after which again asks me if I understand. This time I responded, "Yes, I understand now."

Tom hits me even harder and knocks me off the chair and screams, "You still don't get it. We need 100% buy in, damn it!"

Tom gets out of his chair and says he needs to calm down and walks around the living room for about a minute. He then takes a grease board and starts drawing up his '50 Slant Defense'. It involves a lot of slanting and blitzing. It's a very aggressive attacking mentality. "We do not let the offense dictate the tempo. We dictate the tempo! We want them on their heels, out of their comfort zone. We attack!" I sat there, loving it.

A few years later, after attending a football coaches clinic, Tom, and a few other football coaches, including me, went to a tavern for a beer. On the way, one of Tom's buddies says to me, "Did you know Tom is a Vietnam Veteran?"

As soon as we go to the bar, I asked Tom what branch of the service he was in. "Marines," he answered in an intense tone. Then I asked, "So, when were you in Vietnam?" Tom gets visibly upset and asks, "Who told you that?"

The other coach admits to telling me. Tom says, "I told you I don't talk about that, damn it. I was there during the Tet offensive, and we need to change the subject." I made the mistake of continuing to press Tom and asked, "What was it like?"

Tom slams his fist on the table, glasses tip over, beer is spilled everywhere, and he looks at me, his eyes on fire and yells at the top of his lungs, "I told you: I don't want to fucking talk about it! Bring it up again, and I'll kick your ass." I never brought it up again!

I never was able to ask Tom again about his military service because his life was cut short in December of 1987. Tom, his wife Margery, and their two daughters, Amanda and Melissa, were driving in the mountains outside of Pendleton on their way to cut a Christmas tree, when a large tree fell and landed directly on their pickup truck's cab, instantly killing all except for their daughter, Amanda.

Many of his coaching friends from the Portland area, myself included, traveled together for the four hour drive to Milton-Freewater, Oregon for the funeral. It was heartbreaking to see three coffins, two were the standard adult size and a much smaller coffin for a child.

There was a large crowd, well into the hundreds, at the church. It was impressive to see the number of former football players from Baker, Burns, David Douglas, Molalla, and Pendleton high schools, who came to the funeral all wearing their football jerseys in respect.

Tom's coffin was draped with an American flag. Many coaches and former players had no idea Tom was a Marine and Vietnam Veteran.

Tom Doud, his wife Margery, and their daughter Melissa all died together in December of 1987.

BOB HOFER   Army

I met Coach Hofer in the '80s when he was a varsity football coach and History Teacher at Oregon City High School. Bob was a very good varsity Offensive Coordinator, Defensive Coordinator, and a Head Coach at several different high schools all over the State of Oregon.

In the off season, most high school football coaches would attend coaching clinics and the largest and most popular one was in Seattle, Washington. It was an opportunity to see and hear legendary college and professional football coaches. It was also an opportunity for all of us young coaches to drink, and in many cases, drink too much.

I learned a lot about Bob from those coaching clinic/drinking sessions, but I would not learn until about ten years ago that he was a Vietnam veteran.

Over the years, I had invited Bob to our events, but he always graciously declined. I was finally able to sit down with him recently. After chatting about those coaching clinics and drinking fun, Bob says to me, "This month I celebrate one year of sobriety, I've been diagnosed with PTSD and have been getting therapy at the VA, plus AA meetings. It's helped a lot. When I came back, I drank. Drinking was my band aid."

After telling him I was happy to hear that, I started with my usual first question, "Where are you from?"

Bob laughing says, "All over. I was born in South Dakota, but our family moved around as my father was an inspector for the Corps of Engineers. I attended ten different schools in twelve years and graduated from high school in Riverside, California in 1970."

"How did you end up in the Army?"

"I was drafted, had a low number. But I figured it would be okay because after serving, I could go to college on the GI Bill. I tried to join the Air Force because I wanted to fly. Passed all the tests, but failed the vision test. Walking out of the recruiting station, the Army recruiter yells, 'You can fly helicopters in the Army, you don't need perfect eyesight.' So, I believed him and joined the Army.

"After testing my eyesight, they told me my vision was not good enough," laughing. "Because my tests scores were high they sent me to NCO school at Fort Benning, Georgia. Learned to jump and rose to the rank of 1st Sergeant during training."

"I could never do that, too afraid of heights."

"Me too, but I had no choice. Before jumping out of a plane, they would tap the side of your leg and you do a practice jump.

"The first time in the plane during my turn, I was shaking and wondering how I would ever jump out. I felt the tap on my leg and instinctively jumped out. It was awesome, couldn't wait to do it again.

"After that I was sent to Vietnam in the beginning of summer in '71, attached to the 1st Calvary, and we were sent over to replace the 101st Airborne who were pulling out. I had just turned nineteen. It was beyond strange because just two years earlier, I learned how to drive and now I'm calling air strikes, flying in helicopters all around the Cambodian border, the coast, and in the Delta. We were based close to Saigon, but we sent for support wherever needed.

"To be honest with you, I don't want to talk about more than that. The majority of my tour was spent in the jungle, and we experienced a lot of stuff." Bob paused and respecting his wishes, I asked, "any funny stories?"

Bob laughed and said, "There's always a lot of those. We were guarding the big guns in Ka Katum when we were hit with a mortar attack. The first strikes hit behind us and our guns, the second hit right in front of us. We knew we were being bracketed and my buddy, Lee and I ran, like everyone else.

"We ran straight to the mess hall as it looked safe. The shooting stops so we decide to just wait in line for chow. The cooks came out and thought we were crazy. Every mealtime everyone allowed us to cut to the front of the line because now everyone thought we were crazy."

"What about leaving Vietnam and going home."

"Well, we were pulling out of Nam and my tour was ending soon. The Army offered me five thousand to stay another year. That was a lot of money to me so I told them I would think about it overnight. I was assigned guard duty and that night we were mortared again and that made my decision easier.

"When I gave them my answer, they told me it would take three weeks till I would rotate out. Later that very day we received orders that we were going out in the jungle again and told we would be gone for three weeks. I was called out and rotated out, three days after making my decision.

"It was crazy, going from a firefight in the jungle to being greeted by protesters in Oakland, screaming "baby killers" over and over. What's funny is I went to an anti-Vietnam protest in '68 with a buddy to pick up chicks.

"When I got back, I heard from a friend who was playing football at Eastern Oregon University. He called me and talked me into coming up to try out. I made it and the football coach was able to waive the out-of-state tuition, so I could afford to come. Even with the GI Bill, I could not have afforded without some help.

"During my junior year, my counselor called me in and asked me what I wanted to do my life. I said that I had no idea. She responded by telling me that my tests scores said I could be a teacher. I said okay. I was majoring in sociology and psychology and started taking education courses and after graduating got a Master's in history.

"My first year of coaching was the defensive back coach at Eastern. I taught and coached at Hermiston, North Valley, and Oregon City high schools, then was the Head Football coach at Eagle Point for four years. My wife wanted to move to Canby to be closer to her parents, so I was hired at Canby High School to teach history and was the defensive coordinator for years until retiring."

After interviewing Bob, I called a couple of coaches who worked with him at Canby and learned that his road to getting help had been long and extremely painful especially for his wife and children.

I have had many, many discussions with spouses and adult children of veterans who have experienced combat. They, like myself, have similar childhood experiences of the difficulties veterans have and how their families suffer with them. My Korean War veteran father drank for fifteen years before he realized he need to stop. I, like Bob, finally sought the help I needed and was able to work through my problems of anger.

The thing my dad went through and what Bob went through and were called upon to do is not their fault. What we need for every veteran who has sacrificed so much for our country is to apologize for not giving any veteran, such as Bob Hofer, the help and support they deserve.

Bob Hofer is still living at the age of 70.

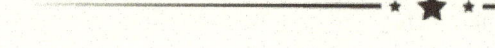

ED BURTON   Army

In the summer of '81, I was hired as a freshman football coach for one of Oregon City High School's (OCHS) middle schools by the varsity head football coach, Don McCarty. At the summer football coach's retreat in Seaside on the Oregon Coast, I met the varsity offensive line coach and head wrestling coach, Ed Burton.

For three days, we had meetings all day, with lunch and dinner breaks, and then another meeting in the evening. They had a great coaching staff; many would go on to become head coaches themselves. They all turned the football program into a league and state power. They were tough!

I would not learn that Ed was a Vietnam veteran until I brought veterans to OCHS in 2001 to speak to students. The administration decided that they wanted to have an annual Veterans Day Assembly and asked Ed to organize and MC the Assembly.

I invited him many times to come speak to high school students with us, but Ed always graciously declined. I learned from other coaches that Coach Burton never talks about his time in Vietnam.

The assembly honoring veterans was student driven with Coach Burton at the helm. It was an exceptional and very emotional assembly with over two thousand students in the main gym who were very respectful.

Most of the Oregon high schools who have held annual Honoring Veterans assemblies in the past have required the teachers to vote on whether or not to have the assembly every year. The votes were always close as the baby boomer teachers mostly voted yes, and the younger teachers voted no.

Coach Burton and many others fought for years to keep this tradition alive. But in the fall of 2019, the majority vote ended the assembly. As too many of the baby boomer teachers had retired and were replaced by new young teachers, the total voters voting no came to have the majority. There main reasoning was in their words, "Not relevant anymore."

This was not a question of Ed Burton's loyalty to OCHS for decades even though he has probably done more for OCHS than any teacher or coach in the over one hundred thirty-five-year history of the school.

The staff, teachers, and administrators of Oregon City High School and district need to know that ending the Veteran's Day assembly hurt Ed a lot because he saw it as a slap in the face not only to him, a Vietnam veteran, but to all the other men and women who served our country and deserved to be recognized.

He told me on the phone later that it really hurt when they said it was not relevant anymore. That it brought back memory of his experience that happened when he came back home from Vietnam.

But first, in order to understand Ed better, you need to know more about him.

"I was born in Longview, Washington, and my dad first worked on the Bonneville Dam, but after we ended up moving to Modesto, California looking for work. I attended a large high school that was later split in half when a second high school was built. The two schools were divided into poor vs. rich.

"My parents split up when I was in eighth grade. It was a rough upbringing, not a pleasant life. I was one of those kids who never wanted to go home after school. So, I went out for sports. I played football, basketball, baseball, and track.

"I never would have made it through if it weren't for my football coach. He took care of me, got me summer jobs, bought my books, and so much more. He really took care of me; I'll never forget him.

"My sophomore year at Modesto, I got hit so hard that it knocked the snot out of me. I became so angry that I promised myself, I'll never get hit that hard again. Immediately my attitude changed. I played angry and tough trying to hit everybody I could on every play. The game could not last long enough.

"But it did end, and I was left thinking about what I would do after high school. A friend mine was going to Chico State, so I decided I would go too. I borrowed some money, drove to Chico, and enrolled the second semester in January of '61.

"At first, they wanted me to play quarterback, but when the starting tight end got hurt, I jumped in and played and also played some wide receiver too.

"I guess I was good because before my final semester my college, coach got me a free agent tryout with the Buffalo Bills in the summer of '63. There were well over a hundred rookies in camp, and all were extremely competitive. After two weeks of training camp only seven of the first rookies remained.

"Every day, new guys would join camp as they had been cut by other teams and given tryouts for Buffalo. One veteran lineman reported twenty-five pounds overweight and was cut as he stood on the scale.

"Football was no fun anymore; we were just cattle for slaughter. I lasted four weeks, and the day before the first game, I was called into the head coach's office. He said, 'I have a plane ticket to Ottawa, Canada for a try out or a plane ticket back home.'

"I grabbed the ticket home. I returned back to school and started to finish, getting my teaching credentials. Another reason I retuned was my girlfriend was back home.

"My coaching career started while I was finishing up school. I coached the freshman football team, then joined the boxing team, ran track, and even played baseball. My first teaching job was at a high school with a lot of rich kids. You could always tell the rich kids' cars from the teachers' cars in the parking lot.

"I was the varsity offensive line coach and an assistant wrestling coach. I was still boxing, and after boxing practice, I would go to wrestling practice for another two hours. I loved it and the wrestling coach was a legend.

"Then on the first day of school, in September of '65, me and three other teachers were drafted. Because their draft boards were in different counties, they all received occupational deferments. I went to my draft board in Modesto, and the sergeant asks, "Are you a Dairy Farmer?" Because they are the only ones in this county who qualify for a deferment.

"Six weeks later, Cassius Clay (Muhammad Ali) sued the draft board and was granted a deferment for religious reasons. I thought about how I could do the same, but I didn't have money to fight it. So, four days later I reported to Fort Ord. I was ten years older than everyone else and was close to finishing my Master's degree.

"There was some kind of disease going around and we were all ordered to stay in our dorms but could sit outside on the grass. While there, I used to sell quarters for phone calls. My girlfriend Penny would drive down often, and we would sit on the grass and talk for hours."

Ed was an easy interview as he just kept telling me his story with very few pauses. "At boot camp I started shaving my head. Hell, I was going bald anyway. Halfway through our training, our DI was shipped out and they made me the DI because of my athletic coaching experience.

"After training was finished, I wanted to stay as a DI, but no, I was assigned infantry. After a short stint at a naval station, I was transferred to Fort Dix and put in charge of eight gyms, coached the wrestling team, and competed also. I won the Fort Dix championship at 191 lbs. (87 kg).

"Penny drove out and we got married. After that, I was ordered to Turkey to run a gym, but while waiting for top secret clearance, I'm ordered to Vietnam. I went to talk to my CO and asked, "What happened to Turkey? I want to go to Turkey." He yells at me, "Bullshit! You are going to Vietnam!

"Penny and I drove back out west to Travis Air Base, and I was flown to Vietnam. My MOS for the first six months was really sweet. We were stationed and worked at an Army R&R resort. Busloads of soldiers would come every day from the Mekong Delta.

"There were speed boats, water skiing, ping pong tables, games, and a PX (trading post) where you could buy a can beer for ten cents. We would take the troops on tours of Saigon. I watered skied every morning and every late afternoon."

Surprised, I said, "Wow, I never knew this was available to our troops."

"Yes, it was a sweet dig. I should back up. On my second day in Vietnam, I received two yellow booties in the mail. My wife was pregnant, and I wrote her back saying I would be home for the birth. Penny also wrote that she went to her doctor and told the doctor she was going crazy and needed me back home. The doctor laughed at her and said, 'You'll be just fine, go back to your teaching job.'

"During the month of November, I became friends with a captain, and I told him I need to get home for the birth. He agreed to send me on a temporary courier job, flying me home for three weeks, but I needed my CO's signature. My CO yelled at me, 'Listen private, if anyone is going home for Christmas, it's me, not you.' He was being a real dick.

"So, my captain friend set up a new job that would be taking a large canvas container, top secret, not to be opened. But the day before I was supposed to go, another soldier was caught in Hawaii because they opened a container in customs and in it was just his clothes and personal stuff.

"On January 25, I got a legitimate trip, but again needed my CO's signature. I forged his name. I told all the guys to cover for me. PFC Jerome Crockem, from Louisiana tells me, 'Coach, if anyone gets close to finding out, I'll kill him.' He was crazy and a good friend," Ed laughs.

"On January 28, I flew out of Da Nang, and the plan was that I was assigned to guard some kind of decoding machine for the entire trip. From the San Francisco Airport, I called Penny to pick me up.

"She had no idea about my plan of course, and I heard her drop the phone on the floor. We stayed up all night talking. On January 30, Penny's birthday, we went for a walk and her water broke.

"At the hospital in the waiting room, I get a call from a friend who tells me to turn on the TV. I do and see that the VC are attacking us all over South Vietnam. And I see fighting in the streets. Penny decides to walk out of her room right then, sees this on the TV, and yells out, 'Wow!' and gets very upset. I help her back to her room.

"She is panicking and for some reason her contractions stop. The doctor orders her home, and I have to make arrangements to fly back to Vietnam. The next day, the baby starts to come. We jump in the car- her dad drives- it's a forty-minute drive to the hospital.

"When we arrived at the Naval hospital, we had police following us with sirens on. We pull up to Emergency. Both her dad and I get out of the car, run to the back seat, and run headfirst into each other, just like and old Keystone Cop's comedy.

"The police are laughing at us and help get her into hospital. Less than thirty minutes later, she delivers a baby boy. I get to hold my baby. With Penny and baby still in the hospital, the next day I fly back to Vietnam.

"It gets crazier. Arriving in Da Nang, I'm ordered to get on any flight available to Saigon. I find a flight on a C-130 loaded with ammo, and the only seat is in the cockpit. Without any warning, the pilot turns the plane, drops suddenly, and lands on an airstrip in the middle of the jungle with one small hootch on one side.

"We are ordered to unload the ammo and load the plane with wounded civilians. The pilot refuses, and they agree to load as many as possible on top of ammo crates. I'm ordered to give up my seat and stay there. The pilot pulls me aside and tells me, 'I'll slowly taxi down the runway, when I wave run and jump into the plane.'"

"My luck continued: I get back to base and my best friend tells me nobody knew I was gone. It was destiny, just amazing.

"But then reality started to set in because I found out we were locked down for five days. I'm now assigned guard duty up on the roof of the compound overlooking a cemetery. I also learned that almost everything was destroyed.

"The R&R center was bombed and destroyed. The PX was burglarized and destroyed. All the boats were either sunk or stolen. The VC had even stolen one of our jeeps with a .50 caliber on it. There was even a picture of our compound that got on Life Magazine."

Ed pauses and his always upbeat positive voice changes, "My first combat experience, first firefight. Not fun. I was not prepared for this. I hadn't shot a gun in over six months. I got my pick of weapons, a Thompson sub-machine gun, a grenade launcher, and a pistol. It was not fun."

Before I could ask Ed another question, he starts right up again. "Well down the road, I got to meet Penny and little Derrick in Hawaii for six weeks of R&R. My time up was June 1, but they were able to get me home sooner. Flew into Oakland and was greeted with protesters but that was nothing compared to what would happen to me later.

"In July, I went back to San Ramon High School because it was the law to get my old job back. The principal was not happy to see me and told me, 'I have to give you a job back in the district, but it won't be your old job.' He assigned me elementary school PE, rotating between five grade schools and no coaching.

"While I was there, a handful of teachers came to the office. They came in and approached me, and one of them spits on my shoes," Ed says with a tone of hurt and anger.

"It hurt, but eventually I got a job at a different school, Biggs High School, where I was teaching five different subjects. And I was probably the worst teacher as I would take up most of the class time answering students' questions about Vietnam. But I coached three sports. I also finished my Master's degree at Chico State and scouted for their football team.

"That spring, I drove north into Oregon and dropped resumes off at every high school. I was hired by coach Thurmond Bell, teaching English, coaching varsity offensive, and also an assistant wrestling coach. My first wrestling season, we took second place at that year's state meet. Your school Ken, Milwaukie, were state champions.

"Next, I was hired as the head wrestling coach at Oregon City High School in '77 and was the offensive line coach for Don McCarty."

I couldn't help myself and said, "And the rest is history." That got a good laugh out of Ed. "My last question is: how did you deal with the memories of your experience in Vietnam?"

"I drank too much; I was drinking a case and a half of beer a day. That started over there and continued back home. Penny turned me around. Without her, I don't know where I'd be. When a soldier goes to war, the whole family goes to war."

"I've always said, the wives deserve a medal."

"Then Penny deserves a lot of them," Ed stated with love in his voice.

I know Ed still hurts from when the Veterans events stopped at his high school. He, like I, knows that veterans are not irrelevant and that all veterans should be commended for serving their country with valor. They should be praised and celebrated.

Ed Burton is still living at the age of 81.

DAN ROM   Marines

Dan was a fellow PE Major at Portland State, and we were in many of the same classes. I would run into him over the years at football coach's clinics as he was also a high school teacher and head football coach. It was only a few years ago that I learned he was a veteran.

Dan grew up in Portland with his twin brother and graduated from North Catholic High School (De La Salle North Catholic High School today) in 1964 where he played football. His father passed away when they were just ten years old.

"When were you drafted?"

"I was working at Armour Meat Company when I received my draft notice in '65. I didn't want to be in the Army, so I enlisted in the Marines."

"Why the Marines?"

"I read a Leatherneck magazine in high school and was intrigued by their history and traditions. I was also impressed by the Marines raising our Flag on Iwo Jima and the battle at the Chosin Reservoir. They never left anybody behind. Also, my stepbrother, who was much older than I, served in the Marine Corps during WWII and Korea. He had retired from the Corps while I was in high school.

"I went to boot camp in San Diego on October 5, 1965, then ITR. During ITR we were given leave to be home at Christmas then back to complete the rest of ITR. From ITR, I was assigned my MOS and was trained on the job as a supply man.

"We then received orders to Camp Pendleton's Staging Battalion where we were met by other Marines from around the US. By this time, we all knew we were headed to Vietnam. On March 12, 1966, we embarked on the USNS Gordon from San Diego. Seven hundred and fifty Marines boarded for our journey."

"Did you get seasick?"

"No, I was very lucky. Many others did. I was told to grab a top rack in our birthing area. The racks lowered down on chains and were stacked five high like bunk beds but much narrower. Many Marines got sick especially early on and were throwing up over the side of their beds. Me being on the top bunk was fortunate.

"From San Diego we traveled to Hawaii, where the 3rd Brigade of the 25th Infantry Division joined us. Then we stopped in Okinawa and dropped off one of our sea bags and then headed for Vietnam.

"The Army Brigade was dropped off first, and we went on to Da Nang. At Da Nang, we were loaded on Mike Boats for our trip. When we got there, the boats stopped short of the landing area.

"While we were wading through the surf to the beach carrying our sea bags on our shoulders, other Marines who were wading out to the Mike Boats would shake our hands and thank us for replacing them so they could go home. Once on the beach, we were given our orders, and I was assigned to H&S Company 2nd Battalion 3rd Marines.

"I was assigned to Battalion Supply. I learned to drive a mule (M274 Utility Platform Truck) in order to move supplies, mostly C-rations and ammunition around the area and to the landing zone where we would put it on helicopters. I also learned how to direct a helicopter into a landing zone.

"Almost daily, we would convoy to Da Nang to get supplies that had been ordered and also provide security at night. The first operation I went on was Operation Allegheny where a recon unit was ambushed. A company of Marines were lifted in, and I was attached to Command Group to help provide security and help with resupply and medevac our casualties.

"It's just crazy how fast a relative calm can change when a firefight erupts. Your adrenaline will go from zero to a hundred in a second. I saw my first combat during that operation and got a Chicom (fragmentation hand grenade) that didn't explode. We found large amounts of ammunition and weapons and found a mockup model of a 105 mm Howitzer made of wood and bamboo. I participated in several other operations around the Dai Loc area.

"In November, the battalion moved to Dong Ha which is on the DMZ. I participated in many operations that staged out of Camp Carroll. I went to Da Nang around Christmas and was able to see the Bob Hope Show.

"I also contacted Malaria before our battalion was going to Okinawa. I was sent to recoup at a hospital and when I returned, they were afloat, and I was assigned to 'Charlie Med' the 3rd Medical Brigade.

"My job there was to collect and tag weapons and gear from the casualties. Once while taking a shower we had some rockets hit, and we grabbed our fighting gear and took off toward the nearest bunker naked.

"On my last operation our commander was killed just outside of the camp while going to the aid of a recon unit that had been ambushed. On a side note, in 2019 that commander Colonel Ohanesian's wife died, and her daughter invited members of our battalion to her funeral at Arlington.

"In July, I was transferred to 2nd Battalion 4th Marines and was there till I rotated back to the states in October."

"Did you get out of the Marines then?"

"No, I made Sergeant in April of '68 while I was stationed at Camp Pendleton. I was transferred to Guam where I was assigned to the Armed Services Police. My job was a patrolman, and we had no responsibility on the different military bases.

"Guam was not a big island, but it had a large military presence. Military on Guam were mostly Navy and Airforce with a small Army and Marine unit. Our responsibility was to aid the Guam police and to provide traffic control and security when Polaris missiles were moved from the ammo dump to the submarine base.

"Our other responsibility was to deal with servicemen when they were on liberty. We broke up lots of fights and disagreements among the militaries.

"I received orders back to Vietnam in May of '68. I was assigned to Force Logistical at Red Beach and then transferred to 3rd Tank Battalion in Quang Tri. At Quang Tri, I was assigned S-3 (operations officer). I led a rifle squad that patrolled in our area of operations."

"How did you deal with the memories?"

"I started drinking heavily and got in a lot of fights. I was angry at the world. This went on for four years. After playing in a seven-man football championship, I got so drunk, I was arrested, and spent the night in the drunk tank. I vowed to myself, never again. I continue to have bad dreams at night.

"I got married on June 21, 1974. I had always wanted to coach, so I enrolled at Portland State in September of '74 and majored in Health and PE. When I graduated in '77, I couldn't find a PE job, so I substituted and enrolled at University of Portland to pick up my Master's and a social studies endorsement.

"I graduated in the summer of '78 and was offered a job at Roosevelt High School where I became a teacher and assistant football coach. I was the head football coach for approximately ten years. I taught social studies at Roosevelt till I retired.

"I have also coached football at Central Catholic, Lakeridge, and finished my coaching career at Clackamas High School. I was also a realtor until 2018."

When he finished, I said to him, "I don't remember you as an angry man in '74 at PSU."

"I had to learn to keep my memories in check. It was like locking them in a box where occasionally they would creep out. Early on I didn't know about PTSD. I have been diagnosed and am now getting help.

"After my crazy years, I wanted to just settle down. It has not been easy. I hired an assistant coach and found out he was a Vietnam vet. He was in the Army who had been there, and we were able to share our experiences.

"Over the years when he would teach about Vietnam, he would invite me in, and we would team teach for several days. The students learned a lot and were very appreciative. At our last reunion, I purchased several T-shirts for our wives that said, 'Marine Wives are Going to Heaven.' At our reunions everyone's wives met, and my wife was surprised that all the husbands shared similar experiences.

"In August of '67, my best friend Ron, who I went through boot camp, ITR, OJT, Staging Battalion, and who was also shipped out on the Gordon with me, got seriously wounded when he was shot in the leg and in his chest. He carried the round in his chest the rest of his life. His leg was also amputated several times and eventually was removed completely.

"This was difficult for me as his parents were like my mom and dad. They lived in Ontario, California. I was always invited to their home at any time. I next saw Ron when I was in Camp Pendleton. He was recovering and rehabbing at Oak Knoll Naval Hospital in Oakland, California.

"I would drive up at least once a month to visit, and he and several other amputees would go out for one or two 'adult beverages,' or three, and shoot pool.

"A time or two someone would give them some crap and a fight would begin. Ron told me to stay out of it unless one of them was knocked down. I only had to help once."

Dan paused and got emotional, "You know, every one of those amputee veterans wanted to go back to be with their buddies in Vietnam."

"When Ron and his first wife had their first child, he called me and asked if I would come down for his son's baptism and also asked me to be the child's Godfather. He also said they were going to name their baby after Ron's father and me.

"I was honored and humbled. I accepted and took a bottle of Chivas Regal twelve-year-old scotch and after the service I gave the bottle to Ron and told him that on his son James' twenty first birthday, we would open the bottle.

"Twenty-one years later, my wife Malinda and I, and our children, drove up to Ron's house where we had a wonderful steak dinner and opened the bottle, and toasted James' twenty first till the wee hours of the morning. What a great time. Unfortunately, Rod died of a massive heart attack in February of 2001."

After a respectful silence Dan looked up and me, and I asked, "Do you have any funny stories you can tell me?"

"Oh yes. Do you remember the anti-war protests that got ugly at Portland State? Well, that was when I was drinking, and I was so angry that I gathered a bunch of rocks, put them in a pack, jumped on my motorcycle and rode down to there and threw them at the protesters. A policeman grabbed me and asked what I was doing. I told him I was throwing rocks at hippies; he then told me to hit one for him. So, I did."

Dan Rom is still living Canby. He and his wife Sharon have been married for forty-eight years.

MIKE ZAGYVA   Marines

Mike retired after a forty-year career in education as a middle school principal and was loved and well respected by everyone: students, staff, teachers, parents, and the community of Canby.

"I was born in Aurora, Illinois in September of '49. My Grandparents immigrated from Hungry to Ellis Island in 1913. My father was a Navy Gunner's mate and earned a Purple Heart at Peleliu, South Pacific, during WWII. My mother worked as a migrant language tutor at a local school, and during the war she made hand grenades in a war factory.

"After the war, my father attended college on the GI Bill and majored in engineering. I'm going to now act like a proud son. My father was an engineer for the Apollo space program. He was the lead engineer in designing the L.E.S. (Launch Escape System)."

"How did you enter the military?"

"A good friend on the draft board told me in May that my number was No. 3, and I was going to receive a draft notice and be ordered to report in June. Me and four other buddies decided to just join because we didn't want to ruin our summer. I told them, 'Let's join the Air Force.' One of the guys yelled, 'No, we have to join the Marines.' So, we all joined the Marines."

"Tell me about boot camp."

"In September, we flew down to San Diego and were greeted at the airport by several DIs who proceeded to yell at us the entire time walking through the airport. I remember a bunch of Navy guys just laughing at us. It took me thirty seconds to figure out "Oh shit, what did you get yourself into, Zagyva?" Mike laughed.

"But I wouldn't trade my Marine Corps experience for anything. After boot camp, I'm sent to DLI, Defensive Language Institute, and I was never told why. I was just standing in line and told 'you are going to learn Vietnamese and be an interpreter.' After that, I was sent to Vietnam in '69."

"Anything you feel comfortable sharing about your time in Vietnam."

"Ken, what I'm about to tell you, I've only shared with my son and only with him because he served in the Army in Iraq and Afghanistan. I felt he would understand. I'm very proud of him. John is a Clackamas County Deputy Sheriff. I wouldn't be telling you this if it wasn't for the fact that last week, I found out I have cancer. It's time to get this off my chest.

"It was December 20, 1969, and I was on point while were doing patrols for a number of months. We were setting up ambushes around a village that the VC had recently attacked. A firefight breaks out. It's red tracers, friendly fire. It was the RVN and both sides send up green flares for friendly fire.

"A little while after the firefight, we hear one gunshot go off in the village. Because it was night and very dark, we wait until the morning to go into the village. When we do go into the village, we find out the gunshot was the VC executing the village chief.

"This little Vietnamese boy approaches me and starts telling me everything that happened. He was speaking very slowly so I could understand him. The boy told me a lot of helpful information and gave me a note that the VC had left on a tree in the village.

"I was so young and dumb because I interviewed this boy in front of everyone including the Vietnamese villagers. I told my commander everything."

Mike pauses and looks away. "We left and came back to check on the village two days later. Nobody would talk to us, and everyone ignored me. We looked everywhere for the little boy but could not find him. Nobody would even look at me let alone speak to me. To this day I don't know what happened to that little boy.

"I never should have interviewed that little boy. This has haunted me my entire life and to this day, I cannot get out of my mind seeing the village chief's body.

"That event changed me forever. Words do matter. When someone tells me, 'This is over the top,' or 'I have something to share with you but don't tell anyone else.' I will never share. I will never break that confidence. I want them to know, they can trust me. My entire career in education and military I had to know exactly what the rules were before I made any decisions."

Mike posted this on Facebook on Memorial Day in 2022. He gave me permission to use it:

Lance Corporal Douglas W. Young, USMC
KIA by "Friendly Fire" from ARVN Ambush
Dec. 20, 1969
West Hartford, CT

Our Platoon (2nd) was watching all the entrances and exits of a village north of Da Nang. A VC hit squad assassinated the village leader. We heard the AK 47 fire. At the same time Young's Platoon (3rd) was covering our backs walked into an ARVN (South Vietnamese Army) ambush. We saw the red-on-red tracers, green flares which indicated "friendly forces" and yelling cease fire on the radio net. Then we heard the Corpsman calling in the medevac to take care of the wounded. Later we found out he was hurt as well but "his" Marines came first. Young, who was walking point, was killed instantly. The ARVN's never worked in our Area of Operations (AOR) because of such close proximity to US Marine ground forces. It was a tragedy that should have been avoided. RIP Doug, you are not just a name on the wall.

"There were a lot of firefights and ambushes and prefer to not talk about them. I just wanted his story told."

"You could tell me a funny story if you would like."

"Okay...," Mike laughed. "You've heard about men in combat who never shoot their weapons in the heat of battle? I remember us giving guys a bad time because they would forget to pull the pin out of a hand grenade and just throw it.

"I still laugh about this one. I was at camp Brooks north of Da Nang and the night before shipping out, I sprayed painted 'Zag is gone' on every hooch. I learned while boarding a second plane that MPs were one flight behind me with orders to arrest me and bring me back for destroying government property." Mike laughed again.

"How were you treated when you came back home?"

Mike looked away and just stared for about ten seconds. "We were greeted by the protestors yelling all the same stuff at us. I made a mistake of driving to the State Capital in Salem to check out an anti-Vietnam War protest, and I saw a guy waving a VC flag. That was the closest I ever came to killing someone. I was so angry, I told myself I can never see something like that again.

"Another time was in my first semester at Oregon College of Education, now Western Oregon University, a professor asked me in front of the class what I did last year. I said I was in Vietnam. He said something negative to me. After that word got around and many students and professors learned I was a Vietnam veteran. Then the comments and harassment started. I didn't do anything about it. I just kept my mouth shut, went to my classes.

"I was apologized to once in my life. I was standing in uniform several years ago at the dedication of the Canby's Vietnam Helicopter Memorial when a man approached me and said, 'I was a protestor back then, and I want to apologize. I'm sorry.' He just walked away, and I was kind of stunned.

"After graduating, I got my first teaching job starting out at only $7,200. I told my wife we just couldn't make it on that, so I joined the Oregon National Guard to make a little extra money. I applied and was accepted into Intel as a Warrant Officer. I eventually became the Command Chief Warrant Officer and retired after a total of forty-three years in the military."

"What would you tell young people today who might be considering joining the military?"

"Look outside the box. There's a great big world out there that's a lot bigger than that small bubble you are sitting in. The military has many opportunities, adventures, and seeing other parts of the world. It will also pay for college, and you will make lifelong friends. Just this morning I met for coffee with two friends I served with. I never planned this career, but I'm very grateful."

Mike emailed me a speech he gave at the Canby Kiwanis Club and gave me permission to include it:

> Good afternoon, my name is Mike Zagyva, I served in Vietnam in Comm and as a Vietnamese Linguist with the 3rd Marine Amphibious Force. Earning the USMC Combat Action Ribbon. Today, I am going to talk about two specific changes on how our society has evolved in honoring and supporting our veterans and those wearing the uniform.
>
> After serving in Vietnam, I came home went to school on the GI Bill. After getting my first teaching paycheck, I figured this is not going to work. We needed to eat four weeks a month not three. So, joined the Oregon Army National Guard.
>
> Our plan was for only a year or so but ended up retiring as a Chief Warrant Officer 5 holding the positions as the Oregon Command Chief Warrant Officer, Deputy J2, and Intelligence Branch Chief. I also retired in '04 with the Canby School District where I was a teacher, and an Elementary and Middle School principal. In '06 Oregon's 41st BDE was mobilized for Afghanistan. I remember telling Marcia that I wore the uniform for almost 30 years and needed to step up to the plate.
>
> We were in the kitchen, and she said, 'I understand why you are doing this, and I don't like it, but will not be one of those wives to lay guilt trips.' I therefore volunteered and was slated to be an Intelligence Officer with the task of training the Afghan National Army in Herat, near the Iranian border. I was injured in a Combat Training exercise during the train up in Shelby, MS a week prior to deployment and sent home.

I was then asked to work full time for the Oregon Guard. I spent over 40 years wearing a uniform either full or part time with the last 8 years full time. Then brought back for another three years as a DoD civilian working for the Defense Intelligence Agency's Joint Reserve Intelligence Program. Most of my experience was with the Indo/Pacific Command, especially with Joint Forces-Korea.

We all have heard the stories of how the Vietnam Vets were treated upon returning home. I am going to share just a few of those. I rotated out of Vietnam in late September 1970. I grew up in West Salem. Three days after I was home, a friend and I were driving past the State Capitol and the first thing I saw was a demonstration with people waving Viet Cong flags. I think I understand the issues now with the Confederate flag. I won't share what happened when I confronted the individuals, but I have never been to any demonstration since. I enrolled at the OCE, now WOU, in January 71. In my first Phycology class the instructor was asking all the students what courses they took that Fall. When it came to me, I made the mistake of saying I was in Vietnam during fall term. Based on the responses and attitude of those around me and the professor, it was the last time I shared I was a Vet.

When I started teaching in 1974, a secretary at the school made it clear where she stood on Vietnam. There were three other young male teachers who were Vets there, an Infantry Squad leader, a door gunner, and Navy Seabee, and we all looked at each other and never talked about the military. When I joined the Guards in 1974 my first unit was an Aviation Intel. We were standing outside near the highway in the chow line and when people would drive by, they would honk the horn, lean out the window and flip us off. After a while, the chow line was moved into the hanger. I was a smoker at the time and learned not to go into the 7/11 store in Canby in uniform. I did it once on my way to guards and was hassled and made fun of. I was a brand-new teacher and figured it would not look good for a third-grade teacher being involved with an altercation. So once again I kept quiet and walked around the individuals without saying anything. At that time even the VFW and American Legion did not want anything to do with us. Especially after the fall of Saigon. These are just a few of the incidents.

After WWI, WWII, Korea, and Vietnam, our society used the terms Soldier's neurosis, shell shocked, and battle fatigue in describing those service men/women who had experience trauma and may have had a hard time readjusting to civilian life. The hard truth was you were expected to deal with all of it on your own. "Suck it up and move on."

During this time when you were discharged from the military it was a handshake and pat on the back. One day you were in the jungles of Vietnam and a couple days later walking around as a civilian. After a great deal of hard work and dedication by some medical professionals the term PTSD was introduced, and the VA recognized the condition in 1980. Now when discharged from the military there is an outstanding support system as you transition back to society.

They say time heals all wounds. After the decisive victory of Desert Storm, we began to see a positive change. I remember reading Gen Colin Powell's book on leadership. In one of the chapters, he shares that after Vietnam a number of up-and-coming officers got together to address certain issues that plagued the military. He mentioned names like Franks and Schwarzkopf. Attitudes began to change. In the civilian world, those Vietnam Veterans were now community and business leaders. Because of their leadership roles, attitudes also began to evolve, and the general public started to appreciate the sacrifices. Veteran Memorials began to take shape.

I cannot take any credit for Canby Vietnam Era Memorial. That goes to the original committee members started by Mike and Irene Breshears. They began the project in 2001 and finally dedicated in 2011. I was in uniform full time then and was the liaison officer with the Oregon Guard and committee. The Guard provided the keynote speaker, the honor guard, band, and a Blackhawk display. The Blackhawk was flown by Canby Graduate, Scott Anderson. Becoming involved with the dedication ceremony started a healing process.

In talking about Veterans and their dedication, I would be remiss if I did not acknowledge the families of those who serve. I must admit I had no idea. I remember my father a WWII vet, Purple Heart recipient, hugging me when I left for Vietnam, in tears, saying he spent three years in the South Pacific so his children would not have to go to war. I did not understand until our youngest son enlisted in the Army as a Cavalry Scout. He landed in northern Iraq during the initial invasion. At that time, they would be able to call home hopefully at least once a week. Most of the calls were to his lovely wife and newborn son, but at least once a month he would call us.

The calls were in the middle of the night. Marcia would jump out of bed and treasure our 3 min phone call. Then she would cry herself to sleep after. Seeing what a positive experience I had with the Oregon Guard; John enlisted in the Guard after his active duty. Then in 2014, his unit was mobilized for Afghanistan. He left his job as a Clackamas Deputy Sheriff, a wife, and FOUR young boys. It has been said it is harder for those at home when a loved one is deployed. That is true. Today he is the Command Sgt Major in charge of the Guard troops helping the hospitals in Oregon.

Our family is proud of its military service, from ancestors wearing the Union uniform at Gettysburg, to great grandfather with Blackjack Pershing chasing Pancho Villa on the US/Mexican border in the early 1900's, WW1 in the trenches, WW2 both grandfathers in the South Pacific. Myself in Vietnam and John in Iraq and Afghanistan. And now passing the first baton of many to grandson, Cody, John's son last Thursday who will be following in his father's and grandfather's footsteps and enlisting in the Army and leaving for boot camp next fall.

Finally, I hope I can say this without much emotion, and I am positive all Vietnam Vets would feel the same. I would gladly go through my homecoming experience again knowing our sons, our daughters, and grandchildren will never be in those types of situations.

I want to thank you for this opportunity to share. God Bless you and your family, and may God protect our troops. Thank you.

I talked some more with Mike in June of '22 and learned he did not have cancer after all. However, he had gone through a couple of operations on his right foot because he had developed a bone infection and twice they have removed part of his foot."

He said to me, "It was from a parasite only found in the jungles of Vietnam that had been dormant for fifty years. That's the VA's theory anyway.

"I know we were exposed to Agent Orange a lot. I remember walking on brown leaves surround by dead trees. The dust would kick up and cause you to cough." Mike just shook his head.

Mike is still living at the age of 73.

SAM WHITEHEAD   Marines

I've known Sam since the early '80s when I started teaching and coaching at MHS and whenever old football coaches get together after not seeing each other for many years. We immediately talk football and all the great memories.

Sam was the offensive and defensive line coach for Gresham High School's varsity football team. Back in the '80s, Gresham's football team was an impressive, tough, hard hitting state power, and they had a great group of coaches.

We played them in the state playoffs in the fall of '85. Milwaukie was 10-0, ranked second in the state, and Gresham also 10-0, and ranked first in the state. We faced off in the second round of the playoffs. Gresham beat us 6-0 in a defensive struggle. For Gresham, it was a great win that after all these years still feels great, but for Milwaukie it still hurts. But that's sports.

Sam immediately starts off the conversation about that game. "I never forget how hard hitting that game was. Standing on the sideline, I felt if I was watching a college football game." Sam gets very excited talking about this. "Sparks were flying. And the one-on-one battle between Ben Lytle and Chris Hicks was epic! I've never seen two great high school football players go at it like that."

Both Ben and Chris were named to the All-State football team. Ben was first team offensive guard and first team inside linebacker, while Chris was also first team linebacker, but second team offensive guard. They faced each the entire game while playing both offense and defense.

When he finished speaking, I said to him, "Did you know that Ben Lytle is my stepson from my first marriage?"

"No, I never knew that. Wow."

"He now goes by Benjamin Blair. And he is the co-author and editor of Volumes I and II and this Volume III, too."

After that we agreed to have another interview sometime in the future. For two years off and on, I would call and leave messages wanting to interview him.

A couple of times he told me, "We will make it happen, and I'll talk about Namville." But it took his wife, Jane, and his best friend, former teacher and the head football coach at Gresham, Gary Stautz, to pressure Sam into talking to me.

"Let's get started. Tell me about your mom and dad. I understand he was a veteran."

"My dad, Gus Whitehead Jr., served in the Navy as a radar man on a sub-chaser in the South Pacific during WWII. His ship was sunk in the Solomons, and many were lost. One uncle was killed during the war. He was in the Navy as a front turret gunner on the USS Idaho. I also had several other uncles in the Marines who fought in the South Pacific.

"My mother, Maxine, was a stay-at-home mother as that was very common back in the day. She did not like me playing football and only agreed to letting me play if I joined the band and choir. She wanted fine arts in me," laughing again. "I played the French Horn and was even in a brass quartet.

"I played football and wrestled at David Douglas High School for two legendary coaches, Marv Hiebert and Delance Duncan. My junior year I played a lot but was the backup tight end all season.

"During warm-ups before the state championship game, the starting tight end gets hurt, so I ended up starting my first varsity football game in the state championship which we won by the way. My senior year, I took fifth in the state in wrestling in my weight class.

"Grandma always asked me, 'Are you going to serve?' I graduated in '67 and always wanted to be a PE teacher as I was inspired my ninth grade PE teacher who was a Marine. He taught me discipline. I went to Portland State to play football and got married, but transferred to Mt. Hood Community College to wrestle, but also mostly to save money.

"It was a requirement to take at least fifteen hours to have an education deferment, but because I did not, I received a letter stating, 'Greetings, you have been drafted.' I was able to finish my sophomore year though.

"I joined the Marines because my uncle Bill Call really inspired me. Bill served in the Marines during WWII on Iwo Jima and again during the Korean War at Inchon and the Chosin Reservoir, and you wrote about him in Volume II.

"I'll never forget my first night of boot camp at MCRD (Marine Corps Recruit Depot) in San Diego. Man, it was a whole new world. I was in culture shock. After boot camp, we were shipped overseas for jungle training and then I get a Dear John letter from my wife.

"I arrive in Vietnam in December of '69 right on the coast just north of Da Nang. Our base was surrounded by Concertina razor wire and sand. Once a month, helicopters would spray powered tear gas on the sand that surrounded our base. If anyone walked on the sand, it would kick up the dust, and you couldn't breathe, and it would suffocate you.

"If the wind ever kicked up, we would get it in our eyes even while wearing gasmasks. We were bad to the newbies though, had them walk through it," Sam laughs.

"Our bunker was up front, and at night, we would have a three-man rotation on alert. During the day, we would go on patrols outside of the wire." Sam showed me some color pictures he had taken, and in one was him and his platoon walking through a rice paddy.

"After four months, I was promoted to Lance Corporal, and soon after to Corporal. A week after that, Platoon Sergeant.

"So, there were three small villages outside our wire. We felt so bad for the kids who were always hungry. We'd throw sea rations all the time to them over the wire or toss them to kids while driving down the highway to Da Nang.

"Our job was find out where the NVA and the VC were, and what kind of numbers. We'd go through villages and look for supplies that were used to support NVA and VC. We could keep the NVA away with our firepower. The VC were ruthless; they would kill civilians.

"Something I feel the best about was the 1st Marine Division's first year of trying to build relationships with the villagers. They would build bridges over canals or put up buildings for villagers. We would give clothes donated from churches stateside to the Montagnard children, it was an orphanage in Da Nang. We received a Presidential citation for that. I'm proud of what we did.

"Once, we went into a place where lepers live. This cute little boy, a leper, just clings to me, and I was scared. We learned that they had dry leprosy, and it is not contagious. Wet leprosy is contagious. But it was a rewarding and impressive experience.

"Going home, I was flown to Okinawa, for one week and issued new clothes, all smaller sizes, because I lost a lot of weight. Then the Freedom Bird to a military base in Southern California. I had to take a taxi to Los Angeles International Airport, and I wore civilian's clothes, but with a Vietnam service ribbon on my chest.

"I get out of the taxi, and I froze. I'm shocked; too many people. I'm in culture shock. A guy walks up and asks if I'm okay, and I answer no. He walks me to my gate and luckily, we avoided any protesters.

"I land at Portland Airport, and it was a Sunday. We drive down 82nd Ave. because it has lots of car lots. I had sent money home for savings and had $4000 in savings. I buy a '65 Corvette for $4000. Today, worth $125,000.

"The next day on Monday, I went to an insurance agent to get car insurance. The agent gives me a look showing he is turned off that I'm a Vietnam veteran. He said it was a six-month waiting list to get approved. I lost it and slammed the table, shoved it into his chest and walked out.

"I enrolled at Warner Pacific and wrestled and was in the top twelve national both years. We were National Champions my senior year. I'm hired at Gresham High School in '74 to teach PE and coach freshman football and wrestling. And the principal who hired me was a Marine too."

Sam then showed me lots of Vietnam pictures he had taken and an impressive big binder with pictures and letters from Gresham Alumni. It was put together by Gary Stautz and given to Sam as a gift when he retired. Sam let me borrow it, and what I always assumed about him was true: he was a well loved and respected teacher and coach.

Sam and his wife Jane have been married forty-nine years and their anniversary was the day of our interview. They have three children Jill, Bonnie, and Katherine.

Sam is still living at the age of 72.

DAVE WOOD — Army Medic

Dave was an athletic trainer at Portland State from '73 to '77, also majoring in PE and Health with a minor in Sports Medicine when I first met him.

Dave used to tape my ankles and wrists before football practice and games. He was a friendly guy and had a great sense of humor with many one liners and an infectious laugh. It wasn't until about ten years ago that I learned Dave was a Vietnam veteran and a medic.

I interviewed Dave at his home in February of '22. It was the first time I had seen him since the early 2000s when Dave was my son Anthony's PE Teacher at Ackerman Middle School. While I really enjoyed seeing him again, this was an emotional interview for him.

"I actually had anxiety going on since yesterday as I was wondering what kind of questions you would ask me." I told him what I have told so many veterans, "I'm sorry. I have learned that what I do is like picking a scab off and opening old wounds. I know it may hurt, but everyone needs to be remembered. And most importantly, I'm very grateful to you all."

"I was born in March of 1950 and attended and graduated in '68 from Marshfield High School in Coos Bay on the Oregon coast. I played football, basketball, and baseball, except my junior year. I went out for track that year because my close friend and neighbor sold me on the idea. Do you have an idea who I'm talking about, Ken?"

"Oh my gosh, Marshfield in '68. Is it......." Dave in a raised and excited voice yells out, "Steve Prefontaine! In fact, less than a month before he was killed in the car accident, we went to a party together to catch up."

Steve Prefontaine, University of Oregon, was one of the world's great distance runners and a '72 Olympian.

"My dad, Ron, was a WWII Marine, 6th Marines. After the Japanese bombed Peral Harbor, he and a couple of friends walked from Silverton to the Top of the Hill restaurant in Aurora, Oregon, ate breakfast, then hitchhiked to Portland and joined the Marines. They told the recruiter, 'We want to kill Japs.'

"He was badly wounded on Guadalcanal and lived with shrapnel in his body and scars from phosphorous burns." Dave pauses and in a sad tone said, "But, he beat me down badly. He beat me down badly. He beat me down badly!" Dave's voice volume raised each time he said it. The last time he sounded very angry, and then there was a silence before he spoke again saying, "He was a powder monkey and never talked about it. He only spoke a little to me when I came back from Vietnam.

"I attended Southern Oregon University on a partial football scholarship and played wide receiver for coach Al Akins. He was using the run and shoot offense when Mouse Davis was still running it at the high school level. But I had bad grades and during my sophomore year in '69, I got drafted.

"My test scores were high, and I qualified for OCS (Officers Candidate School). But I felt if I was going to be in military, I might as well get something out of it. So, I became a medic and was sent to 91C Clinical Medical training. It was tough. We had to read tons of textbooks and mostly nurses training. It was intense training, learning how to sew up wounds, and amputation training at Valley Forge General Hospital."

"Were you exposed to many Vietnam veterans' amputees?"

Dave becomes very emotional, and eyes get watery. "Many amputees and many quad amputees." Dave gets choked up again and starts shaking his head, "Just a head and a trunk, most wanted to commit suicide."

Dave goes quiet, and then after a pause starts again. "It was supposed to be yearlong training but was cut short, as Medics were badly needed in Vietnam. They sent the bottom half of the students of my class all to Vietnam, and I was in the bottom half. We were sent to Fort Lewis and before being sent, I gave shots to soldiers at Fort Lewis, using the shot gun.

"We flew into Cameron Bay in '70, and I was first sent to Quang Tri, a few miles from North Vietnam for a short time, but then transferred to the 91st M.A.S.H. Evacuation Hospital in Chu Lai about twenty miles from Da Nang for the rest of my tour.

"A lot of the time, I sewed up lots of wounds and it sure helped being educated." Then Dave gets really emotional and sad. "Piles and piles of body parts, body bags, the screaming. The wounded pissing and shitting pants, blood everywhere." He stops talking and looks away for a moment. I don't know what to say, and then Dave starts talking again. "We would work thirty to forty hours straight whenever there were mass causalities. No breaks.

"Many times, I went with the copters to help pick up the wounded. I had to prioritize the wounded over who got help first. It was, 'Get this guy to preop right now.' We were all a team--doctors and nurses working together. I can still see all the litter stands with IVs hanging down. It was so depressing. I just pushed myself; I had to go on.

"They handpicked medics to see if you could handle working in the ER (Emergency Room). Most couldn't, but I could. I was never afraid of hard work. Hell, I pulled green chain in a sawmill as a teenager.

"One of the scariest times for me was when me and a doctor removed a M79 round lodged in the neck of an Army captain while still on the chopper. He didn't make it. The demolition guys came up behind us with big shields thinking it was going to go off. I was scared to death."

Dave paused again and then changed the subject. "Chu Lai has a beautiful white sand beach. I did a lot of great snorkeling on my down time. At the same time, it was a freeway of helicopters. It was also called Rocket City. Sometimes at night, we would sit on the beach a watch artillery strikes up in the mountains and watch all the tracers in the sky."

I then asked, "How were you treated coming back home?"

In a disgusted tone of voice, "Yeah, we were screamed at, cussed out, all that crap. So, I learned to keep civilian clothes in my duffle bag, and I would change into civilian clothes.

"I know I have PTSD really bad, but I failed every PTSD test, because I just couldn't finish it. They wanted me to write down incidents that bothered me. It was a lot of paperwork filling out forms. I never finished and they're still in our closet.

"But it all got worse during Covid, watching the ER's on TV in New York brought back a flood of memories." Dave gets very emotional again and started choking up again. "I have the fight or flight syndrome. The nightmares are getting worse, and I've scared my wife many times. One night I woke up pissing in the closet.

"I have had the same dream for years: I'm at the funeral of a dead soldier back in the states, and he's lying on a stretcher covered with bloody rags." Dave gets emotional again.

Dave changes the subject to say, "I sewed up an eyebrow cut on a tough PSU wrestler, but both of us never told anyone," Dave laughs.

"Oh, and I have a hell of a high school football game story for you. I was working at Putnam High School and was the athletic trainer at all the home football games. During a game, a really tough Putnam kid gets hurt and comes out of the game. He begs the head coach to put him back in.

"I check him out and tell them he has a broken collarbone. The EMT (Emergency Medical Technician) approaches us and tells me, 'You have no business diagnosing an injury, stick to taping ankles. The head coach tells me basically the same thing. The kid goes back in and goes down the very next play and is taken to the hospital.

"On Monday, the principal calls me into his office to chew me out for butting into something that was none of my business. I found out later the kid had a broken collarbone.

"I started a very impressive health curriculum at Ackerman, was even called down to Salem (State Legislature) to discuss dealing with blood and AIDS. I was always called down to the woodshop several times to help with cuts, including a time when someone cut off a hand."

Dave Wood is still living at 72 years old, and his wife, Leslie, also a PE teacher, and an All-American in Field Hockey at Southern Oregon University.

THE BROTHERS JOHNSON

| MICHAEL W. JOHNSON | Marines |
| ANDREW S. JOHNSON | Army |

Michael informed me he only attended one of Milwaukie High School's Living History Day events many years ago and never returned because another veteran, a Major in their assigned classroom, spoke the entire session. This was a big problem in many classrooms in the early years.

Teachers were instructed to divide the number of veterans in their classroom by the hour and inform them the amount of time they had to speak. This hopefully would allow every veteran the opportunity to speak. Most teachers did a good job, but some didn't. I would get a handful of calls from upset to disappointed veterans.

I'm sorry I didn't learn about this happening to you, Michael, back then, because after meeting and talking to him, hell, I would have assigned a classroom all to himself.

Andrew, Michael's younger brother by two years, brought Mike to this interview as Mike lost his sight when badly wounded in Vietnam. It was very obvious from the very start; they were extremely close, and both had a great sense of humor.

This was the most fun and entertaining interviews I've ever done. These two were 'Outlaws.' Terms they used to describe themselves as young men growing up in Oregon City. They were hard working, tough, farm boys and high school wrestlers who loved to fight a lot and would get in fisticuffs with each other and neighborhood kids often. Once their father, Walter, broke up the two of them fighting with a two-by-four.

Andy told me, "My father yelled, 'You want to fight? Okay, how do you like this.' And he starts hitting both of us with the two-by-four. We ran away as fast as we could, and then our dog a very protective Border collie attacked and bit him." Both Mike and Andrew laughed out loud.

"Our dad, Walter, was a WWII veteran who served in the South Pacific. We knew he served in New Guinea with the Army Corps of Engineers building roads and airports, but he never talked about it except for a few funny stories.

"The one in particular we remember was about shooting and roasting wild hogs. Seems the wild hogs would dig tunnels through the jungles and tall elephant grass, and they would hunt them.

"Our dad would crawl into one end with his Thompson submachine gun while the other soldiers would start at the other side of the area and make lots of noise to drive the hogs down the tunnels toward our dad.

"When the hogs ran towards him, he would open fire. One time he had to shoot six hogs, he said it was either that or be run over as there was only room in the tunnels for either him or a hog. They had a huge barbeque that evening." Both brothers laughing out loud again.

"My grandparents had seventy-five acres out in Redland, Oregon, and my parents had five acres attached to the seventy-five that his grandmother gave him upon returning from the war. We were very poor and our mother, Stellabeth, was a stay-at-home mom.

"She was known as the neighborhood mom because all the neighbor kids, both our sister's and our friends, were always playing at our house. Dad worked at the West Linn Crown-Zellerbach paper mill running the Yard Dept. as assistant foreman on the Willamette River Falls.

The Yard Dept. was in charge of everything which moved in, around and outside of the mill. From all the raw material to the paper mill equipment used to make the paper and including the finished paper rolls. He was on call twenty-four seven. So many times, we accompanied him at night to keep the mill running. Part of our work ethic we inherited from him.

"We didn't know we were poor at the time because everyone we knew were pretty much in the same predicament. We always had clean clothes, sometimes patched hand-me-downs. And living on the farm, we had plenty to eat. Our folks always fed anyone who knocked on their door and were always helping one neighbor or another to get by.

"Once a young couple who were renting the forty-acre farm across the road lost their job and had to move to find work. So, they dropped off their new baby for my mom to babysit for a while until they got settled again and they never returned, called, or wrote for over two years.

"We had three sisters, Barbara, Beth, and Jane and now little April. After they returned, we never heard from them again. We often wonder to this day whatever happened to our little sister April. Never heard from them again!"

"When were you born?"

Mike, "I was born on June 18, 1948."

Andy, "May 16, 1950, in the old Oregon City hospital on Washington street, our dad, and his siblings, on the farm in Redland."

"And where did you graduate from high school?"

"Both of us from Oregon City High School Jackson Campus. Me in '66 and Andy in '68. We both wrestled all four years at OCHS, and Andy played offensive tackle on the football team as well. For every Wrestling meet Andy's senior year, we had to draw straws for the three heaviest weight classes as we didn't have anyone on the team who weighed over a hundred sixty pounds.

"Our coaches were Wally Sparks and Chet Newton who wrestled for the US Olympic team in the 1920s. Chet taught us a lot of great wrestling moves, and Wally was the line and strength coach for the football team, so he got us in tip top condition."

Andy with pride in his voice said, "My son, Erik, was also a great athlete and won the Scholar Athlete his senior year for the Portland area, played football for Ed Burton.

"He also played football for the Air Force Academy his first year and just retired from the Air Force after twenty-five years of service as a Lieutenant Colonel with over six thousand flying hours. Mostly combat flying with many medals and awards, one being the Distinguished Flying Cross. Almost all during the war on terror."

"So, you both had early morning chores and late afternoon chores?"

"Of course, we had early morning chores; feeding & milking cows and goats, rabbits, chickens, chopping firewood and stocking the wood box daily, etc., and then evening chores every day on our farm.

"We spent our summers picking berries, beans, and even potatoes for the local farms in the area. It's how we bought our own clothes and school supplies each year. We didn't spend it on anything else. For things like that we walked about three miles to the store in Redland and picked up beer and pop bottles to buy BBs and .22 shells and an occasional can of pop or a candy bar. I guess we were the original adopt a highway program for our area.

"We even built two outbuildings on our farm as twelve and fourteen year olds, and they are still standing to this day!" Mike said.

"So, Michael, you graduated from high school. What did you do next?"

"I got a job at Crown-Zellerbach and worked for about a year. A friend talked me into joining the Marines, and we joined on March 1, 1967.

"I'm sent to Vietnam right after infantry training in August of '67. I was with a rifle platoon. We went on search and destroy missions for weeks at a time, and sometimes choppers would take us up in the mountains to drop us off. You had to jump from the chopper onto six to eight feet tall razor-sharp Elephant or Cogon grass and hoped you didn't land on bungee sticks," Mike laughs.

"Oh, have you heard about the rock apes? We were out on patrol and held up in the mountains in a patch of large boulders. It was pitch dark, and suddenly we see these guys silhouetted up on top of the boulders above us. We thought they were Viet Cong, but looking closer their arms were too long and their legs too short. Then all of a sudden, they started throwing rocks down at us. It was then that we realized they were rock apes!

"There were also snakes. There was one, the Green Bamboo Viper, that we called a 'Three Stepper'. If it bites you, step one: sit down, step two: put your head between your knees, and step three: kiss your ass goodbye," laughing.

"One time as we came out of patrol, one of my buddies had one hitching a ride on his backpack. We had him take it off and set it down which caused the snake to quickly retreat under the pack. We lifted the pack and killed it. Then cut off its head and pried its mouth open which immediately the fangs automatically sprang out.

"Even a dead snake can still kill you if you mess around with its dead head. Gives new meaning to Grateful Dead fans," laughter.

"Another time we were at a remote firebase, and the bunkers were infested with these smaller Indian cobras about three feet long. We couldn't even use the bunkers and had to sleep out on top of the bunkers.

"The snakes were inside holes, so we couldn't get them out. Once in a while, one or two would come out and head for the wire and we would open up on them with or M16s. But most of the time the snake got away and came back again during the night and crawl over us in the dark to get back inside the bunker.

"One night, I woke up with something touching the side of my head, so I asked one of my buddies if it was one of those cobras. I thought for sure it was about to bite my face. My buddy said he didn't see anything.

"It was pitch dark, so I decided I should just grab it and throw it before it bites me. I reached up and grabbed it, and low and behold it was the strap of my metal pot. We were more than a little spooked of those snakes in the bunkers.

"It was pretty common for snakes to crawl on you at night, but most were not poisonous. One night I had what must have been one over three feet long crawl over me. I tried to stab it in the head with my K-bar (Vietnam War knife), but it was faster than me and jerked its head out of the way. Luckily, it had a round head, so it probably wasn't poisonous, but you don't know so it scares the crap out of you!

"There were also very large alligators or crocodiles, we weren't sure which. But when you're wading across a river up to your neck, holding rifles over the head, you're always thinking 'where the hell is that twenty-foot-long croc right now?' Makes you move as fast as you can to get across and out of the water quickly.

"Then of course you had to deal with the leaches you just gave a ride to. We used to burn them off with lit cigarettes or a lighter. We also saw many large pythons and would open up on any we saw, but at night it wasn't a good idea to be shooting and giving away your location. I also remember seeing tigers drinking water from the rivers.

"We were soaking wet for weeks at a time, the worst part of crossing the rivers were the leaches. In an area called 'Leach Valley,' they were so pervasive that they issued you condoms and earplugs to wear so they didn't crawl inside of your urinal tract and ear canals.

"After each river crossing, we would strip down and burn the leaches off with our cigarettes to get them to release. Taking care of our feet was another issue. Since we walked everywhere, it was a constant battle, and so was having dry socks."

"So, Mike, tell me about when you were wounded."

"We were on another two week seek and destroy mission and were into the second week and were sitting on a ridge top when we got hit by small arms fire from the bottom of the valley below.

"The hillside and ridge, all the foliage was gone from previous bombardment and most of the trees were all broken, and the vegetation was gone. It had apparently been napalmed too.

"We see that the small arms fire is coming from a Viet Cong reinforced bunker complex at the bottom of the valley only some three hundred yards below us. So, we call in an air strike and artillery bombardment of the bunkers.

"So, I'm digging a fox hole to get down into since, as I said, this bunker complex is only about three hundred yards below us, and the handle on my E-tool breaks off, and my fox hole is only about two feet deep on the high side and six inches deep on the downhill side.

"I hear the jets start to make their bombing runs, and I crawl in with my back against the high side and my feet against the low side, put my flak jacket over my upper body, pull my metal pot down over my face and put my chin against my chest. The bunker is hit with multiple two-hundred-fifty-pound bombs and artillery rounds and destroyed.

"The blast sends shrapnel up our way. As I said, I'm crouched as low as I can, get in my shallow fox hole, holding my helmet and bent over. When everything settles down there is a red-hot piece of shrapnel the size of a large knife blade about two inches wide, ten inches long and half an inch thick all jagged on the edges laying right next to my shoulder, changing colors and glowing white, blue to red hot. I was lucky that day, but not the next.

"The next day, we get orders to hike into a fire base about sixteen klicks from our current position. So, we chop our way down the ridge and hike to where they fly in resupplies.

"We load back up with food and lots of ammo. We head out and along the way is a dried up rice paddy, and we start to cross it keeping separated by ten to fifteen yards as you're trained to do.

"I'm carrying my M79 grenade launcher on my shoulder and about sixty to seventy M79 rounds in my backpack and stuffed into empty claymore bags hanging on my web belt around my waist. Each weighs about one pound each so it's heavy. I have a .45 caliber handgun too with ammo too. That plus two bandoliers of M60 .30 caliber machine gun rounds crisscrossed over my chest. Plus, all my personal gear and MREs. We are heavily loaded down.

"We are walking across this rice paddy when I see a hand grenade in the trail on the ground in front of me. I grab my M79 with my left hand to hold it on my shoulder and then bend down to pick up the grenade up with my right hand. I see the spoon is still attached but the firing pin is dropped down, which means it about to explode.

"I turn to my left and throw it but, it explodes about a foot out of my hand, shrapnel all through my body, but all my gear I'm carrying, and my flak jacket, protect my vital organs and upper torso.

"Several pieces did hit me in my face, and I lost my right eye, part of my cheek bone, and multiple teeth. It went behind my nose cutting my optic nerve, so I lost sight in my left eye too, and lost my right hand since it was mostly blown off.

"The flak jacket and all that extra gear around my torso saved my life.

"After a minute or so, I wake up with the medic cutting off my clothes, I'm spitting up blood and broken teeth. He yells, 'Don't swallow! Just spit out your broken teeth!" I remember hearing the sound of the helicopter coming in and thinking how great the wind from the chopper blades felt since it was so dam hot.

"Then being loaded on board and it tilting as it took off, and I don't remember anything else until waking up in the hospital in Da Nang. After about a week or two, I'm sent to a hospital in Okinawa, Japan.

"The Marine Corp personnel detail responsible for notifying the families of wounded or deceased soldiers went to my grandparents' home, not my parents,' for some reason unknown to me, to tell my family the news. My parents are called and when they arrive, as they walk up to the house, my grandpa in his grief yelled to my parents, 'Mike's dead!'

"The doctors only gave me a ten percent chance of living, so my only guess was they thought it was appropriate to tell my folks I had died already. After a couple of weeks in Okinawa, I was able to call my parents on the phone, which shocked them. I was able to tell them I'm still alive, but in lots of pain.

"One night while in the hospital in Japan, I was dreaming I was still in the jungle and had to go to the bathroom. I'm not really awake sort of sleep walking in the hospital. As I get out of bed, I feel this metal bar and wonder to myself, 'how did this metal bar get out here in the jungle?'

"I had no idea I was in the hospital, and two Japanese orderlies grab me to put me back to my bed. But in my mind, when they start talking to me in Japanese, I believe I'm being attacked by a couple Viet Cong. I hit one orderly with my right stub and knocked him on his ass." Both brothers are laughing hard.

"Then some nurses run up to me, and one yells in English, 'Johnson, get back in your bed!'" I say to her, 'What the hell are you doing out here in the jungle?" Both brothers are laughing, "You don't argue with nurses. I wake up and ask, 'Where am I?'

"I was lucky when I came home, no public airports, so no protestors. But I remember going to a bar or tavern for a beer and some people would try to educate me about Vietnam. I told them, 'You are so full of crap your eyes are brown. Why don't you go over there yourself and learn what really is happening?' They all just had no clue. It was not even worth the time talking to them."

"How did you deal with it all, memories?"

"I mostly had to get on with my life. I had to learn how to do everything such as how to walk around blind, how to feel your way around and navigate city streets using a blind man's cane. I had more important things to worry about." I was deeply impressed with Mike's tremendous positive attitude.

"I had to make a living, so I attended Clackamas Community College in 1972 and earned an Associate's in Science degree to become a machinist. I was hired on and worked at Proto Tool in Milwaukie for fifteen years until they moved the plant to Texas.

"I retired when they moved the business out of state. I decided to fish and hunt a lot; salmon, trout, bass, deer, elk, and turkey, you name it. I still go fishing and hunting and still love to shoot my guns.

"I'm a member of the Douglas Ridge Rifle range out toward Estacada and shoot there on a regular basis. We use pistol scopes so the person assisting can aim at the target while standing behind me, and I hold the rifle and fire when instructed when I'm on target. A lot of trust building with various family members.

"I'm so grateful to my father who fought the VA for several years trying to get me my benefits. They kept saying no, over and over again, until they finally gave me the benefits I deserved."

It has been almost fifty years since the Vietnam War officially ended. the government also failed to make good on its promises to those who served. Many of the veterans I have spoken with tell me of the indifferences they met not only with civilians but also with the government. How they had to fight for, and are still fighting for, benefits. Too many veterans are still dealing both physically and psychologically with the effects of war, even today.

I have also heard many Vietnam veterans tell about their treatment by the VA as, 'delay, deny, until you die.' Our veterans deserve better. Veterans like Mike who has sacrificed so much for their country should be treated better.

After Mike finished speaking, I asked his brother Andy, "So Andy, did you join the Army or were you drafted?"

"That's a hell of a story. See, I was all gung-ho about joining the military because of what happened to my brother. I wanted revenge!

"That was until my parents and I drove down to the hospital in Oakland to see Mike. We went through the Amputee Ward at the Naval Hospital in Oakland, California… and it was shocking! The number of men, many just boys about my age, with no arms or legs, nothing but a head and torso was heartbreaking.

"I thought, wow, this is the real carnage of war, and I want no part of this. So, I enrolled at Clackamas Community College to get an Associate's degree, but mostly to get a deferment. My draft number was No. 37. I like to say it was the only lottery I ever won.

"My first draft notice came in '69, so I went down to the induction center in Portland to get tests and a physical. A DI walks in and points to half of us in the room and says, 'You are going to be Marines.' I was scared shitless!

"We are taken to another room. And there an officer asks, 'Are any of you in college right now. I raised my hand, and he said, 'Go home.' I took my grades a lot more seriously after that.

"I became an automotive technician, graduating with the first graduating class at CCC in 1970, and I earned good grades, actually on the honor roll. All through high school, I didn't get very good grades, and I worked a lot.

"I was all about cars. I loved cars and built several hot rods. I worked at Danielson's Thriftway in Oregon City and also worked at the Texaco Service station at 7th and Washington. And worked on the weekends for my uncle's construction business carrying lumber, from the ninth grade through my days at CCC.

"After graduating from CCC in 1970, I start a cement foundation business with my cousin until the Spring of '71 when I received my second draft notice. I told you my draft lottery number was No. 37, and I thought you would get a new number every year. Well, NOT!

"I'm twenty years old and go out to visit my parents and my mom hands me a draft letter from the President. I only have seven days left before the date listed in the letter to report to Fort Lewis, Washington for basic training.

"I gave my '63 two-door Chevy impala to my sister. Then I sold my share of the Cement Foundation business to my cousin. Basically gave it away! We were making good money, clearing two to three thousand a month, and now I was going to get eighty-six dollars per month as a private in the Army.

"After boot camp, I'm sent to AIT (Advanced Individual Training) for 4.2-inch Mortar man training as my MOS, both at Fort Lewis in Washington. After completing AIT, I received orders sending me to Vietnam in September of '71.

"We have thirty days leave, so I go home for a while and go deer hunting with my now blind brother and my dad. Before going on leave though, a few of us decided to go to San Francisco for a week to party before reporting into the transfer station in Oakland.

"After three days we are flat broke and decide to sleep on park benches in Golden Gate Park. That San Francisco fog comes in the early morning and the newspapers covering us get soaking wet, and it was cold at the end of September.

"We decided to report in early and the DI at the desk wrote a big 'Red D' on my papers. I asked what it meant, but he won't tell me. We just wait and do KP duty every day and others come and report in. The other guys we went through basic and AIT training are just waiting for when our names are called out every day and when we will be shipped out. I wait and wait, but my name is never called out.

"Why is my name not called, I wonder to myself. So, I finally go ask and I learned my papers were filed in the Deferment file. So now, they panic and don't know what to do with me. Three days later I'm sent to Fort Dix, New Jersey for thirty days. Every day, they call names out again and if your name is not called, they give you KP duty, or some other menial task to do which isn't pleasant.

"Well, I hide in the back and when my name isn't called, I would sneak back inside and just play cards all day. While there, a couple of us decide to go AWOL to see New York City. I put my civilian clothes into my duffle bag and go to the bus station.

"There are MPs everywhere, so we change clothes in a restroom, and buy a bus ticket. Since we had experience from San Francisco, we slept on benches again in Central Park. We go back and they never even missed us," laughing again.

"My name is finally called, and I'm sent to Panama for Advanced Jungle Infantry Training for Vietnam and issued, for some reason, winter clothes. Luckily, they issued us jungle fatigues when we got to Panama.

"Garrison duty was like hell, and Panama was hotter than hell. For PT, we had to run five miles to the beach and back in the sand every day for six months. Then I learned our base is going to be inspected, and we have jeeps and trucks in bad shape. I'm approached because of my auto mechanics education and asked if I could get every vehicle up to par to pass the IG inspection (Inspector General).

"I made a deal with them for no more running every morning, as I needed all the time available to work on all the vehicles. I also hand-picked four other guys to work for me. I'm told if we pass the inspection, we will not have to run at all the rest of our time stationed there. We passed and the Lieutenant in charge lived up to his end of the bargain, we never ran PT again.

"I have a funny fist fight story. Another soldier was giving me crap, and I had enough of it. He was on the base boxing team, so we squared up to fight down at the motor pool. Before I knew it, he hit me so hard I went down like a sack of potatoes.

"I cut my forehead when my head hit the pavement, but I jumped back up quickly only to be knocked down several more times till I used my wrestling skills to do a takedown and with him on the ground. I was bleeding, but I had won the fight.

"I had to go up to the base infirmary to get some stiches. Afterwards, when an officer was questioning us about the rumor of a fist fight, I told him there wasn't any fist fight. But he saw my bruised and bloody face and didn't believe me. So, I told them I was hit with a ball pin hammer that flew off the handle, bounced off the wheel seal I was putting in, and hit me in the forehead.

"The officer responded, 'That's something else. That hammer must have bounced a long way. That's the same story I got from the other soldier.' We covered for each other, but it was not planned. We became good friends after that.

"The best part of being stationed in Panama is I met a beautiful Panamanian woman, Virginia, with long black hair and brown eyes. I was not allowed to date her one-on-one for the first date though. She could only go out with me if there were three other girls with us. It was the rule, no choice.

"Her father was a civil engineer for the Panama Canal. Her best friend who we met through was the niece of the Dictator of Panama, and her dad was in charge of all of the country's casinos. We dated for a while and ended up getting married on January 13, 1973. Next year will be fifty years."

"How were you treated when coming back to the states?"

"Lots of the typical yelling and name calling only because we had to wear our uniforms whenever traveling on orders back then, and I was never in Vietnam. The Hare Krishna's were at all the airports back then and were mostly just annoying.

"After coming home from Panama, I worked one summer in the Dakotas as a cowboy on the ranch my sister and her husband were managing since I wanted to introduce my wife to them. We would have stayed longer, but my wife didn't like the remoteness. It was five miles to the mailbox!

"One day she asked me when we were going on to Oregon, and when I told her I liked it here, she told me we were either going to Oregon or she was going back to Panama. Needless to say, we left shortly thereafter!

"Then I went back to college at OIT (Oregon Institute of Technology) in Klamath Falls and got my bachelor's degree in Diesel Technology.

"Was hired on by the Cummins Distributor and spent the next forty years working for them, traveling the territories in the Pacific Northwest, Alaska, and Hawaii and around the world from Southeast Asia and Europe.

"Started as a management Trainee for seven-fifty per month in September of '75, and retired on December 31, 2015, as a Vice President of Sales.

"Both of us agree that we grew up a lot being drafted and sent off to serve our country. We left as rowdy young guys fighting and raising hell, but once we experienced the world outside of our little town, we became better citizens and lived to give back to our community verses only thinking about what we might get from it.

"And while we hated being away for several years of our lives, I think it made us who we are today and are much better because of the experience, no matter how hard it was to live it out at the time."

Mike and Andy are still living at the ages of 74 and 72.

THE BROTHERS ANGELL

GRANT ANGELL	Army, Green Beret
CURT ANGELL	Air Force

Grant attended most of our Milwaukie Living History Days from '98 until they ended in 2010. He then joined us at Reynolds High School when they took the program over. Grant, and a couple of his close Vietnam veteran friends helped us out every year at Reynolds.

I am most grateful to Grant for is his help in getting the Milwaukie High School Flagpole Memorial built. The school district had passed a bond levy to build a number of district improvements, and Milwaukie High School was getting a new Auditorium and Fine Arts Center.

In the front of the Auditorium, a new flagpole was to be installed. I approached the MHS Administration because we wanted a memorial built to remember Milwaukie High's fallen alumni.

Not making much progress, I turned to Grant, and he became a driving force behind funding and building the memorial. Anyone who knew Grant knew if he wanted something done, he would not quit until it happened. He was able to convince North Clackamas School District to participate in fundraising efforts to build the memorial.

We dedicated this beautiful memorial with a ceremony in the spring of 2009. It was located on the west side of campus in front of the auditorium. The sides are marble with the engraved names of all Milwaukie High School alumni who were killed in action or died while serving our country.

I was able to learn a little more about Grant from his younger brother, Curt, also a Vietnam veteran.

Grant was born in May of 1946, in White Plains, New York. Their mother, Barbara Angell, hosted a home economics program, Morning Marketing on KRON-TV in San Francisco.

When they moved to Portland, Oregon, she was the host of the first five-day-a-week local program in Oregon and the second live local program ever to air on KPTV called, What's Cooking?. She had a wide variety of guests on her new, retitled show Northwest Home where she interviewed guests, including former First Lady, Eleanor Roosevelt, food icon Duncan Hines, and George Liberace.

Their parents decided to name their first born after the father, Grant Curry Angell, but did not want Grant to be a junior, so he gave him the middle name McCormac Barbara's maiden name.

During WWII, their father volunteered for service in the Army but was turned down because of his eyesight. Ironically, he ended up being drafted a short time later. He earned a Purple Heart during the Battle of the Bulge and returned to the states where he met a Red Cross volunteer named Barbara.

"Grant graduated from Milwaukie in '64 and then attended Multnomah Junior College and was drafted in '66. In the Army, he became a Green Beret in the 1st Special Forces Group."

"Did he ever tell you about his experiences in Vietnam?"

"No, he would never talk about Vietnam. All I ever heard was the great R&R stories," Curt laughs. "But some of them might not be appropriate for this book. After serving in Vietnam, Grant served at the White House during the Nixon presidency."

"So. Let's talk about you, Curt."

"Well, I was born in Berkeley, California in July of 1950. I go by Curt but was named Curtis. Whenever I got in trouble, our mom would yell 'Curtis D. come here right now!'"

"What were your high school years like at MHS?"

"All four years I was in various choirs, and my senior year, I sang in the Acapella choir. I was a First Tenor." Curt laughs and says, "Here I was over six feet tall, and my voice didn't change until my senior year. My father encouraged music and made me learn to play the clarinet, then guitar.

"Anyway, my junior year at Milwaukie, I signed up for the Air Force so I could enlist once I graduated. I was able to make some choices for jobs I wanted to do in the Air Force, so my first choice was a transport aircraft loadmaster, and my second choice was aircraft maintenance.

"After graduating in '68, I enjoyed working different jobs locally and on April Fool's Day 1969, I got notified that I was to report for basic training at Lackland Air Force Base in Texas on April 7.

"After being in basic training for a couple of weeks, I reported for my flight physical to qualify for loadmaster training, but I was told I was too tall to be on flying status, so I went to aircraft mechanics school at Chanute Air Force Base in Illinois. Upon finishing my training, I was stationed at McChord Air Force Base in Washington.

"Instead of working as a mechanic on the Lockheed C-141 aircraft, I was assigned to the technical order library. We were responsible for updating the technical information carried aboard each C-141. I made changes to the six-volume aircraft library, which directed how all maintenance was to be performed.

"In '73 there was a critical shortage of C-141 flight engineers, so the Air Force began recruiting efforts to fill those positions. In order to qualify, an NCO had to be an E-5, Staff Sergeant, and meet certain education requirements. I applied, was accepted, and after I was given a medical waiver for excessive standing height, I then went to training to become a C-141 flight engineer.

"In '74, toward the end of Vietnam War, I flew into Saigon's commercial and military airports, Tan Son Nhat International and Bien Hoa Air Base, evacuating Americans out of Vietnam. My last flight to Saigon was shortly after a C-5 crashed. It had taken off and climbed to about twenty thousand feet when the aft pressure door failed. The crew managed to return to the airport, but crash landed.

"Things were pretty chaotic when we parked, and we had to wait for things to calm down before taking off. Our typical ground time was three hours and fifteen minutes, but we always tried to shorten it if we could get all the evacuees on board.

"One trip prior to that final evacuation flight, we were waiting on the tarmac at Tan Son Nhat and an ARVN jeep drove by us very slowly with its .50 caliber machine gun aimed towards us. They then turned around at the end of the parking area and drove by us again with the gun turned around aiming at us again."

Curt then told me all the impressive assignments he was involved with during his Air Force career.

"We evacuated fifty-two children out of Cambodia before it fell to the Khmer Rouge. Evacuated many Americans from our embassy in Iran right before it was overrun, evacuated dental students from Grenada, flew out some of the bodies from the Jonestown suicides, evacuated Marines from Lebanon after the terrorist bombing, and evacuated Americans out of Clark Air Base in the Philippines as Mt. Pinatubo erupted."

"Wow. That's amazing," I responded.

"There's more. We dropped the 82nd Airborne in Panama while getting fired on from the ground. We were the lead aircraft and weren't able to drop all the troops on the first pass, so we flew around for a second pass. The three other planes dropped all their personnel, they followed their training and stayed in formation behind us while we dropped the remaining paratroops. This led to the Air Force changing its airdrop policy.

"I retired in Oct 1, 1992, as an E-8, Senior Master Sergeant, having held it longer than any other rank I had held in the Air Force.

"After retiring, I flew commercially on Boeing 727-200s, for the small passenger carrier America Trans Air. I then transitioned to Emery Worldwide Airline and was based out of SeaTac Airport on the DC-8 and flew night freight both nationally and internationally. I flew there until August 2001, when the airline closed.

"After being with Emery for a year, I met a pro-union guy who was trying to convince us all to join the union. I ripped him for the quality of the communications he had written to us. Actually, his work was bad. Low and behold, he convinces me to edit his work. Our pilots end up joining the Air Line Pilots Association, and I was elected as Vice-Chairman of the union.

"When the airline closed down, I went back to college and got my Master's degree in Human Resources and worked in HR (Human Resources) at Fort Lewis for the Department of the Army, then at Sand Point for NOAA (National Oceanic and Atmospheric Administration), and finally the State Department till retiring in 2013."

Grant Angell passed away in February of 2018 at the age of 71.

Curt Angell is still living at the age of 72.

INSPIRATION AT ITS FINEST

KIM PHUC PHAN THI   'Napalm Girl'

My wife and I attended one of the most inspirational presentations I've ever experienced at Westgate Baptist Church in Portland, Oregon on Friday, May 10, 2019.

The speaker was Mrs. Kim Phuc Phan Thi, who was the nine-year-old girl who had been badly burned by a napalm bombing in June of '72 during the Vietnam War. The Pulitzer Prize-winning photo taken of her running down the road in pain and agony with her clothes burned off is considered one of the most important photos from the past century.

There is no way I can do justice to her story and life journey in a small section in this book, therefore I highly recommend reading her book *Fire Road: The Napalm Girl's Journey through the Horrors of War to Faith, Forgiveness, and Peace*. It's outstanding and a must read and I'm in awe of her.

Instead, I want to share with you the emotional meeting with Kim Phuc Phan Thi and Bill Chisholm, Army, Korean War, Two Purple Hearts, Chosin Few whose section is in this Volume II.

Bill was badly burned by napalm bombings from our own Navy Corsairs and because of that, he was extremely apprehensive to go with us. In the end we were able to bring him because we told him her presentation would possibly bring some healing.

A few days before, I had contacted the church and told them about Bill and asked if they could please pass this information on to Kim. Hoping the two of them could meet.

The presentation started with a short highlight film about Kim, and it started right at the beginning with the actual black and white footage of the jet approaching the small village and the bombs dropping and the explosions of fire balls.

Bill put his hands over his ears, put his head down and his whole body began to shake. Both Malinda and I put our arms on his shoulders to comfort him. But, when the film was over, Kim started speaking in this soft, loving voice, Bill opened his eyes and took his hands away from his ears. He told me later that he was going to get up and walk out after the film ended.

Kim shared her unbelievable story of surviving while in constant physical pain, the many surgeries, and treatments. She also spoke of being used for propaganda purposes by the communists, as well as her amazing faith. Kim was left for dead in a hospital morgue for three days and doctors believed she survived because of the cold in the morgue.

344

Kim's life changed forever when she found a bible hidden behind some books in library in Hanoi. She became a Christian and hid her new faith for years. On the way to her and her husband's honeymoon in Moscow, they left their plane during a refueling stop in Newfoundland and asked for political asylum in Canada.

She got a big laugh when she told us, "I received a phone call from Oprah Winfrey inviting me to be on her talk show, and I didn't know who Oprah was." She was the most loving, positive, inspiring, caring, amazing woman and speaker. Lots of laughter, tears of sadness followed by tears of joy.

At the end of her presentation, she asked Bill Chisholm to come up on the stage, and we followed him. She introduced Bill to the audience, and then Kim and Bill hugged for what seemed like an eternity. Both cried and so did everyone else. It was a very special moment for all.

Afterwards Bill said, "Meeting her was one the most healing experiences I ever had."

Kim Phuc Phan Thi is still living at the age of 59, and is married to Bui Huy Toan. They have two children.

WILLIAM HANH VUONG   South Vietnam Army

For the last few years, I've always addressed the Major as Major Vuong, and he kept requesting me to address him as William. My excuse was always "I'm sorry, it's how I was raised."

Six years ago, I met William at a store one afternoon as he was walking towards me in the same isle. I noticed he had on a dark green beret with a military patch, so I approached him and asked, "Excuse me sir, were you in the South Vietnamese Army during the American war." He responded "Yes, I was assigned to the American Army."

I then told him about me taking veterans to high schools to talk and would he be interested in joining us. William was interested and invited me to his and his wife's Vietnamese restaurant HA VL. The very next week, I went there for lunch and visited with him. The Vietnamese soup is the best I had ever tasted.

William agreed to attend Reynolds High School's Living History Day the following November. We also invited William and his lovely wife, Christina, to our annual Welcoming Dinner with all of the out-of-state veterans. I told them we would pay for everything, but they brought with them a huge pot of one of their soups. It was so good that within a short time there was a constant line of people getting seconds.

Christina was starting to get quite the positive reputation for her soups. They opened up a second restaurant called Rose VL Deli and soon it became a favorite and highly rated eatery.

My wife and I went there for lunch many times, and I would tell William, "I'm writing a book about all the veterans I've known over the years. I would love to interview and include you." He would always respond "I don't know, I'll think about it."

He finally agreed after I brought Chosin Few veteran, Bill Chisholm, to lunch at his restaurant one day. While we were eating, I said, "I would be so honored to include both of you in my book I'm writing, but you both keep telling me no."

What happened next kind of shocked me. Bill said to William, "I have always told Ken, no, I don't want to talk about it. But if you agree to be interviewed, I will too."

They both agreed and shook hands promising to tell me about their experiences. That very next week I was finally able to interview Bill. His story is in Remembrance Volume II in the Chosin Few section.

For William's interview, I emailed him some of the questions I would ask him. The only question I was concerned about was, "Are you able to share any of your experiences in the Communist re-education camps (POWs, hard labor)?"

I did not receive an answer from him. Then in March of 2018, I met him at Rose VL Deli, and we sat at a small table while I asked him questions.

"I was born in 1940 during the Japanese Military occupation of Vietnam. My great-grandfather and grandfather were both governors of provinces Binh Dinh and Ha Dong during the French occupation. The French colonized this part of the world in 1887 and lost control to the Japanese Imperial Army in 1940.

"My grandfather was sent to France to become a doctor and stayed there for twenty years." Because of this their family was considered upper-middle class. I asked, "Did your parents share any stories from the Japanese Occupation?"

"Yes, they told me the Japanese soldiers were very mean and cruel. Young women were raped the entire five years they occupied Vietnam. They would confiscate raw rice after every harvest, and many starved. There were many public beheadings also.

347

"After the end of WWII, Ho Chi Min set up a puppet government and many of Vietnam's political figures and the rich were killed. Then the French returned to re-establish their colony and the war with France lasted from 1946 to 1954."

I asked, "How was the French treatment of the Vietnamese?"

"The French raped our women also. In a public square, they would place a tall pole standing upright and cover it with grease. They would make people try to climb it and beat them with clubs when they slide down or failed. In school, we were forced to learn French, learn the history of France, and sing French songs including their National Anthem."

"What kind of student were you?"

He responded quickly, "I was always first in my class, always great grades."

I asked, "Concerning the American war in Vietnam, how did it all start for you?"

"I started working with the American CIA as an Assistant Camp Commander and Translator for American Special Forces in 1962 in the Kon Tum Province. One of my jobs was to translate the military manual before sending it out to the field.

"I was also the ARVN representative to the US advisory team. I was the only interpreter (Chief Interpreter and Translator) in charge of the highest manual. A few years later I worked for my advisor, Major Norman Schwarzkopf, who I became good friends with.

"In 1965, I escorted five-star General Westmoreland and Henry Kissinger to Kon Tum Province. In '67, I was moved to the US Embassy in Saigon because they needed a qualified person to run intelligence for II Corps.

"When the Americans pulled out in '75, my staff and I were trying to withdraw and get back to Saigon but were ambushed by Viet Cong. My driver was killed, I had to move his body over while being shot at and trying to escape to safety. As I drove away, my left forearm and wrist was hit by bullets. I was very lucky."

William's American connections landed him in a Vietnamese prison for ten years. Christina raised their six boys until William was released as a prisoner of war in 1985. I next asked him about his experiences in the POW camp after the war ended.

"The Communists called them 'Re-Education Camps' because their goal was to brainwash us." William then looked me straight in the eye and gave me the most determined look. A look that reminded me of the look some of the great competitors I coached gave me when it was time for them to compete.

After about ten seconds, William stated in a strong, intense voice, "They could not brain wash me!" He pointed his index finger to his head and said, "Mind Control." I was very moved and impressed.

"The guards were uneducated from the jungles. The first three months, I was interrogated every day. I told them the same lie every day that I was only a foot soldier, I didn't know anything.

"They would point a gun at my head and yell, 'We will kill you if we find out you are lying.' I would always open my shirt up and say, 'Go ahead and kill me, I don't care.'"

I asked him if he was beaten and tortured and all he said was, "They were very mean and cruel." I did not push my question further.

"What kind of labor were you forced to do?"

"We worked in rice paddies and the jungle from six in the morning until six at night, mostly seven days a week. Sometimes we got Sunday off if the guards thought we worked hard enough all week. Every day we had to cut five bamboo poles, eight to twelve meters long and carry them to our camp. They were used to build barracks. We moved camp about every three months. We had to clear the side of a mountain so manioc or cassava (root vegetables) could be planted.

"First of all, the mountain from the top was cleared by cutting down small and big trees in the jungle and then let them dry. The trunks of big trees were pulled down by prisoners to the ground then cut up to be used for lumber. The dried leaves and branches were burned and used as fertilizers.

"Each prisoner was required to dig eighty-five holes per day in the hot dry season in Summer. Each hole dug was twenty by twenty by forty deep." William gave me a look of frustration.

"It was impossible. How can we do that kind of labor without breakfast, just two small meals per day. One small bowl of corn or maybe a very small scoop of rice, plus four pieces of sea salt and half small bowl of watery powered manioc soup.

"But even though we were all starving, I was very disciplined in what I ate. You see, everyone who ate the food prepared for us got malaria and dysentery and died within two to three months. I would only take a couple of sips of the broth to keep hydrated. I knew how to survive in the jungle, what to eat and what not to eat.

"Many POWs would step on small fish in the rice paddies and eat them raw or they would catch rats, mice, bugs and eat them raw. They would get sick and die. I had very strict discipline." William points to his head again with his index finger, "Mind Control."

"I promised myself that they will never break me, and I always had hope that this would end someday. I never gave up hope." He smiled and pointed to his head again, "Mind Control."

I asked him, "It's extremely obvious to me that you are very, very mentally tough. How have you dealt with the memories and PTSD?"

"Ever since my release from the re-education camp, I have had nightmares every month even now. My wife is the only one who knows what I've been through."

While I was interviewing him, his wife, Christina kept coming out of the kitchen many times to check on her husband. She looked very concerned.

Finally, she said "Time to take a break, eat some soup, and we can finish this at a later date." I responded, "How did you know I was thinking the same thing." I cannot tell you how good that soup tasted.

We were unable to finish our talk, but William said he would email me the rest later. As I drove home, I thought Major Vuong might be the mentally toughest, most disciplined, and determined human being I've ever known, and I've known quite a few people with similar qualities. With all due respect to the many mentally tough football players, wrestlers, and veterans I have known.

A few days later I received the email from William with the rest of his story. I'm so grateful that William emailed me the rest of his story:

> When I was in Vinh Phu prison in Hoang Lien Son Province in North Vietnam, I did not know when I would ever be released as well as all the political prisoners who were sent to the North. After I was released from the prison in the North and sent to the South, I learned that there was a political negotiation between the USA and the Vietnamese Communist government. All prisoners will be released without notice or order in advance. It was a top-secret issue.

One day in 1982, all prisoners in Prison in Vinh Phu Camp 5 were assembled for roll call, then most of the prisoners were freed and sent back to South. 148 of us were left behind and continued in prison. I was freed in 1985 in Saigon, South VN. My wife and six sons were living in Kon Tum Province far away from Saigon about 900kilometers, and I did not let Christina know I was freed.

My friend Dr. Trần dinh Tung and Nguyễn van Dung wanted me to be in their hospital An Binh for a physical checkup and I stayed in this hospital for 30 days. This hospital was immediately confiscated after April 30, 1975, by the communists. After gaining weight and my health improving, I let Christina know I was released. The reason why I did this because I did not want, she and my six sons to see my skinny body.

I then reunited with my family in Saigon continuing our starving life. Every morning I'd take a bus to Cholon town in Saigon seeking families who need to learn English for their family's reunion in USA or Canada. So, I had a teaching job earning for my family while Christina sold secondhand clothes on the pavement at Hải Ba Trung Street in Saigon.

During the war, I met Major H. Norman Schwarzkopf at MAAV camp, the American Military Advisors for ARVN 22nd infantry division/II Corps in Kon Tum Province. He was major serving in Qui Nhon Province and came here for a meeting where I met him with the military advisory team.

Suddenly in 1992 I was informed that General Schwarzkopf wanted to see me by my coordinator Jeff Mac Murdo who was serving for IOM in Saigon while I was teaching for this program. Jeff then took me to the Rex Hotel in Saigon to see the retired five-star general. It was a nice surprised of reunion with him, but I was so scared and secretly knew that if the communists found out about this, they would put me I prison again.

I saw and talked with him for about 15 minutes in the corner of the lobby hiding. Nobody could see us. With him was his female secretary and reporter Dan Rather. In the next day I met him again at the top balcony of the Rex Hotel. There we visited for an hour. The general complained to me that his team hired a helicopter of the communists to fly over to Qui Nhon remote area where he served during his tours in Vietnam in 1965 and 1966. He said to me "I had to pay the communists $35,000 dollars for the trip - "goddam it" HANH"!

"We laughed and then we said goodbye to each another. That was the last time I ever saw him, and I still miss him, Ken."

In 1986, four of William's sons fled Vietnam. They were many of the boat people who sought prosperity outside of Vietnam. Luckily, through his father's connections, they were able to gain immigrant status to travel to America. Unfortunately, William and Christina could not attain refugee status, and were stuck in Saigon. After seven years they were able to rejoin their family.

They are an American success story. He graduated from PSU, taught English to high school students as the Vietnamese Educational Bilingual Specialist for Portland Public Schools School for fifteen years. The entire family is heavily involved with the Boys Scouts, and William is also the Vietnamese Community of Oregon Advisor.

Thirteen years after coming to America, William and Christina were able to realize their dream of starting a restaurant. They opened the HA VL Restaurant and now have another the Rose VL Restaurant. Their Vietnamese soups have won many awards and are very popular in Portland.

If you go to their restaurant, get there early because they always sell out of their soups by noon. Oh, and the Vietnamese iced coffee is wonderful!

LEST WE FORGET

I decided to end this book with 'Lest We Forget'

This was an extremely emotional task for the Gold Star families and me. It took some time getting a few to talk. All were very helpful, but it was a difficult conversation. Some cried, some were still angry, and all remembered their family loved one's loss as if it happened yesterday. I'm very grateful to them all.

MILWAUKIE HIGH SCHOOL GOLD STAR ALUMNI

I attended Milwaukie High School's annual Gold Star Assembly every year as a high school student and every year as a teacher. This assembly, a tradition that has continued for over seventy years, honors the lives of former Milwaukie High School students who made the ultimate sacrifice in our country's wars. The tradition was started after World War II by a student who had lost her brother in the war.

It's a silent assembly in which students are released from classes and they move in silence to the school auditorium and quietly take their seats. When they enter the auditorium, the lights are dim. On stage are over fifty students, each holding a lit candle.

Then after a speaker says a few words, the names of Milwaukie students and one teacher who have died in wars are somberly read aloud one by one, and a candle is extinguished for each name. It's a truly beautiful ceremony, and every year all the students are very respectful.

To most Americans, and even our students, they are all just names of KIA's or MIA's or a causality while serving. But to others, they are friends and family. They deserve more and I wanted to include some of them in this book, so I tried to find more about them.

We were kindly given all of the resource information, as well as letters people wrote on the walls of the fallen few below by the Clackamas County Fallen. Their website goal is to in their own words: "Simply to curate these public stories for educational purposes, so that the Clackamas County residents who lost their lives in the Vietnam War, will always be remembered."

HALLIE 'BUD' WILLIAM SMITH — Class of '59

Basketball, baseball, student body president, Air Force, fighter pilot, born on October 17, 1941. His parents owned The Candy Store on Main Street in Milwaukie. After graduating Bud attended Lewis & Clark College.

Date of birth: 16 October 1941
Date of casualty: 8 January 1968
Home of record: Portland, Oregon
Branch and Rank: Air Force, Major, Pilot
Unit: 7th Air Force, 460th Tactical Reconnaissance Wing, 16th Tactical Reconnaissance Squadron
Awards: National Defense Service Medal, Vietnam Campaign Medal, Vietnam Service Medal
Location of name on the Vietnam Wall: 33E, 94
Location of service: South Vietnam, Pleiku province

Major Bud Smith remains listed as Missing In Action, to this day. As of this writing (2022), Bud Smith's remains have yet to be recovered. However, his navigator's remains were recovered and identified using DNA matches, in 2006.

I was able to speak with Jay Lillie, Milwaukie class of '58, who told me, "Bud Smith was the ultimate nice guy! Smart, very upbeat, friendly to all, athletic, member of so many clubs and teams at Milwaukie. A natural to be Student Body President. Belonged to the same Hi-Y club and summer baseball teams. His Vietnam MIA bio says he was on a mission in the mountains west of Danang."

From THE CLACKAMAS COUNTY FALLEN

****

Wife's tribute

He was a wonderful person, and I am still proud to have been his wife for four short years.

****

A friend that will never be forgotten. I will never forget the last time I saw Buddy and Judy. I was on a family trip with my parents on the Oregon Coast. We were looking out our window and we thought we saw Buddy and Judy walking hand in hand near the beach. The reason we figured out it was definitely Buddy was because he had his Lewis and Clark jacket on. We debated whether to bother them as we knew that Buddy was on leave and their time was short. It was a good thing my dad and I ran to catch up with them. Who would have known how short his time really was? They were really glad to see us as we wished him good luck and hugged and kissed him good-bye. Thank goodness that memory will always be in my mind. I was nine years old and that was the last time we saw Buddy. We miss you a lot!

****

You will NOT be forgotten

Thoughts of you always bring a smile to my heart. How fortunate I was to have met you in college, married you after we graduated and had four wonderful years together before you were sent to Vietnam in 1967. There is rarely a day that goes by without a happy memory of our short life together. The last time I saw you, you were 25 years old, and I am now 70. Will love you forever.

****

Not Forgotten

For more than 40 years my mother has kept her POW/MIA bracelet with Capt. Bud Smith's name on it. Growing up I always saw it as she explained to me what it meant. I even showed it once in a high school history project on Vietnam in the 1990s. I then had him in mind, when, as a young Airman, I wrote an essay for the Air Force Times called, 'Sometimes, I Forget.' Because she never could find his name on the

Vietnam Wall (the bracelet only had 'Bud' as his first name), she/we held out hope he had returned home safely. Today we searched for him online and found out his full name, his story, and that he is still missing. Putting a face to his name and reading the tributes from his wife and friends humanizes this worn metal bracelet that my mother has kept close. Our prayers are that he did not suffer when he paid the ultimate sacrifice for his country. We will certainly remember him forever. He is not forgotten.

****

Still remembering your sacrifice

I never met Captain Smith. As a junior high student in 1973, I purchased an MIA/POW bracelet. Seems like I read a newspaper article and thought it would be a good way to support the troops. I took my obligation to wear the bracelet until he returned home very seriously. I wore it for 10 years. When the troops began returning home, I would search the newspapers for his name. I am so thankful for the internet because I have become able to learn a little about Captain Smith. I cried at the Vietnam War Memorial and felt honored to make a rubbing of his name. To any of his remaining family, I hope you will find comfort that Captain Smith is still thought about and respected today. I am now 53 years old, and I will always remember him.

****

You will never be forgotten

Hi sweetheart,

There isn't a day I don't think of you and miss you. I will always love you and feel blessed to have been your wife for 3 years and 11 months to the day. The American government has approved an excavation of your 1967 crash site in South Vietnam. They will be searching for any remains with a team of professionals during the dry season of 2015. I still attend MIA meetings in Washington D.C. every year and I will honor you as long as I live.

Hallie 'Bud' William Smith remains Missing in Action.

WARNER 'CRAIG' JACOBSON   Class of '60

Date of birth: 4 June 1942
Date of casualty: 22 June 1968
Home of record: Fresno, California
Branch and Rank: Army, Captain, Field Artillery Unit Commander
Unit: Americal Division, 3rd Battalion, 16th Artillery, A Battery
Awards: National Defense Service Medal, Vietnam Campaign Medal, Purple Heart
Location of name on the Vietnam Wall: 55W, 18
Location of service: South Vietnam, Quang Nam province

I was able to talk with Craig's younger brother Scott and he told me, "Craig was born on June 4, 1942, and was a 1960 graduate of Milwaukie Union High School. Craig was ten years older than me.

"He was very popular at Milwaukie High school especially with the girls," Scott laughs. "Everybody liked him, and he had a great sense of humor. After high school, he attended the University of Oregon and was in the ROTC program. Craig graduated with honors and joined the Army as a Second Lieutenant and sent to Vietnam in January of '68.

"My dad told me he was at the kitchen sink looking out the window when he saw a military vehicle pull into the driveway. He knew right away Craig was killed. They were told by a couple of officers that Craig was killed instantly by a sniper and was slumped over in the helicopter.

"Nobody knew he was shot and killed until after the helicopter had landed. Dad said that after hearing the news, my mom ran to the bedroom, threw herself onto the bed and cried.

"I was spending the night at a friend's house and my older sister was attending Western Washington College. My mom called my friend's mom and told her there has been an accident and to send me home immediately.

"I knew right away, Craig had been wounded, never even considered he died. When I got home, the Officers were gone. Mom said while crying, 'Craig's dead.' I turned to dad and asked if that was true. My dad had tears running down his face, hugs me for the longest time, and cries. It's the first time in my life I ever saw my dad cry.

"We watched him come home at Portland's Airport. There was an observation stand. We watched his casket slowly come down the conveyer belt and the six pall bearers in their dress blues carry his casket to the hearse. We followed them to Lincoln Memorial for his funeral.

"In 1996, I was doing an electrical wiring job at a home in Camas, Washington. I was coming downstairs when the homeowner, Dana, asked me to grab her coffee mug and bring it downstairs. It was a University of Oregon mug. I asked her if she went there. She said, 'Yes in the early sixties.'

"I asked by chance if she knew my brother Craig Jacobson. Dana collapses to her knees in shock and says, 'We dated. We were girlfriend and boyfriend, and I attended his funeral."

"What are the odds?" Scott said in disbelief.

Warner 'Craig' Jacobson is buried at Lincoln Memorial Mausoleum.

DAVID F. POPP Class of '61

Army, Airborne, Helicopter shot down, daughter Cynthia graduated from MHS in '84

Date of birth: 5 April 1943
Date tour began: 14 November 1968
Date of casualty: 14 March 1969
Home of record: Milwaukie, Oregon
Branch and Rank: Army Reserve, Chief Warrant Officer
Unit: 1st Cav Division, 1st Squadron, 9th Cavalry, Trp B
Awards: National Defense Service Medal, Vietnam Campaign Medal, Vietnam Service Medal, Purple Heart
Location of name on the Vietnam Wall: 29W, 39
Location of service: South Vietnam, Tay Ninh Ridge

I spoke with David's daughter Cynthia who told me, "I remember going to my first Gold Star Assembly at Milwaukie as a freshman. It was very emotional, but I remember feeling very proud that my father was being remembered.

"Sadly, I have no memories of him, but I do know that he left for Vietnam on my second birthday. He was MIA in March of '69 and they found his helicopter in January of '70 where it crashed and recovered his remains.

"For years I've have tried to find out what happened and why. The second helicopter flying with them saw nothing. They said it just disappeared. The jungle canopy was so thick, they couldn't see anything. The Army told my mom different versions, not reality. This was very hard on the family.

"I've put a lot of my life into healing from all this. I've attended healing retreats, counseling, and even traveled to Vietnam with Vietnam veterans. Some of the veterans took me on a side trip to find the crash site as they had the coordinates, but the jungle was too thick. On top of a mountain, we could only look down at the area, but it was really helpful for me."

David's wife, Coralee, told me, "I graduated from MHS in '64 and was best friends with David's younger sister, Ruth. She was one of four sisters. Ruth mailed a picture of me to David who was an Army paratrooper stationed in Brussels.

"We met when he came home for R&R, and it was love at first sight. I just loved everything about him. He was so handsome, funny, and adventurous, even took me hunting. We got married in January of '66 and Cindy was born on November 12, 1966.

"David got out of the Army and went to work for his father's dry cleaning business and did not like it. His goal was to fly a helicopter for Oregon Fish and Wildlife, so he reenlisted to become a pilot. After he went MIA, I learned that he volunteered to go to Vietnam. I thought he was ordered. He knew I would have been against him going.

"How I heard the news was, I was driving home and saw a car in front of our home and two soldiers at the front door. I drove by and didn't return until later. Of course, they came back and handed me the telegram that he was missing in action.

"It hit me so hard especially because there was nonexistent information. At first, I let myself believe he lived and maybe found a Vietnamese lady and they found an island to live on. I'll always remember him."

From THE CLACKAMAS COUNTY FALLEN

****
A Brave Marine
I was with you on LZ Sierra, you served your country with honor. Semper Fi my comrade in arms
****
A note from a Great Niece.
David Fred Popp was the great uncle I never met. I hear such wonderful things about him from my grandmother (his sister) who misses him very much. She remembered him as handsome, brave, a dare devil, and sometimes embarrassing because he would always tell boys that they could not date her in school. She remembers once when he got into a fight at school and she ran home telling her parents "They're killing David!" And off went my great grandma and great grandpa Popp to the rescue. I never met them either. I am sure he is with my great aunt Nancy Popp whom I never met and my great aunt who I have met but died a few years back. My grandmother misses him very much and don't worry she is taking care of great aunt. Love, the great niece you never met.

David F. Popp is buried at Willamette National Cemetery.

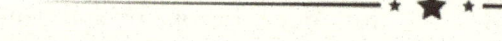

WAYNE CONRAD REINECKE   Class of '64

Date of birth: 8 May 1946
Date of casualty: 12 January 1967
Home of record: Milwaukie, Oregon
Branch and Rank: Navy, Petty Officer Third Class, Aviation Antisubmarine Warfare Technician Third Class
Unit: 7th Fleet, Cvsg 59, Hs 8, TF 77, USS Bennington
Awards: National Defense Service Medal, Vietnam Campaign Medal

Location of name on the Vietnam Wall: 14E, 17
Location of service: North Vietnam, Binh Dinh province

Third Class Reinecke was a member of Helicopter Anti-Submarine Squadron 8, Carrier Anti-Submarine Group aboard the Aircraft Carrier USS BENNINGTON (CVS-20). On January 12, 1967, he was a crew member of a Lockheed Viking Anti-Submarine Helicopter (SH-3A) over North Vietnam when his aircraft crashed. His remains were not recovered. One shipmate reported that he died from friendly fire.

From THE CLACKAMAS COUNTY FALLEN

****

Shipmate V-1 Div. USS Bennington CVS-20
I will never forget. I was there with this hero. Same squadron, air crew, flew side by side. Thanks again and again
****

Shipmate V-1 Div. USS Bennington CVS-20
Wayne, you picked a strange day to help Clayton after his on deck crash the day before. you went with him because he was your friend and he didn't feel well yet. the only reason for the flight, was a milk run to send mail and pickup up a 1st class petty officer then return. your crew was supposed to be in stand down after your deck crash but they released your crew because it was a simple mission. I was on duty in Prifly Control Tower waiting for your helo to return. I was standing under the speaker when your pilot called Mayday and he said he had failures and was coming in hot. he never made it the ship was close enough. My Division officer saw your help go down and i went out on the side deck to count lights, i only saw 3 out of 5 possible, we launched a SAR helo, without warning and we didn't have control of the SAR they opened fire on the floating helo....my mate you and clayton died from Friendly fire, the skipper was bringing the ship around to pickup the helo and crew. it was found out the next day, that a Ltjg in CIC who had control of the SAR thought you crashed on land and ordered the shooting. That night haunts me now . for your rest and peace of mind i managed to find your sister

and Clayton's sister and explained to both families what happened and put the 2 ladies together to help sort and ease your loss. Rest Mate
****

Gone From Us, But NEVER Forgotten.............
Went to see you today Wayne as the Vietnam Traveling Wall came to visit here on Oak Island, NC. As a fellow shipmate and the historian for the USS Bennington Association, I remember 12 January 1967, as it was a few days after Bob Hope and his Christmas show were aboard. SH-3A Tail # 149909 from HS-8 aboard the old girl (BENNINGTON CVS-20) went to a watery grave with you and Clayton Kemp. We NEVER had the opportunity to meet but please know that you will NEVER be forgotten as long as there is one member of the ship that remains on this side of the turf. To you and Clayton, "thank you again shipmate" for your service to our country.
****

48 years ago this tragic event happened but there isn't a 12 January that goes by and you both are not thought of. I'm happy that your sister and Clayton's had the opportunity to meet before. I had always wished that it would happen. As the historian for the USS BENNINGTON Association, I've made sure that the info was added to the Time Line History of the ship for historical purposes. You shall be remembered always.
****

Fellow aircrewman in HS8, my best friend at the time.
Well my friend, it's been a long, long time. Your and Kemp's dying on that dark night was unnecessary. Your pilot, I forget his name, came into the aircrew bar in Sasebo and sat down next to me and cried because your death was his fault. He transferred out soon after. Heard he went to jet jockey training. Your copilot seemed oblivious to his shortcomings on that flight. Several years ago came across a MIA site and was surprised to see your name on it. Wrote the guy who was wearing a MIA bracelet with your name and told him what happened to you. That you're not missing, just resting on the bottom of the South China Sea in a broken bird. Evidently Kemp had been writing letters back home about all kinds

of made up stuff that our squadron was doing. His folks seemed to believe you two died on some secret mission instead of pilot error.
Rest easy old friend, I've not forgotten you.
****

What a surprise to find this site regarding my nephew Wayne. It's hard to believe that it's been 39 years since we were informed of the accident.

Wayne Conrad Reinecke remains Missing in Action.

———————————— * ★ * ————————————

LARRY IANNETTA   Class of '64

Attended Central Catholic HS transferred to Milwaukie High School his Senior year to graduate with friends, Army

Date of birth: 2 May 1946
Date tour began: 24 January 1968
Date of casualty: 29 March 1968
Home of record: Milwaukie, Oregon
Branch and Rank: Army, Specialist Five, Single Rotor Turbine Observation Utility Helicopter Repairman
1st Cavalry Division, 227th Assault Helicopter Battalion, B Company
Awards: National Defense Service Medal, Vietnam Campaign Medal, Vietnam Service Medal, Purple Heart
Location of name on the Vietnam Wall: 47E, 1
Location of service: South Vietnam, Thua Thien province

This was a very emotional interview for Anthony Iannetta.

"Larry was born on May 2, 1946, and my brother was six years older than me. I really looked up to him and admired him. He was a real nice, very loving, gentle, traditional type kid, and very sociable. He was very handsome and a lady's man. He took care of me, looked out for me," said Anthony. Anthony got emotional and apologized.

"He was going to play football his senior year at Milwaukie but broke his leg during the summer. But to understand our family, I have to take you back to my grandfather. He came from Italy at the turn of the century and married an Italian lady who died from the Spanish Flu. After my grandmother passed, he put his children, my father was one of them, into a Catholic orphanage. Grandpa was a strong Catholic.

"My dad lived there until being forced out in the eighth grade. My dad lived on the streets of Spokane during the '20s. He got a job working on Gran Coolie Dam and then the Bonneville Dam. Dad was a very simple, humble hard-working man. Dad had no high school education.

"My dad was good friends with Art Lacy, who bought a B-17, flew it to Oregon and displayed it above his gas station for decades. Dad worked as a welder for Cranston Machine Shop. He met my mother and had my sister Anita. She was twelve years older than me. Six years later, Larry was born, and I was born in '51.

"He believed in FDR (Franklin D. Roosevelt) that we are all in this together. His hardships made our family very strong. We moved to rural Oak Grove, Oregon with my uncle Armin who bought some lots with a shack on it. We built a home next to the shack. He slept in the garage so we could sleep in the house. The roads were still gravel.

"Mom was very patriotic as her brother, Don, was a belly gunner on a B-17 during WWII. They flew out of Italy and was shot down during a Pulaski bombing raid. He was MIA for over a year. We found out later, he was captured and rescued by an all-women Italian underground group. The POW camp was not very well guarded, just by boys, Brown Shirts. The women took him over the Alps to safety.

"We all attended St. John's Catholic school until high school and my Dad wanted Larry to attend Central Catholic. We were super Catholic. Both of us were altar boys. He talked my dad into letting him go to Milwaukie High School his senior year to be with his friends.

"We had no money for going to college, so Larry joined the Army to become a mechanic. The Army paid for him to take correspondence courses from the University of Maryland to get his math scores up so he could take mechanics school training. Larry wanted to be an Airline mechanic after serving.

"Larry was stationed in Germany and volunteered to go. He had such a strong sense of duty. He felt he had to go." Anthony becomes very angry and says, "He didn't have to go. Why did he go?"

He was sent to Vietnam on January 24, 1968, as an Air Chief mechanic for his helicopter and a door gunner on flights. Anthony again gets emotional and is silent for a few seconds before he continues.

"I was in my freshman English class at Putnam High School when the principal and my older sister walked into the classroom to take me home. They never said a word. We walked in silence to her car. Dad was sitting in the back with tears running down his face. That was the first time in my life that I saw my father cry.

"The whole ride home nobody spoke. We got home and Mom was home alone. She walked up to me and said, 'Larry's dead.' My dad just grabbed me and hugged me hard and started sobbing.

"My dad relied on his faith to deal with Larry's loss, always saying, 'He's in a better place.' Mom struggled the rest of her life. She cried herself to sleep for many years."

From THE CLACKAMAS COUNTY FALLEN

****

It's been a long time
It has been 46 years. Long time, much has changed. We are friends with the Vietnamese now. New wars have started, in Iraq and Afghanistan. The Rolling Stones are still touring, after 50 years. Camp Evans was turned over to the 101st Airborne in the fall, we moved to An Loc near the border across from Saigon, living in a rubber plantation. See you soon.

Larry Iannetta is buried at Willamette National Cemetery.

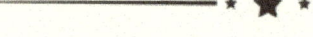

MARTIN DIETRICH   Class of '64, Army

I was able to talk with Martin's younger brother Paul Dietrich.

"Marty was born in '48, and we all grew up on a farm in Oregon City out in Beavercreek. Our Dad, Charles, was a WWII veteran who landed on the beaches of Anzio and fought against the Germans in Italy until being wounded. His parents, immigrated from Berlin, Germany at the turn of the century. My mom, Dorothy, was one-hundred percent German. While they lived on the farm, she actually cooked on a wood stove and was a great cook.

"Our dad was an amazing man, a jack of all trades. He drove a team of six horses hauling gravel out of a quarry as a teenager in the late twenties. He logged some during the Great Depression using a chain saw with a six-foot blade and helped build the old Oregon City court house in '36. He was great at growing vegetables on our farm. But, they sold the farm and we moved to California and my dad went to work for the Government.

"My sixteen-years-older-than-me brother, Ralph 'Butch', served in the Army from 1950 to 1964. But after he became disabled with severe kidney problems, had to leave the Army in '64. His health issues would lead to an early death in '71.

"Marty was a great big brother. He was six years older and always helped me, helped me with my homework, and basically looked after me. He loved planes. He would build Balsa wood airplanes and showed me how to build them. Marty joined the Civil Air Patrol as he wanted to fly. He had a summer job in '62 to '64 loading the fire bombers in Santa Rosa used for firefighting.

"We moved back to Oregon, in Milwaukie off of Oak Grove Blvd. and Marty attended Milwaukie High School his senior year. After graduating he attended college as a freshman but was worried that his average grades would lead to him being drafted, so he decided to join because he wanted to fly.

"On July 18, 1967, I was home when a State Trooper came to the door to inform us of Marty's death. The Army had an escort man bring his body home from Alabama. The escort man actually spent the night in our home. He handled all the arraignments for Marty's funeral and burial at Willamette National Cemetery.

"It was hard on all of us, but my mother is the strongest woman I've ever known. She only cried in private. My parents were old school tough. You had to just move on.

"Marty loved flying helicopters. He told me, 'Helicopters don't fly, they just beat the air into submission. It's like rubbing your stomach, patting the top of your head, and flying the helicopter at the same time.' After saying this, he would always laugh.

"His death hit me hard, and I started getting into a lot of trouble. I dropped out of high school and pressured my dad into letting me join the Army in '72. They had lost two sons from serving and my mom was not for it. We were at the kitchen table and Dad shoved the papers across the table to Mom. She signed it. I am convinced that if I had not joined the Army, I would be in prison today. It saved my life. I made a successful career out of it.

"About a year after Marty's death, my mom told me that she had a dream and she said, 'Marty came to me last night and told me he's okay and happy and in a better place. I feel so much better.'"

Martin Dietrich is buried at Willamette National Cemetery.

WILLIAM BLOCK   Class of '65, Army

Date of birth: 13 July 1947
Date tour began: 8 January 1968
Date of casualty: 12 February 1968
Home of record: Milwaukie, Oregon
Branch and Rank: Army Selective Service, Private First Class, Light Weapons Infantry
Unit: 25th Infantry Division, 1st Battalion, 27th Infantry, B Company
Awards: National Defense Service Medal, Vietnam Service Medal, Vietnam Campaign Medal, Combat Infantryman Badge, Purple Heart
Location of name on the Vietnam Wall: 39E, 2
Location of service: South Vietnam, Gia Dinh province

I was able to talk with Dr. Jim Block, Williams's older brother.

"I need to start with my parents to lend some understanding about our family. My father, Harold, flew a B-17 Pathfinder during WWII out of England where he met and married my mom, Lilian, an English war bride. She was from the Comkee area, which was heavily bombed. Her family's first home was destroyed during a bombing raid. The area is now a Memorial Park. I was born in September of '45 in London. My mom was pregnant with me while living in the subway tunnels during the bombing raids.

"In May of 1946, after the war's end, when I was six months old, we boarded the Queen Mary for New York. We traveled all the way to Oregon moving in with my dad's parents' house on River Road. My brother, William John Block, was born on July 13, 1947. His middle name was chosen to honor our mom's dad and her brother who was in an elite Irish unit who landed on beaches of Anzio where he was killed in action.

"Bill was a typical, playful, happy-go-lucky boy. My parents eventually bought a home in Oak Grove. Mom stayed at home until we started school and then she worked in downtown Portland at J.K. Gills. It was my job to prepare meals to be cooked after Mom or Dad got home. Dad worked at a bakery and was allowed to bring home the donut holes. This was before they started to sell them. But Bill preferred eating out at the first fast food restaurant. They had a Wiz Burger hamburger that only costed nineteen cents. We would go there after sports to get one.

"On a side note of interest, my dad helped his friend Art Lacy bring the B-17 to Milwaukie. I remember playing in the plane above the Bomber gas station. Being two years older, I was always looking out for Bill. We loved playing sports and both of us played basketball and baseball for Oak Grove School. We played on many great teams.

"At Milwaukie High School, we both played basketball and baseball. It was when that famous football coach who went on to coach in the pros was our football coach, but I can't remember his name."

"Mouse Davis, I played for him at Portland State," I added.

"Yes, he was loved by many at MHS. Bill played basketball with the great Rick Whelen who went on to play at Oregon State University. They were both drafted, but Rick was recruited to play basketball for the Army. Bill was really good at working on cars and was a mechanic. He loved cars. His first car he bought by saving his own money was a '64, 357 Chevelle SS.

"He was drafted and inducted on August 2, 1967. Our grandma was so upset with the news she had a heart attack on her drive over to say goodbye. My grandpa, offered to drive him to Canada or just join the Coast Guard. But Bill refused. He felt it was his duty.

"He was assigned to the 25th Infantry Division, 1st Battalion, 27th Infantry, B Company. The 27th were called the Wolfhounds. Bill was killed during the Tet Offensive at 12:00 on the 12th of February 1968 in the Gia Dinh province near the Cambodian Border.

"Mom was visiting a relative's grave site when at the moment Bill was killed she collapsed and knew at that moment her son was dead. We have no explanation for this.

"I was attending college at the University of Chicago when a Chaplin and an officer came to tell my parents. My parents had fought Bill's going to Vietnam as he was scared of guns. They even took him to a psychiatrist to confirm this. My dad contacted Oregon Senator Wayne Morris to help, and he tried. We all felt since he was a mechanic, why couldn't he do that?

"We believe the Army retaliated by putting him into the infantry. As soon as he got there, he was assigned to Point. His best friend learned about Bill's death in the Stars and Stripes paper before we knew.

"Dad did not handle this well at all. A friend of the family Les Peake who owned Les Peake Memorial handled everything. But my dad forced Les into opening the metal casket to see Bill's body. It was the first time I saw my dad cry. He was unable to even identify him, but I could because there was a birth mark on his temple. There were no visible wounds, but I noticed that the lower body was gone.

"How did your mother handle this?"

Without any hesitation, Jim responded, "She's English," and then laughed. "You know 'stiff upper lip'. She never cried in public only in private.

"To this day, I'm haunted by what he could have become had he not died. This just tore our family apart in terms of our future, but we lived. Bill gave me a gift to look to the future, and I pushed myself to get my doctorate and pursue a career in Academics.

"Both mom and dad went into a long very quiet period. Dad was never the same. Mom eventually recovered.

"Later, I was drafted, but refused to go, and I believed they were going to arrest me. Mom went to the Portland recruiting office and had to prove that her son was killed in action in Vietnam. I was allowed to continue college working on my Master's degree and then my Doctorate."

I was able to speak with Tom Dietz, Class of '65, about Bill.

"Bill and I both attended Oak Grove Elementary. We played baseball together in grade school and he was good enough to continue playing at MHS, where he lettered. Besides baseball, Bill's other love was cars. After graduation from Milwaukie, he attended Multnomah Junior College, which we all called MIT; Multnomah in Town, and received a degree in auto mechanics.

"My high school memories of Bill are deeply rooted in his basement. His family had a pool table, and we all spent many hours after school honing our pool skills. It also helped that his mother was such a welcoming presence. She always made us feel at home whenever we came over. On the weekends a favorite pastime was cruising Yaws, the Speck, and Broadway. The fact that Bill had a car made this possible.

"Bill and I and another friend all became eligible for the draft at about the same time in '67. The other friend and I joined the Navy reserve, which had only a two-year active duty requirement, and more importantly, no waiting list as the reserves did.

"We urged Bill to join up with us, but he had some pretty strong feelings about the Navy uniform and opted to be drafted instead. I do not have any details of Bill's time in Vietnam, except that he was there for a very short time before being killed."

I spoke to Loren Gramson, Army, Vietnam about Bill

"Bill was a typical young man of the early '60s. I never met a nicer guy. I was drafted and met Bill at Portland's Induction Center on August 7, 1967. We became best friends. Hell, we were just kids.

"Also with us was Milwaukie High School great basketball player Rick Whelen. He was drafted with us, and we all reported together. Rick was a great basketball player at OSU. But Rick was not sent to Vietnam because the Army wanted him to play basketball for them. I actually walked on at OSU freshmen's basketball team and made it. I walked away from school later that spring as I was all shook up over several friends who had been sent to Vietnam.

"We spent nine months at Fort Lewis together. And we would sit around and talk about cars and girls and lament where we were. It seems like it was just yesterday.

"When he was told he was going to Vietnam, Bill told me, 'I'm going to get killed, I just know it.' Of course, I would tell him not to talk like that, that's not the right attitude to have, but he repeated it again. Bill was just not cut out to be a soldier, he was real quiet and fun loving. Such a tragedy.

"I still have the picture of me, his mom and dad, his brother Jim, his girlfriend Gay, and Bill looking sharp in his uniform. We were all saying goodbye as he boarded the plane. Everyone is smiling. The last picture I took was Bill and his mother hugging. Little did we know, this would be their final goodbyes.

"Bill told me again, 'I'm not going to make it home.'

"The day I arrived in Vietnam was the same day Bill was killed, February 12, 1968. It would be six weeks until I found out. This has haunted me for decades. One day I started reading the names of KIAs in Stars and Stripes. It was right in the middle of the Tet Offensive, and it was getting really nasty. Then I saw Bill's name and it hit me like a sledgehammer.

"In '75, I contacted the Class of '65's ten-year reunion committee as I wanted to find any living relatives of Bill's. I learned his father had passed and his mother moved to California to live with Bill's brother Jim. Jim and I were able to connect, and we are friends to this day.

"About my time in Vietnam, when it was my time to go, my parents could not take me to the airport, my brothers took me. My parents were never the same. Getting on that plane was the hardest thing I ever did. I was in the Mekong Delta, and it was wet and damp all the time.

"I remember walking over brown leaves and seeing all these dead trees. Twenty-five years later, I had a VA doctor tell me why I was having health issues, but if he wrote down the truth, he would be fired.

"Coming home, I landed at Portland Airport around one in the morning. There were no protesters, but I'll never forget this little girl about two or three years old looked at me and smiled. I smiled back. Her mom jerked her daughter around and she turned their backs to me. Then it hit me I was wearing my uniform.

"How do you boil down what you remember about someone into a few paragraphs? I don't know. I will do my best to be brief. And I can't help but include some thoughts about that time and place and a comparison to today."

I received a letter from Bill's girlfriend at the time Gay (Lively) Adams. She gave me permission to have it in the book.

> William J Block was a young man with hopes and dreams. I'm sure that all young men and women do. He was a guy who always took responsibility for himself. He had brown hair and a ruddy complexion from his English ancestry and wonderful eyes. He was tall with broad shoulders, built for strength that was all the more evident after he came home from basic training.
>
> He mirrored his dad in that way. He held himself to a high moral standard and had strong ideas of right and wrong. He was not boastful or conceited. But he expected himself to do things in the right way.
>
> That said, if he made a mistake he didn't try to blame it on circumstances or someone else. He stood tall, squared his shoulders and faced it. Nor did he dwell on it. He learned his lesson and moved on. He was an easy person to talk to and to know. Very honest and straight forward with an easy humor. He was very tuned in to other people. We didn't go to school together, but I surmised he was at least somewhat popular in high school. We couldn't go anywhere in the city together without someone honking their horn at him to say hi. And he had several tight friendships.
>
> Bill knew he had a duty to serve in the armed forces and that he would need to complete that. In those days, the draft left no real choice on that matter. You could go to college or try to use some other loop hole to delay it, but you were obligated to go thru the physical for the draft – and if you passed, you were given a number and had to serve when called.

.You could claim to be a conscientious objector or try to escape to Canada to avoid it all - there were many who did that. But that was not something Bill would do. Bill never had a desire to be a warrior nor any idea of glory from being in the service. But he never shirked from his feeling of responsibility to serve either.

He wanted to do his duty and come home. His dream for after he came home was to settle down and have a family, and to build a house with a round door. As to making a living, he wanted to do something with his hands – maybe become a mechanic as he liked to work on cars.

He told his mom that I was the girl he wanted to marry. I knew his time in the Army would change him, but that was not what I worried about. I wanted him to come home safe and sound. I wrote him a letter almost every day starting with when he went into basic training, and I promised to wait for his return.

In one of his letters to me written during basic training he wrote "They are trying to change me into an animal, and I won't let them." In my reply I said, "Learn what they are teaching you about how to survive, and come home to me." He was always on my mind. Like many soldiers, I know he knew fear and worried he wouldn't make it home. But he still would not turn away from his duty. Courage is not the absence of fear. It is what you do in spite of it.

Bill's parents went to the Governor of Oregon for help to get their son reassigned from infantry to another area. They were successful, and Bill was offered a chance to move to a different division. But he refused. By that time Bill was bonded to those he served with. I've learned a lot since then about the brotherhood that grows between soldiers. He was dedicated to standing with his unit no matter what the cost. Brave, loyal, responsible, dedicated. Who knows what Bill might have accomplished in his life had he lived.

When Bill's mom called to tell me he was missing in action, I fell silent. I went numb. I thought about that empty place the world would have by not having Bill still here. In that moment, I didn't let myself feel. I held on to the hope that he was still alive somewhere. I stayed in that state of mind right up to when they found his body and brought him home. I think I went into a sort of shock after that. It took a long time for me to deal with my pain.

I am told Bill got to Vietnam right in the midst of the Tet offensive. It was February 1968. At the time, I don't think anyone realized what a turning point that was in the war. From the time he left to go there, I watched all the newsreels looking for his face.

I think he was only in Vietnam a week before he went missing. And the protests against the war were at full force. People who showed no respect for our country treated those who served with disdain. It caused unbelievable pain to those who served and to those who loved them.

The protestors called the soldiers all kinds of names and chanted "down with the establishment," and men were often referred to as "male chauvinist pigs." It was as though the protesters blamed all those who served for the war. It is not the soldier who makes that decision. And with the draft in place, other than turning against their country, those young men had no choice on serving or not.

The actions of those protesters showed me they did not understand the courage and character of a man who would live out his duty to his country. The things they said will always hurt my heart. They were out in full force at Bill's funeral, too. A huge crowd, yelling, jeering, pushing. It was all a blur to me. Still is. It took years for me to get my balance back after Bill died. For a long time I thought I would never return to myself or fall in love again. I will never forget him and the love we shared. Bill taught me a lot about what to appreciate in a man.

There are many Vets from the Vietnam war who now do all they can to ensure there is support for our soldiers when they come home from war or even just from serving in the armed forces. They don't want our service men and women to ever go thru what they did when they came home from Vietnam. I see It as a part of the legacy of all who served in those days - and as a tribute to them. I hope it is a tradition that will never fade. I see it as a reflection of at least some of the lessons we learned from that war.

I pray our leaders, military and civilian, do not take the decision to send our young people into danger lightly. And we need to do all we can to protect and honor our soldiers. The way our exit from Afghanistan was handled fills me with anger. It was so disrespectful of our service personnel. These people who serve are surely one of our most precious and valuable resources.

Today, our military people are not in harm's way because of the draft They are there because they feel a responsibility to serve and protect the country they love even if it costs them their life. My father served in World War II and used to say, "I may disagree with what you are saying, but I will fight to the death for your right to say it."

They were willing to give their life so we will continue to be free and so we will not have another World War or another 9-11. When all is said and done, Bill and those that served in Vietnam all share that same level of dedication. My husband also served in Vietnam. All who serve whether in the past or today, deserve our respect, our thanks, and our admiration. We are all forever indebted to them.

William Block is buried at Wilhelm's Portland Memorial Mausoleum.

RODNEY 'KEITH' ARNOLD — Class of '65

Keith left behind a young wife. Keith's call sign was "Dustoff".

Date of birth: 14 August 1947
Date tour began: 19 March 1970
Date of casualty: 25 April 1970
Home of record: Milwaukie, Oregon
Branch and Rank: Army Reserve, Helicopter Pilot
Unit: 1st Cav Division, 15th Medical Battalion
Awards: National Defense Service Medal, Vietnam Service Medal, Vietnam Campaign Medal
Location of name on the Vietnam Wall: 11W, 48
Location of service: South Vietnam, Binh Duong province

From THE CLACKAMAS COUNTY FALLEN

****
My Cousin Keith, UH1-H Huey Pilot, 15th Med Bn, 1st Cav Div. Keith, as these years have passed, I have searched for you in your friends and myself, finding our love and admiration for you, a common bond. I know you are with Uncle Glenn, and what joy it brought him to see you

again, as he missed you so very much. The pride I feel for you was first felt by him, passed to me as a precious gift, your memory to be held strong, to be held safe. I heard a Huey flying over my home the other day, and thinking of you, I went outside to glimpse it. Standing in my back yard I watched that sleek bird with a single light toning, head west toward the ocean...and I waved to it, and said 'hi' to you out loud...I think you heard me. I think you also know how proud I am of you, and how proud I have always been, to be your cousin. God Bless you always, and thank you for staying near to me.

CRASH INFORMATION ON U.S. ARMY HELICOPTER UH-1H TAIL NUMBER 68-16429 [From vhpa.org]

> The crew of UH-1H (68-16429) was performing a test flight. The purpose of the test flight was to perform an N1 topping check. The aircraft departed Phuoc Vinh at approximately 1030 hours and proceeded to the units test flight area south of the Song Be bridge, RVN. At approximately 1100 hours, according to witnesses on the ground, aircraft 68-16429, which was heading in a northeasterly direction, began violently spinning to the right at an altitude of approximately 1200 feet above ground level. Witnesses also stated that at approximately 700 feet above ground level the aircraft began to recover from the spin and that at approximately 400 feet above ground level the aircraft again began to spin, finally crashing in a rubber plantation 8,000 meters to the southwest of Phuoc Vinh. The three occupants of 68-16429, pilot WO1 Rodney K. Arnold and passengers SFC James H. Brooks Jr. and SP6 James T. Conway, survived the initial impact of the crash but succumbed to their injuries subsequent to the accident.

Rodney 'Keith' Arnold is buried at Willamette National Cemetery.

MICHEAL GREELEY   Class of '66, Marines

Date of birth: 22 March 1948
Date of casualty: 26 May 1967
Home of record: Milwaukie, Oregon
Branch and Rank: Marine Corps, Private First Class, Rifleman
Unit: 1st Marine Division, 3rd Battalion, 5th Marines, K Company
Awards: National Defense Service Medal, Vietnam Campaign Medal, Purple Heart
Location of name on the Vietnam Wall: 20E, 116
Location of service: South Vietnam, Quang Tin province

I was able to talk to Michael's brother Mark Greeley, MHS Class of '68.

"Michael was a good brother. We were typical brothers who fought, argued, and played together a lot as we were just two years apart.

"I remember our grandpa giving my brother Michael a 1956 Oldsmobile and he turned it into a hot rod. He put in an Oldsmobile Rocket V8 engine with a VM transmission back in the turbo hydro days. It was the fastest around. I helped him a lot.

"We would cruise Broadway, Specks at Foster and Powell and the old Tic Toc. Michael raced others a lot and claims he never lost. He was a great guy who was well liked and had no enemies except those he beat racing," laughing.

"The Marines came to our home and told my parents that Michael was killed in action. We were a large family with lots of laughter and that changed overnight. My parents would never talk about it. My cousin, also a Marine, escorted his body home from California. He identified his body and told mom, 'You don't need to see his body.'

"His body was taken to Peake Memorial in Milwaukie, and Mom was so distraught that she tried to open the casket with a screwdriver to take the screws out. Peake Memorial had to grind the screws down. It was so hard on our family. Every year we visit his grave at Willamette National Cemetery. In fact, we have a total of twelve relatives up there.

"We were told by the military Michael had been shot in the back of the head by a sniper while he was trying to rescue a wounded Marine. The Marines told us he died instantly, but my parents received five letters from his Marine buddies he served with. One of them wrote that Michael lived for about five minutes, and they were all there for him.

"It was hard on us all. I still miss him."

I was also able to talk with Michael's other brother Mitchell Greely, Class of '72.

"Michael was six years older than me, and my best memories of my older brother was he loved cars and working on them. Our grandpa gave him his Oldsmobile. Bill took the chrome off, painted it grey, which was a popular color back then. The he turned the car in to a hot rod. He would take me for rides in it and I loved it.

"I kept the hood ornaments for years, but sadly they were destroyed when my storage shed burnt down a couple of years ago."

From THE CLACKAMAS COUNTY FALLEN

****
Dear PFC Michael Greeley,
Thank you for your service as a Rifleman. It has been too long, and it's about time for us all to acknowledge the sacrifices of those like you who answered our nation's call. Please watch over America, it stills needs your strength, courage and faithfulness. Rest in peace with the angels.

****

NOT FORGOTTEN

Michael, Although we never met, I just want you to know you are not forgotten. You gave the ultimate sacrifice, your life for what you believed in. Sleep well my friend and thank you for protecting our freedoms.

****

Michael Greeley is buried at Willamette National Cemetery.

--- ★ ---

DONALD SCHAFER   Class of '66, Navy

Date of birth: 15 April 1947
Date of casualty: 1 May 1968
Home of record: Milwaukie, Oregon
Branch and Rank: Navy Reserve, Seaman Apprentice
Unit: 7th Fleet, USS Genesee
Awards: National Defense Service Medal, Vietnam Campaign Medal
Location of name on the Vietnam Wall: 53E, 40
Location of service: South Vietnam, Quang Tri province

I was able to speak with Don's sister Barbara Schafer Beauchemin, Class of '73.

"Don was one of my three older brothers, Robert and Ken. He was the oldest, eight years older than me. I was the baby of the family. To me, he was the ultimate big brother, he always had my back. He was the enforcer and kept my other brothers from picking on me.

"He was a natural leader. We lived across a field from Albertsons, and Don started working there as soon as he was old enough to get a job. He was very reliable, a very hard worker, and he worked as many hours as possible a week he could get after school.

"We had a cousin who was killed in Vietnam whose funeral we attended in Colorado. Don found out there he was drafted so he joined the Navy.

"To this day my brother, Ken, who was three years older than me, and I cannot explain what we experienced at school the very day Don was killed in Vietnam. We were sitting together during a break, and I felt this strange, bizarre feeling come over me. Everything felt off.

"Before I could tell my brother, he said, 'I felt something very strange. It felt weird like something is wrong.' I told him in disbelief that I felt something strange too. It wasn't much later that my mother came to school and took us home and told us the horrible news.

"The military had come to our home earlier to tell my parents. Of course, none of us were ever the same. My father took it the hardest as he felt cheated and missed Don his entire life.

"His body was lost in water at first and was finally found and retrieved many days later. Dad was a dentist and our dentist, and he was able to identify his badly decomposed body with Don's teeth.

"It wasn't until 1982 that we received Don's duffle bag. Nobody in our family would touch it especially Dad. I finally got the courage to go through it. His dirty clothes were in there and I just lost it crying.

"I remember my freshman year at Milwaukie High School, I asked the teacher if I could hold Don's Candle during the annual Gold Star Assembly. The teacher in charge told me no, and I still don't know why.

"But many Milwaukie high teachers told me I had the same mannerisms as Don. That always felt good. I still miss my big brother."

From coffeltdatabase.org and eaglespeak.us

SA Donald R. Schafer was a seaman apprentice serving on the USS Genesee (AOG-8), a gasoline tanker. On May 1, 1968, the Genesee arrived at Tan My and anchored alongside a pipeline buoy. US Army LARC-801 came out to assist the Genesee connecting to the pipeline. Genesee crewmen SA Donald R. Schafer and DC2 Harley Cowans climbed aboard the LARC and hooked the ship's hoses to the connection on the buoy. Those on board Genesee witnessed the LARC explode and burst into flames. The stunned observers saw one of the men blown through the air and into the water. The LARC was completely engulfed by a lake of fire as the motor whaleboat from Genesee got underway to rescue the crew. SF3 Tony Neil, aboard the whaleboat, dove into the flame-covered water to attempt a rescue. Swimming under water and pushing the flames away with his hands when he surfaced for a breath, Neil located the LARC's driver, SP4 Tommy Miller, who was without a life jacket and badly burned. Neil managed to get the burned driver back to the ship. The others on the whaleboat fished Cowans and another LARC crewman out of the water but could not locate Schafer. By this time, LCM-92 and 18 other LARCs were on site searching for the missing seaman but without any luck. Army units recovered Shafer's body a week later. An investigation determined that a spark from the LARC's exhaust caused avgas from the leaking hose line to ignite, destroying the LARC, killing Shafer and injuring three others.

Donald Schafer is buried at Willamette National Cemetery

LARRY E. DIKEMAN   Class of '67, Army

Date of birth: 14 August 1948
Date tour began: 24 February 1969
Date of casualty: 31 May 1969
Home of record: Milwaukie, Oregon
Branch and Rank: Army Selective Service, Corporal, Armor Intelligence Specialist

Unit: 9th Infantry Division, 3rd Squadron, 5th Cavalry, B Troop
Awards: National Defense Service Medal, Vietnam Service Medal, Vietnam Campaign Medal
Location of name on the Vietnam Wall: 23W, 25
Location of service: South Vietnam, Thua Thien province
I was able to talk with Larry's younger brother Dean Dikeman.

"Mr. and Mrs. Dale A. Dikeman son was born in Portland on August 14, 1948. We moved to Milwaukie, and I was a fifth grader at Hector Campbell Grade School. Larry was a seventh grader at Milwaukie Junior High School.

"Larry had scarlet fever as a child, and this left him with some health issues. We shared a bedroom upstairs. He was a little slower with thinking. He was my older brother, and I was faster and stronger than him and sadly, I picked on him a lot. He was a nice kid, introverted and shy, not involved with anything in high school. I regret not being able to build a stronger relationship or a bond with him.

"Our dad gave him the family's '56 Ford, and we were rebuilding the engine and putting it back in when our mom brings the mail to us. It was Larry's draft notice. Dad told Larry to go back in the house and said he and I would finish up. Dad made a mistake and yelled out the F-word. I'd never heard him cuss like that before.

"Larry graduated from Milwaukie High School in '67 and reported to the Army soon after. He was sent to Vietnam on February 24, 1969. I was not drafted in '69, but I was very nervous because after Larry's death. I did not want to go.

"Larry was twenty years old when he was killed May 31, 1969, when a tree fell on him during clearing operations in the A Sau Valley. South Vietnam, Thua Thien province. The Army came to the house and told my parents. They were broken over his death and never got over it."

From THE CLACKAMAS COUNTY FALLEN

****

THANK YOU
Dear Cpl Larry Dikeman,

Thank you for your service as an Armor Reconnaissance Specialist. Your 49th anniversary is soon, so sad. Memorial Day is coming up, and we remember all you who gave their all. It has been too long, and it's about time for us all to acknowledge the sacrifices of those like you who answered our nation's call. Please watch over America, it stills needs your strength, courage and faithfulness. Rest in peace with the angels.

****

Dear CPL Larry Ernest Dikeman, sir

As an American, I would like to thank you for your service and for your sacrifice made on behalf of our wonderful country. The youth of today could gain much by learning of heroes such as yourself, men and women whose courage and heart can never be questioned. May God allow you to read this, and may He allow me to someday shake your hand when I get to Heaven to personally thank you. May he also allow my father to find you and shake your hand now to say thank you; for America, and for those who love you.

Larry Dikeman is buried at Willamette National Cemetery

DANIEL IRVIN MAMBRETTI

Class of '69, Army

Date of birth: 6 March 1951
Date tour began: 10 December 1969
Date of casualty: 30 January 1970
Home of record: Milwaukie, Oregon

Branch and Rank: Army, Private First Class, Light Weapons Infantry
Unit: 1st Cavalry Division, 2nd Battalion, 7th Cavalry, B Company
Awards: National Defense Service Medal, Vietnam Campaign Medal, Vietnam Service Medal, Purple Heart, Combat Infantryman Badge
Location of name on the Vietnam Wall: 14W, 82
Location of service: South Vietnam, Tay Ninh province

I was able to talk to Daniel's sister Charlene Mambretti Wrisley, Clackamas Class of '65.

"Number one was he was very loved by all but especially our family. Because at that time he was the only boy not only for my parents but for my mother's sister Evelyn. That's right all girls and just imagine being the only boy with seven girls. He also was very loved by many. He had a wonderful personality and was also at one time starting a band. He was the vocalist and had a great voice.

"Danny joined the army, he volunteered with his good friend Donny Anderson on what they called the buddy system where they were assured to be in Germany for the duration and not Vietnam. But sadly, my brother could not make himself parachute from a plane, so he was reassigned and that is why he ended up in Vietnam.

"Needless to say, my brother's friend Donny Anderson never quite got over the guilt because he talked my brother into joining. But I and my family never ever blamed him. It was Danny's choice to not wait to be drafted. Also, Donny's brother Ray was my brother's best friend and he struggled to get on with his life after losing his best friend.

"My brother's memorial service was the biggest to that date for any service member in Milwaukie. There were so many there at St. John's that people were crowded out the door. It was heartwarming, yet heart breaking.

"I often think of what could have been and what he would have accomplished, and I like to believe that he would have been a great person and a loving father and husband too. On a side note, my brother was the apple of my father's eye. No one loved him more than that man, and when my father passed, he did so on March 6, my brother's birthdate."

I also spoke with Daniel's friend David Branham, Class of '70.

"Danny was a real good guy with a great sense of humor. I remember going over to his parents' house for a going away party the night before Danny and his best friend Don Anderson reported to boot camp. They joined on the buddy system, but the Army transferred Don into Airborne and he was never sent to Vietnam. Danny was sent to Vietnam.

"His parents were such good people, and I got closer to them after Dan's funeral. They kind of latched on to me. I joined the Army to avenge Danny's death."

I also spoke with Daniel's friend Chuck Kersey, Class of '70.

"Danny Mambretti was a good friend. He taught me a lot about sports and life. He loved the Yankees and when we watched the game on tv, we had to stand and put your hand over your heart during the National Anthem. He was a good person. My mom would get him birthday and Christmas presents."

In addition, I was able to speak with Kat Beverlye, MHS Class of '72 about Daniel.

"I knew Danny Mambretti, he used to date a good friend of mine. Even though he was a few years older than I, he was always very nice. And when in school, he would watch out for me. My freshman year I kind of got picked on.

"Once Danny saw the kids giving me a hard time, he very calmly walked over to them said something very quiet to them, and they all left. I don't know what he said to them, but they never bothered me again. I will always treasure his friendship. He was one of the good guys."

From THE CLACKAMAS COUNTY FALLEN

****
Remembering my first love.
Danny Mambretti was my first love. I often think of him and wonder what kind of a man he would have grown up to be, if he would have been allowed to grow up. I love him still.
****
My Uncle Danny
Danny was my uncle; my mom's name is Diane Millican (AKA) Mambretti. Though he died three years before I was born, there will always be a piece of him with me. Some people say that I look like him in many ways. Now he is in heaven with his mom Verna, his sister Rosealee, his G'ma Rose and his aunt Evelin. I wish I could have met him. I love you Uncle Danny.
It is now 3/6/2004, Danny's birthday, he would have been 53 yrs. old. Today his father Leo Mambretti passed away from Alzheimer's at St. Andrew's home for Alzheimer's. He was 89 yrs. old. Some might say he wanted to tell his son happy birthday in person. He loved Danny so much, now they can be together in heaven for eternity. I love and miss you Papa :(
****
My Uncle Danny...where are you?
I will never know you-
But I know you so well.
From my mother and her family
your memory lives today.
I respect and honor you for what you have done- giving your life for us to move on.

Thank you, Uncle Danny, for being so brave. I look at your picture and think of what you might have been- how my life might be different if you were around. So I ask you now, Uncle Danny, where are you? I miss you and love you more than you'll know.

****

I Remember!

Daniel, I remember that night in the jungles of Vietnam, Tay Ninh Province. We were in our Night Defensive Position (NDP) and we lost you! God Bless you. I think of you and the others we lost every day! It is almost Memorial Day and what better time to Remember!

****

my mother's love.

Danny, you were my mom's first love. she was only a child, when you went off to Vietnam, but my grandmother tells me about how my mother would run to the window or out to the fence whenever you walked by and wave and holler at you. my mom often tells stories about you and I can tell how much she misses you by the look in her eyes. I recently went up to the Oregon Vietnam wall and rubbed your name. I was about to frame it when I came across your picture online. I gave it to her as an early Christmas present, when she unwrapped it, she burst into tears. I couldn't help but cry with her, she looked at me with such love in her eyes and said, 'that's my Danny'. you'll always be my mother's favorite memory; she talks about you and how much she loved you to this day. I've come to know you even though I was born in 1995, 26 years since you lost your life. I only hope to someday be lucky enough to find love strong enough to last over 45 years like my mother's love has lasted for you.

****

memorial day

I brought you some flowers on memorial day Danny. I know I didn't personally know you, my family did and I'll always be here to remember you.

Daniel Mambretti is buried at Willamette National Cemetery.

IMPORTANT ACKNOWLEDGEMENTS

BENJAMIN BLAIR (LYTLE)   Co-Author, Editor

Benjamin is an expatriate living in Morioka, Japan, where he has been teaching for over twenty years as an adjunct lecturer at universities. He graduated from Western Oregon University with a Bachelor's in Public Health Education, minoring in Eastern Philosophy. He also earned his Master's in Teaching at Lewis & Clark College in Portland, Oregon.

Benjamin is married to Yukari and has two children, Marina and Leon.

Benjamin is my stepson from my first marriage to his mother, Lorraine. I met him when he was in the fifth grade, and I was lucky to have him as a student for four years in Strength Training at Milwaukie High School. I also coached him in football, wrestling, and track and field.

He was extremely intelligent as a youngster, and was a very gifted athlete, and had a strong work ethic. At Milwaukie High School, he was a three-sport athlete. He did football, wrestling (coach Jim Gadberry pressured him into wrestling his junior and senior years, and he ended up advancing in matches at the State Championships), and track and field (4×400m relay, 4×1600m relay, 200m, and shotput).

It was in football however where he excelled. As a freshman, Benjamin started on special teams and was a backup linebacker. He even scored a touchdown as running back in a varsity game. And all this only as a freshman. He started both ways his sophomore, junior, and senior years. He was a natural leader.

He was not only First Team All-League as an Offensive Guard and Inside Linebacker, but was the Three Rivers League Defensive Player of the Year. He was named to the First Team All-State team on Offense and Defense. He played in Oregon's Shrine All-Star Football game and received a full athletic scholarship to play at Idaho State University. But his most impressive honor was being selected the Three Rivers league's Scholar-Athlete of the Year.

After university, Benjamin decided to spend a year overseas, which led him to live permanently in Japan teaching English. We have always kept in touch over the years, and he has always considered and called me Dad, which means the world to me.

Benjamin offered to help me and Bob Christianson co-author and edit Remembrance Volume I, and is the co-author of Remembrance Volume II and III.

Benjamin is so thorough with his editing and writing skills and fact-checks everything. I owe him quite a few beers for all of the misspellings of names that he catches. I'm very blessed, lucky, and grateful for his devotion and impressive work. I'm also extremely proud of him, and I know his mother, Lorraine, is too.

I love you, son!

KELLY SCHAEFFER (NEFF)   Second Editor

Kelly is a former Strength Training student of mine at Milwaukie High School and graduated in 1999. She was very involved in sports and activities. She was an All-League softball outfielder, played soccer, and was the class president.

She graduated from Western Oregon University with a Bachelor of Arts in English-Linguistics, minor in business, in 2003, and earned her Master of Arts in Teaching Degree in 2004. She was the Western Oregon Journal Copy Editor from 2001 to 2003. She taught English Language Arts at Scio High School in Scio, Oregon from 2005 to 2008, and then at Newberg High School in Newberg, Oregon from 2008 to 2018. And from 2018 to 2022, she was a substitute teacher in Portland and West Linn.

Kelly is currently a Language Arts Teacher at Willamette Connections Academy, a youth sports coach, and an editor.

She is married to Colin Schaeffer, a Milwaukie alum class of 1999, who is currently teaching math and social studies there and who was the former head football coach. They have two boys, David and James.

She was heavily involved with our Living History Days at Milwaukie in '96, '97, '98, and worked with her classmates to honor veterans at our high school as well as The Tribute to Veterans at the Veterans Memorial Coliseum in 2000.

As a teacher in Newberg in 2012 and '13, she organized over 800 students and staff from Newberg High School to travel to our Living History Days at Evergreen Aviation and Space Museum. She also attended the Native American Hall of Fame induction ceremony in Oklahoma in November of 2021 where she met many veterans from all three volumes of Remembrance, including and especially her friend and hero, Marcella LeBeau, who was inducted and honored that night.

When I asked Kelly to give me a little background for her to put in the book, she sent me a note. It is just something I want to take the opportunity to brag about as she and I are still very proud of her weight room squat record.

She wrote to me, "I was Mr. Buckles' student for strength training in my sophomore and junior year-- I ended up being a top female squatter in my class- maxing out at 255 lbs. when I weighed only 120 lbs. I made the weight record wall my senior year for softball- outfield: (Bench 135, Incline 115, and Squat 255 = 505 lbs.) I was so proud of myself! I don't think you have to write all that, but I thought I would share that with you because it wasn't easy."

No, Kelly, it wasn't easy, but I knew you could do it! I'm very grateful to Kelly for her helpful editing skills and for taking the time on her own to help promote the books.

Kelly's posted review of Volume I on Amazon:

"I treasure this book! It's my new favorite, and I'm a high school language arts teacher. I am grateful for the stories that Mr. Buckles has immortalized in these pages because they are the true stories of our American Heroes, Our Veterans, written by their trusted friend, Mr. Ken Buckles. It is only because of Ken's vision, his years of dedication and love for these Veterans, for his students, and for history that we are privileged to get to read about and learn from these real, untold stories today. I was one of those lucky students who attended Milwaukie High School for the first 3 Living History Days, and it changed our (the students') outlook on life. It's hard to describe the miracles that we witnessed on those special days-- the people we met, the pride, the honor, the healing, the humanity-- but Ken does an excellent job of capturing that spirit of Milwaukie that made this happen. Thank you to our Veterans, once again, for your vulnerability, courage, and sacrifice so that we may learn from you and live with love for you! You will not be forgotten! Highly Recommended Book!"

MALINDA LETT BUCKLES — My Beloved

Remembering America's Heroes Communications Liaison/Performer

I've been married to Malinda for the past fifteen years. Malinda was a Milwaukie mom and her middle son, Bennie, set us up on a date sixteen years ago.

Bill Call, a former Marine and veteran of WWII and the Korean War, said it best sixteen years ago when Malinda and I were dating, "Ken, bringing Malinda onboard your non-profit is the best move you ever made."

Malinda was born and raised in Atlanta, Georgia, and has lived in Oregon for over 30 years. She has five children, Nick (Air Force veteran), Nikii, Cristal, Bennie, and Moriah, and nine grandchildren, Trinity, Ozias, Delami, Roman, Keylia, Caussius, Tianna, and Tavion.

She loves dancing, singing, and modeled as a teenager, and also acted in two movies, *Just an Old Sweet Song*, with Cicely Tyson, and *Mr. Holland's Opus*, with Richard Dreyfuss.

Malinda got involved with our Assembly of Honors during Living History Days at Milwaukie High years before we ever dated. One of her great additions to our Tribute to Vietnam Veterans event was when she talked every female teacher at Milwaukie High into wearing a mini skirt, go-go boots, and a blond wig. During the assembly they all danced to 'These Boots are Made for Walking'. Everyone loved it, especially the students and they received a standing ovation.

Once we started dating and married, I had her sing for the majority of our veteran related events, and the veterans love her. She has been asked to sing by veterans more times than I'm asked to speak. She has sung at several national veteran reunions.

In July of 2013, I spoke at a Saturday session at the National Reunion for the USS Indianapolis Survivors Association, and Malinda sang a couple of songs. Afterward, members from the USS Indianapolis Survivors asked her to sing the next day during their annual and emotional Memorial Service to those veterans still at sea.

I'll never forget how many WWII veterans and spouses would break down sobbing or crying whenever she sang 'I'll Be Seeing You'. 100-year-old Alice Bruning, a WWII Nurse on a Red Cross hospital ship, approached Malinda after singing that song. And with tears running down her face she said, "My husband sang that song to me on the docks right before they boarded to be shipped overseas. We were married just the night before. Thank you so much for singing our song."

The most important addition Malinda brought to our mission, she recommended that the veterans' spouses be included in events, and I agreed. This took us to another level as we all became a big family, and all looked forward to seeing each other every year.

I'm so grateful for her passionate support, dedication, commitment, inspiration, and love for all that we do and have done. She deserves a lot of credit for getting on me for several years to write and finish all of the Volumes.

Malinda, I love you!

MHS GOLD STAR ALUMNI

The following list is all the names of Milwaukie High School Alumni who died while serving our country in the Armed Forces. They are honored every year at MHS during the 'Gold Star Assembly'. We know of no other high school in Oregon that does anything like this. We are missing important information for many of them. Hopefully, this will lead to collecting and updating this list.

Please go to Remembering America's Heroes Facebook homepage or the Remembering America's Heroes homepage to watch the video 'Gold Star Assembly 1932-1979 — Milwaukie High School'.

Lest We Forget

Talbot Bennett
    Class of '32, Marines, WWII, South Pacific

Richard Umphrey
    Class of '33, Navy, WWII, Fighter pilot shot down during 'Battle of Midway', Married high school sweetheart

Ted Fisch
    Class of '35, Student Body Secretary, Basketball, State Champion Swimmer, Air Corps, WWII, B-17 pilot shot down in Philippines

Jack Levy
    Class of '35, Basketball, Tennis, State Swimming Champion, Maroon Staff, Air Corps, WWII, B-17 pilot shot down at Solomon Islands

Johnny Stein
> Class of '35, Student Body Officer, Maroon and Milwaukian Staff, Air Corps, WWII, B-17 pilot shot down over Germany

Bobby Stein
> Class of '36, Student Body, Football manager, Class clown, Marines, WWII, Died during training at Camp Pendleton

Marvin Walker
> Class of '37, Navy, WWII, Fighter pilot shot down

Mark Estes
> Class of '39, Army, WWII, Died in airplane crash

Bob Landstrom
> Class of '39, Army, WWII

Gordon Carney
> Class of '39, Army, WWII

Robert Donald Russell
> Class of '39, Navy, WWII, USS Neville, Guadalcanal

Owen Bauserman
> Class of '40, Football manager, Navy, WWII, Pearl Harbor, USS Selfridge, Solomon Islands, South Pacific

Alfred Spor
> Class of '40, Army, WWII, 101st Airborne, France

Gene Foidel
> Class of '40, Football (Halfback), Army, WWII Era, Killed in automobile crash at Fort Lewis Army Base, Washington

Mickey Burke
> Class of '41, Football, State Boxing Champion, Baseball, Marines, WWII, Guadalcanal, Left foxhole three times to rescue wounded Marines, rescued two Marines, never made it back on the third trip

Jim Sherwood
> Class of '41, Three sport star Football Basketball and Track, Student Body President, Navy, WWII, Corpsman attached to Marines in Saipan

Randall Townsley
> Class of '41, Football, Army, WWII, Philippines

Jack Jamison
> Class of '42, Football, Wrestling, Navy, WWII,
> USS Vincennes sunk at Battle of Savo Island, Guadalcanal

Wendal Schmidt
> Class of '42, Air Corps, WWII, Airplane shot down

Ralph Mosher
> Class of '42, Student Body President, Army, WWII

Bill Geil
> Class of '42, Band, Navy, WWII, Ship sunk in South Pacific

Robert 'Bob' M. Gribble
> Class of '43, WWII

Gordon Criteser
> Class of '43, Navy, WWII, USS Spence, Destroyer,
> 8 Battle Stars, ship sunk during Typhoon Cobra at Okinawa

Louis Kearns
> Class of '43, Army, WWII, Died in non-hostile incident

Kenneth Wright
> Class of '43, Air Corps, WWII, shot down in Germany

George Dunigan
> Class of '46, Class President, Army, WWII

George Kerr
> Class of '43, Army, WWII

David Wright
> Class of '43, Navy, WWII, ship sunk in South Pacific

William N. Cromwell
> Class of '46, Army, Korea, Chosin Reservoir

Keith P. LaBarr
> Class of '47, Air Force, Korea

Wesley R. Wallace
> Class of '47, Korea

Louis Cavendish Honeyman Jr.
> Class of '48, Army, Korea

Clarence Ruben Berreth
> Class of '47, Army, Korea, Silver Star

Raymond McCoun
> Class of '51, Marines, Korea, Battle in South Korea

Gerald Timm
> Class of '57, Coast Guard, died of injuries from accident at sea

James 'Jim' P. Turney
> Class of '46, Army, Korea

Bud Smith
> Class of '59, Basketball, Baseball, Student Body President, Air Force, Vietnam, Fighter pilot, Jet shot down, Parents owned Candy Store on Main St.

Warner 'Craig' Jacobson
> Class of '60, Football, Tennis, Senior Class President, Army, Vietnam

David F. Popp
> Class of '61, Army, Vietnam, Airborne, Helicopter shot down, daughter Cynthia graduated from MHS in '84

Jere J. Nelson II
> Class of '62, Air Force, Vietnam, Missing in Action

Wayne Conrad Reinecke
> Class of '64, Navy, Vietnam, USS Bennington, Helicopter crashed at Gulf of Tonkin

Larry Iannetta
> Class of '64, Attended Central Catholic HS transferred to MHS Senior year to graduate with friends, Army, Vietnam, Helicopter shot down

Martin Dietrich
> Class of '64, Army, Vietnam

William Block
> Class of '65', Army, Vietnam

Keith Arnold
> Class of '65, Army, Vietnam, Helicopter pilot

Michael Greeley
> Class of '66, Loved working on cars, Marines, Vietnam

Donald Schafer
> Class of '66, Navy, Vietnam

Larry Dikeman
> Class of '67, Army, Vietnam

Daniel Irvin Mambretti
> Class of '69, Army, Vietnam

Cliff Redding
> Class of '79, Navy, Submarine, Murdered on leave

Tom Swanson
> MHS Chemistry teacher, football coach, Normandy, France

Dylan Carpenter
> Class of '05, Navy Corpsman, Afghanistan

Jordan DuBois
> Class of '09, Army, Iraq

The last two alumni veterans' names were added in 2012. Jordan and Dylan were added with controversy. There were some teachers and administration that felt that it was dishonorable to include the two alumni veterans to this impressive Gold Star Assembly because they both committed suicide. I decided to be proactive, so I asked for veterans' opinions on the issue at The 1st Marine Division's and The Chosin Few's monthly lunches. Most of the feedback cannot be printed due to the colorful language. They all stated they would personally visit MHS and demand that the two alumni veterans be added immediately. Well, that was not necessary as I met with the principal and told him how the veterans of both organizations felt about this issue. He agreed and both Jordan and Dylan were added. There was never any question for me that both young men's names should be on this memorial.

In Flanders fields the poppies grow
Between the crosses, row on row,
That mark our place; and in the sky
The larks, still bravely singing, fly
Scarce heard amid the guns below.

We are the Dead. Short days ago
We lived, felt dawn, saw sunset glow,
Loved and were loved, and now we lie
In Flanders fields.

Take up our quarrel with the foe:
To you from failing hands we throw
The torch; be yours to hold it high.
If ye break faith with us who die
We shall not sleep, though poppies grow
In Flanders fields.

~ Lieutenant-Colonel John McCrae
    "In Flanders Fields"